On the Threshold of Modernity

THE JOHNS HOPKINS UNIVERSITY STUDIES IN HISTORICAL AND POLITICAL SCIENCE 109TH SERIES (1991)

1. *Shipbuilders of the Venetian Arsenal: Workers and Workplace in the Preindustrial City*
   by Robert C. Davis

2. *The Ideology of the Great Fear: The Soisonnais in 1789*
   by Clay Ramsay

3. *On the Threshold of Modernity: Relativism in the French Renaissance*
   by Zachary Sayre Schiffman

4. *A Spirited Resistance: The North American Indian Struggle for Unity, 1745–1815*
   by Gregory Evans Dowd

On the Threshold of Modernity

RELATIVISM IN THE FRENCH RENAISSANCE

ZACHARY SAYRE SCHIFFMAN

THE JOHNS HOPKINS UNIVERSITY PRESS
Baltimore and London

Printed in the United States of America

The Johns Hopkins University Press
701 West 40th Street
Baltimore, Maryland 21211-2190
The Johns Hopkins Press Ltd., London

The paper used in this book meets the minimum requirements of American National Standard for Information Sciences—Permanence of Paper for Printed Library Materials, ANSI Z39.48-1984.

Library of Congress Cataloging-in-Publication Data

Schiffman, Zachary Sayre.
On the threshold of modernity : relativism in the French Renaissance / Zachary Sayre Schiffman.
p. cm. — (The Johns Hopkins University studies in historical and political science ; 109th ser., 3)
Includes bibliographical references and index.
ISBN 0-8018-4209-3 (alk. paper)
1. Renaissance—France. 2. France—Intellectual life—16th century. 3. Relativity—History—16th century. I. Title. II. Series.
DC33.3.S35 1991 91-2938
944′.028—dc20 CIP

For My Parents
In Love and Friendship

CONTENTS

	Acknowledgments	ix
	Introduction	xi
CHAPTER 1:	The Problem of Relativism	1
CHAPTER 2:	The Order of History	25
CHAPTER 3:	The Order of the Self	53
CHAPTER 4:	The Moral Order	78
CHAPTER 5:	The Order of the Sciences	103
EPILOGUE	Relativism Resolved	129
	Notes	141
	Index	167

ACKNOWLEDGMENTS

Long ago when I mentioned to a friend, Patricia Jobe, that Montaigne used the term *forme maistresse,* or "ruling pattern," to describe the shape of his personality, she remarked: "What a curious expression! Where does it come from?" Little did either of us realize that her simple question would help inspire years of research into the classificatory way of thinking. So many other friends, colleagues, and mentors have contributed—wittingly and unwittingly, directly and indirectly—to my work that I despair of ever giving them the credit they deserve . . . but I will try.

Hanna Gray and Karl Weintraub introduced me to the study of Renaissance historiography, and for this alone I owe them a considerable debt of gratitude. But they have also exemplified for me the highest standards of intellectual responsibility, standards that I may never be able to equal, though I hope to have emulated them in my own small way.

Michael Hobart has been a constant sounding board for my ideas and an inexhaustible source not only of insight but also of patience. Alan Kors read the entire manuscript, subjecting it to his usual penetrating criticism, from which it has much benefited. Leonard Barkan has been a fund of knowledge about Renaissance and modern literary theory, as well as a personal source of inspiration. I am also grateful to John Salmon, Donald Wilcox, Donald Kelley, Nancy Roelker, and Raymond Waddington for reading and criticizing some of my preliminary papers and articles on the topic. Many friends in addition to Patricia Jobe—Thomas Jobe, William and Wendy Olmsted, Paul Brietzke and Susan Adams, Constantin Fasolt, Robert Rigoulot, Paul Gehl, Marian Rothstein, James Weiss, and the late John D'Amico—created for me the kind of intellectual community in which a book could be written. And I am also indebted to Rebecca Passonneau for her years of moral support.

Several agencies and institutions have provided the financial and material support necessary for the completion of this project. I began research under an Exxon Education Foundation Fellowship at the Newberry Library, and a grant from the American Council of Learned Societies enabled me to continue work at the Folger Library. An Andrew W. Mellon Postdoctoral Fellowship in the Humanities at the University of Pennsylvania provided me with a year unencumbered by teaching responsibilities in which to complete research and begin writing; the Department of History at the University of Pennsylvania provided me with a congenial home during that period. Writing was completed during a National Endowment for the Humanities Summer Seminar for College Teachers, directed by Leonard Barkan at Northwestern University. And a National Endowment for the Humanities Summer Stipend—along with a grant from the Committee on Organized Research at Northeastern Illinois University—enabled me to revise the manuscript and prepare it for publication.

Portions of my argument are drawn from the following published articles: "Montaigne and the Rise of Skepticism in Early Modern Europe: A Reappraisal," *Journal of the History of Ideas* 45 (1984): 499–516; "Estienne Pasquier and the Problem of Historical Relativism," *The Sixteenth Century Journal* 18 (1987): 505–17; "An Anatomy of the Historical Revolution in Renaissance France," *Renaissance Quarterly* 42 (1989): 507–33; and "Humanism and the Problem of Relativism," *Humanism in Crisis: The Decline of the French Renaissance,* ed. Philippe Desan (Ann Arbor: University of Michigan Press, 1991). For the most part, the material from these articles has been recast and redirected for the purposes of the book.

INTRODUCTION

"But our beginnings never know our ends!" T. S. Eliot's parenthetical remark about friendship in "Portrait of a Lady" applies to ideas as well as individuals. The present book originated from an intuition into the structural similarity between La Popelinière's concept of "perfect history" and Montaigne's project of self-portrayal. It seemed to me (sprawled on a couch in my living room several years ago) that no two authors, and no two projects, could be more dissimilar; yet I sensed in both a tendency to divide and subdivide their respective subjects, to describe them in such labyrinthine detail that the reader could easily become lost and bewildered. Montaigne's genius transformed this tendency into the highest literary art, whereas La Popelinière's more prosaic mind merely made it egregious, thus suggesting to me that late Renaissance thought might be characterized by an "individualizing" tendency, an impulse to analyze subjects into their discrete parts.

This inchoate idea was little more than an intuition about the fundamental strangeness of the sixteenth-century mind, an intuition made all the more curious by recent claims for the "modernity" of that mind. In our "postmodern" age, the idea of historical development has emerged as one of the chief characteristics of "modern" thought. Recent historical research has tended to trace the origin of this idea back to the sense of historical and cultural relativism emerging from humanist philology, especially as practiced in the sixteenth century by the so-called "French historical school of law." It has been assumed that the perception of historical and cultural relativism encouraged by legal scholarship was implicitly developmental, that the struggle to understand the diversity of laws and institutions naturally engendered a notion of these entities as evolving in relation to their circumstances. In other words, it has been assumed that the simple awareness of relativism entailed the relativistic view of the world characteristic of modern historicism. Indeed, La Popelinière is regarded as one of the heralds of a "historical revolution" in which all aspects of human activity came to be understood as developing over time.[1]

I have been profoundly influenced by this recent scholarship, which has spurred my abiding interest in Renaissance historiography. Yet my encounter with La Popelinière left me convinced that the strangeness of his mind—epitomized by its individualizing tendency—was far more important for the understanding of Renaissance historical consciousness than its more familiar "modern" aspects. Sprawled on my couch, though, I had no idea where this intuition would eventually lead me, and I originally conceived of it as little more than an introduction to an analysis of Montaigne's attitude toward the past. I could hardly have imagined that it would culminate in an extended essay on the problem of relativism, in which La Popelinière and Montaigne are but two figures in a larger story.

At this juncture three terms require clarification: *relativism, essay,* and *problem.* My argument is predicated on the distinction between the experience of relativism and doctrines of relativism. The experience of relativism represents an awareness of the human world as being filled with unique historical entities, such as laws, institutions, and states; this experience manifested itself in the individualizing tendency characteristic of sixteenth-century thought. It did not, however, necessarily entail a doctrine of relativism, especially not one that attributed the uniqueness of historical entities to their development over time. It did sometimes entail "skeptical relativism"—a way of thinking that used the awareness of diversity to overturn established norms—but even this skepticism represented less a doctrine of relativism than a means of searching for truth amidst complexity. Indeed, my chief concern throughout the book is to show how the experience of relativism underscored the need to find some underlying order or orientation in the world.

Given my historiographical interests, I have only "essayed" a vast subject by focusing on the reaction to historical and cultural relativism, leaving crucial issues in moral and religious relativism—especially casuistry—largely unexamined. And in the manner of a true essayist, I begin with historiography, stray into moral philosophy, and end up, far from my starting point, in epistemology. I would like to think that these meanderings follow the major course of my subject, and that I have neglected its many tributaries through intention rather than ignorance. My aim has been only to chart the crucial, but neglected, issue of how Europeans, and especially Frenchmen, made sense of the complexity of their world once traditional norms had broken down. If we assume that they naturally did so by means of an idea of historical development, then complexity was ultimately non-problematic for them. But if—as I shall argue—the individualizing view of the world precluded an idea of development, they must have found complexity intensely problematic. The course of this book is dictated by their ongoing struggle with relativism, which eventually affected their understanding not only of history but also of moral and natural philosophy.

The experience of relativism engendered a "problem" for those accustomed to viewing the world in traditional normative terms. The weakening of these norms naturally threatened conceptual confusion, a threat that I refer to throughout the book as "the problem of relativism." Although I shall focus on this problematic aspect of relativism, one should not lose sight of its more affirmative side, which provided the opportunity and material for literary and artistic creation. For example, Petrarch's closing in his first letter to Cicero expresses a genuine sense of historical anachronism, a sense of the gulf between past and present: "But these words indeed are all in vain. Farewell forever, my Cicero. From the land of the living, on the right bank of the Adige, in the city of Verona in transpadane Italy, on 16 June in the year 1345 from the birth of that Lord whom you never knew."[2] Petrarch had to struggle with the task of understanding Cicero as an ancient Roman and a pagan. Yet the gulf between past and present provided Petrarch with a golden opportunity for emulating the ancient literary genre of the letter, and the sense of anachronism provided him with his very subject matter. Far from being exclusively problematic, the experience of relativism could become the occasion for creative mental play. Nowhere is this more apparent than in the *Essais*, where Montaigne's shifting perspectives on human diversity provided him with the opportunity and material for self-observation.

That I choose to focus on the problematic side of relativism marks me as a historian from the late twentieth century, an age of newfound (and newfangled) complexities. One of these complexities is expressed by the very observation I have just made, that I see the past through the eyes of the present. And there are also newfangled variations on this complexity, that (for example) my form of consciousness is generated by the dominant mode of "discourse," which serves as an obstacle to understanding the sixteenth-century mode of discourse. These complexities are born of an idea of development that has turned in upon itself, that has begun (as it were) to "deconstruct" itself, engendering a new problem of relativism. There can be no denying the importance of this intellectual turn, which has begun to redefine the style and the substance of historical inquiry; it is evident in the very structural intuition that lies at the heart of this study. Yet I am nonetheless moved to write out of a deep respect for the power of the idea of historical development as an intellectual tool. I have chosen to demonstrate its power and utility in a perverse way—by showing the difficulty of making sense out of a complex world without it.

Mine is the story of an intellectual cul-de-sac, the conceptual dead end that the struggle with relativism led to in the sixteenth and seventeenth centuries. In the first chapter, I cast the problem of relativism—epitomized by the individualizing view of the world—against the background of the "print revolution," humanist education, and advances in legal and historical scholarship. Subsequent chapters pursue attempts to resolve this problem by asserting the order of history (via cultural taxonomy), the order of the self (via moral morphology), and the order of the sciences (via serial reasoning).

This topical analysis also proffers a chronological argument. The attempts by La Popelinière, Vignier, and Pasquier to classify the past were undercut by the breakdown of the classificatory view of the world evidenced in the *Essais*. Montaigne recognized that in a world where one could not know normative truths, one could at least know the movements of one's own mind. This inward turn made his disciple Charron very nervous, because the self did not appear to be anchored to any larger truth. Charron attempted to use Montaigne's relativizing insights as a goad toward a new moral philosophy based on a revitalized system of classification, but he only succeeded in demonstrating how the fuller awareness of relativism precluded classification. With Charron's failure in mind, Descartes advanced further along the path indicated by Montaigne, emphasizing the mind's self-conscious experience of the cognitive moment. But unlike Montaigne, Descartes stripped the cognitive moment bare of all contextual detail in order to reveal its quintessential nature as a logical unit, upon which he could restructure human knowledge. He failed to convince his critics, however, that one could know the richness of the extra-mental world on the basis of a desiccated logical unit. The failure of Cartesianism reified the problem of relativism by separating the natural sciences, unified under mathematics, from the apparent chaos of the human ones. By following the intellectual techniques at their disposal, Frenchmen thus pursued the problem of relativism into a cul-de-sac. No exit would be found until Vico, the heir to legal humanism and opponent of Cartesianism, formulated a science of history that attributed the complexity of the human world to an ongoing process of development.

The idea of historical development is now under attack from a range of critics. Some confuse this idea with the superficial one of "progress," leading them to reject history as a simplistic form of understanding. Others blame it for engendering an abyss of values and beliefs, and seek to reassert the enduring norms expressed by the great authors of Western culture. And still others reject it as a form of false consciousness that privileges the individual, obscuring the linguistic/cognitive structures that make his thought and action possible. These are all serious criticisms. Even the first, which mistakes development for improvement, addresses teleological tendencies that even careful historians sometimes have trouble avoiding. And these tendencies have no doubt contributed to the charge that developmental thinking is a form of false consciousness.

I hope in some small way to address these issues, even though a full-scale analysis of them is far beyond my competence. For those who confuse development with progress, I chart the trajectory of thinking that cannot resolve the problem underlying its development. For those who charge history with creating that problem, I show how the idea of development actually served to resolve an early form of it. For those who seek to supplant historical with structural modes of thought, I argue that the idea of development was born of the failure of taxonomy to encompass the diversity of human reality. Despite new, more sophisticated, structural ways of thinking, we ought not blithely to discard from our intellectual arsenal an idea of proven utility, lest we exacerbate the problem it originally addressed, new forms of which currently beset us.

On the Threshold of Modernity

CHAPTER 1

THE PROBLEM OF RELATIVISM

La Popelinière's List

In his *Dessein de l'histoire nouvelle des françois,* Lancelot Voisin de La Popelinière offered a blueprint for a French history of broader range and deeper reach than any previous effort. He divided his proposed work into three parts: pre-Roman Gaul, Roman Gaul, and the kingdom of France from the Merovingians to the present. Part 1 would concern "the form of government, public and private, of the Gauls living in liberty before the Romans had coveted, undermined, and eventually seized their dominion." It would detail their religion (its priests and rituals), their nobility (its composition, privileges, and lifestyle), the lesser social orders (merchants, artisans, and commoners), and their public institutions (laws, magistrates, and other officials)—"in brief, everything notable about so little known a state." Part 2 would follow the same pattern, but in even greater detail, examining the changes introduced by the Romans in "religion, administration, justice, military discipline, finances, and business," as well as social changes. Part 3 would describe the history of the French monarchy in terms of topics—religion, nobility, administration, and so forth—which were even more detailed than either of the two preceding parts of the work. For example, his history would describe the French nobility in terms of "its duties, power, authority, charters, and privileges; the princes, dukes, counts, viscounts, marquises, barons, and other lords; the officers of the crown, constable, marshals, and others; the peers of France; the royal orders; the *ban* and *arrière-ban;* the fiefs, vassals, renters, and subvassals." The topic of the nobility naturally led to that of military organization, which he analyzed right down to the arquebusiers and pikemen. In short, his "new history" would entail "the representation of everything" one needed to know about France.[1]

The content of La Popelinière's new history is strikingly modern, encompassing virtually the whole range of human activity, but it takes the strange form of an exhaustive list. Perhaps this is only to be expected in what virtually amounts to an outline for a history; but as an integral part of a larger historiographical polemic, the "outline" begins as a narrative. It quickly degenerates, however, into a long, five-page list of all the material appropriate to a history of France. Dividing his subject matter into ever smaller parts, La Popelinière overwhelms the reader with an avalanche of topics and subtopics. By the end of the list, even he has become conscious of its bewildering detail. He concludes the tripartite description of his proposed history with an attempt to simplify the outline in yet another list, albeit shorter, "in order to express more clearly my conception of so novel an undertaking." But this "simplification" takes the even more complex, five-part form of ancient Gaul, Roman Gaul, German Gaul, Frankish Gaul, and the French monarchy. It is as if he cannot restrain himself from further subdividing his subject into its ever more discrete component parts.[2] This impulse is apparent in the very name of his new form of historical writing—*histoire accomplie*—denoting its "perfection," in the sense of "completeness."

To some extent the strange, exhaustive nature of "perfect history" reflects the underlying influence of the Renaissance (and classical) theory of rhetorical dilation, which emphasized the need to enrich discourse with an abundance of examples, expressions, and arguments.[3] This notion of *copia* aimed at the same ideal of completeness evident in perfect history. But "perfection" in rhetorical dilation was necessarily subsumed under the requirements of effective communication; excessive *copia* could overwhelm rather than enhance an argument. For this reason the appropriateness of ideas and examples was more important than the brute fact of their abundance, the conceit being that one could achieve perfection by finding the material typifying a situation. The notion that the diversity of human reality could be typed and classified thus underlay the theory of *copia*; and it is not at all surprising to find that Erasmus's *De copia,* the standard sixteenth-century manual of rhetorical dilation, ends with a classificatory scheme for the organization of literary materials. Such schemata were predicated upon social and cultural norms that Europeans assumed had universal validity.

Perfect history, however, is not simply an example of *copia,* because it is characterized by the absence of accepted norms. Instead of the customary myth of the Trojan origin of the Franks, it would begin with an account of the ancient Gauls. And instead of the heroic deeds of kings, captains, and saints, it would detail the institutional structure of the Gallic, Gallo-

Roman, and Frankish states. Indeed, the expanded scope of La Popelinière's historical vision is hard to reconcile with the traditional Ciceronian commonplace about history as the *magistra vitae,* or mistress of life—where amidst this crowd of institutions are there moral examples worthy of imitation? Without accepted norms regulating the economy of historical expression, La Popelinière had no choice but to make an interminable list of the subjects appropriate to his new form of history, breaking them down into their smallest constituent parts. This activity was consonant, but not coterminous, with rhetorical dilation.

Sixteenth-century authors frequently indulged in the activity of list-making. Of La Popelinière's contemporaries, for example, Louis Le Roy published two lists on historical and political matters, one of them over ninety pages long; and Nicolas Vignier published a gigantic, three-volume chronological list of all the events since Creation.[4] In addition to these relatively obscure thinkers, one can find evidence of compulsive list-making in the two major literary figures of the French Renaissance, Rabelais and Montaigne. Rabelais loved lists, a tame example being the alphabetic one of reptiles in book 4 that begins with "asps" and, after dozens of obscure and fanciful names, ends with "vipers." Aside from outright lists, Rabelais also made use of narrative ones, the most notorious example being the list of ass-wipes in book 1. Lists in general served comic purposes, especially that of ridiculing learned copiousness; but they also reflect the encyclopedic exuberance of an oral culture going into print—the long list of Gargantua's games in book 1 brings together a wide range of popular, everyday activities that had never before been recorded. The narrative lists—generally associated with eating and defecating—also serve to bring the "objective" world into contact with the human body, which provided Rabelais with his point of orientation in existence.[5]

The same kind of activity is apparent in the *Essais,* but to an even greater degree (Rabelais's comic exaggeration notwithstanding). List-making is integral to a work that began as a collection of commonplaces. At the heart of the "Apology for Raymond Sebond" lies a long, narrative list of competing and contradictory philosophical systems. The essay "Of Custom, and Not Easily Changing an Accepted Law" is dominated by a long listing of exotic observances. And the essay "Of Experience," among the most lyrical of Montaigne's compositions, is basically an extended narrative list of his personal habits, punctuated with dense entries like the following:

> Habit, imperceptibly, has already so imprinted its character upon me in certain things, that I call it excess to depart from it. And I cannot, without an effort, sleep by day, or eat between meals, or breakfast, or go to bed without a long interval, of about three full hours, after supper, or make a child except before going to sleep, or make one standing up, or endure my sweat, or quench my thirst with pure water or

pure wine, or remain bareheaded for long, or have my hair cut after dinner; and I would feel as uncomfortable without my gloves as without my shirt, or without washing when I leave the table or get up in the morning, or without canopy and curtains for my bed, as I would be without really necessary things. I could dine without a tablecloth; but very uncomfortably without a clean napkin, German fashion; I soil napkins more than they or the Italians do, and make little use of spoon or fork.[6]

One does not have to look far in the *Essais* to find such passages. Lists—sometimes dense, sometimes discursive—constitute one of Montaigne's major compositional devices. He even described the act of writing in terms analogous to list-making, when he claimed to be putting his thoughts *en registre* and *en rolle.*[7] Implicitly, this "register" served to order the variety of habits, customs, and laws with reference to the touchstone of Montaigne's mind, in much the same way that Rabelais brought the diversity of objects into contact with the body.

The record of Montaigne's thoughts consistently aimed at a higher degree of completeness than Rabelais's intermittent encyclopedic enthusiasms. In this regard, Montaigne's account of himself resembles La Popelinière's account of perfect history. The *Essais* consist of three different chronological strata of composition, delimited by the first edition of 1580, the fifth edition of 1588, and the posthumous edition of 1595. The bulk of the above-quoted passage was written by 1588, with the phrase, "of about three full hours," added before Montaigne's death in 1592. He obviously considered this kind of detail to be important, for he made numerous such additions to the original version of this essay, and to all the others as well. Additions consisted not only of small points of fact but also of examples, as well as discourses on a wide variety of topics; each addition presented another movement of his mind, another facet of his thought. This practice engendered, as it were, a "thick description" of the self having the appearance of completeness.[8] Montaigne endeavored to make the register of his thoughts as exhaustive as possible, in much the same way as La Popelinière attempted to enumerate *every* topic appropriate to the history of France. Indeed, when Montaigne remarked that he and his book were "consubstantial," he was making a statement of the same order of completeness as La Popelinière's declaration that perfect history is "the representation of everything."[9]

We are here in the presence of an epistemic characteristic of late-sixteenth-century thought that governs not so much its content as its form, regardless of the intellectual endeavor. The nature of this characteristic is most apparent in, but not limited to, the activity of list-making. Lists are characterized by discontinuity rather than continuity. Every list has a well-defined beginning and end; its items are set apart from all other possible items by virtue of being in a finite series. Furthermore, its items are also separated from each other, the series being broken down into its component parts.

These internal and external boundaries encourage the ordering of items according to some principle, be it number, letter, or category. A list thus not only emphasizes the discrete nature of its component parts but also gathers them into an organized universe, positing a relationship between them.[10]

The activity of list-making highlights an individualizing tendency in late-sixteenth-century thought, which was merely the reverse side of a relativizing tendency. Lists served to order items that had been torn from their traditional frame of reference, and the more exhaustive the list, the greater the need for order. The compulsiveness of this activity, evident in both La Popelinière and Montaigne, indicates that relativism had become intensely problematic by the late sixteenth century. It threatened to overturn the accepted means of ordering the world and to fragment reality. This problem shaped the development of early modern history, philosophy, and science, areas in which thinkers sought to ease their intellectual discomfort by restructuring human knowledge.

One does not have to probe deeply into the sixteenth century for the roots of this problem. The revival of antiquity had heightened the contrast between the pagan and Christian worlds. The reform movement in the church had divided the Christian world into competing denominations. Overseas explorations had revealed the existence of a strange New World. And the advent of printing had not only accelerated the effects of all these changes but had also created an information explosion. Taken together, these factors conspired to undermine the traditional ways of ordering the world, and thus to heighten the sense of relativism.

The French in particular experienced this problem acutely. Of course, an awareness of relativism was intrinsic to the humanist movement from its Italian beginnings.[11] Leonardo Bruni, for example, had criticized as unhistorical the Petrarchian notion of perennial Rome, which obscured the political and cultural achievements of the Florentine republic. But Florentine humanists nonetheless debated whether their city had been founded by Caesar's or Sulla's veterans. Despite an awareness of their own historical and cultural specificity, they could not entirely free themselves from the pull of a classical norm: their political world bore some resemblance to the world of the polis; their physical environment was filled with Roman ruins; and their vernacular shared many affinities with Latin. Not until the sixteenth century, when humanism spread northward to France, was the primacy of ancient culture effectively challenged. The classical revival made Frenchmen more aware of the distinctiveness of their own culture, with its feudal and scholastic rather than classical roots. And as the century progressed, chronic religious/civil strife spurred them to an ever deeper understanding of their indigenous customs, laws, and institutions, upon which stability might be based. From the mid sixteenth century onward, they increasingly asserted the equality or superiority of French culture to that of antiquity.

This assertion might be dismissed as merely an early example of the proverbial "French cultural imperialism," striving to supplant the classical ideal with a new norm. Were this the case, however, Frenchmen would not have experienced a problem of relativism. That they in particular were exposed to it was due to a combination of factors: advances in legal and historical scholarship, the diffusion of the humanist program of education, and the cognitive repercussions of typographic literacy. These factors helped shape the nature of French intellectual life, from the level of conscious concerns down to the level of unconscious mental habits.

The impact of humanist philology on the study of Roman law in France led to the development of the French historical school of law. Philology demonstrated that Roman law was not universal law but rather the law of a past society. This revelation held forth the possibility that all laws and institutions were relative to their historical circumstances, potentially undermining the existence of any normative standards. These advances in legal and historical scholarship reacted with the mental habits instilled by the humanist program of education, which used a normative view of the world to restrain a skeptical way of thinking. As norms were progressively undermined, skepticism was excited; and those sensitive to the full implications of scholarly developments faced the task of orienting themselves in a world where intellectual traditions were breaking down. This need for reorientation was itself exacerbated by newly acquired typographic literacy, which had the effect of wrenching words, and ultimately ideas, from their traditional oral framework. Taken individually, none of these factors was sufficient to induce the problem of relativism, but taken together they conspired to create a compulsion for order unique to the age, a compulsion that arose from deep within the sixteenth-century mind.

Printing, Literacy, and the Decontextualization of Language

Of the factors contributing to the growing sense of relativity in the sixteenth century, the spread of printing was the most insidious. The skeptical relativism engendered by the Reformation debates constituted a frontal assault on the European mind, as did the cultural relativism enhanced by the discovery of the New World. Yet in both cases, the impact of the assault could be absorbed either by resistance or retreat. In the Age of Religious Wars, when Europeans killed each other over the question of salvation, one could simply dismiss the opposition as wrongheaded. Even those who attempted to convince the opposition of its wrongheadedness—in a debate that unwittingly undercut the established criteria of religious truth—remained convinced of their own righteousness.[12] A similar process governed the European reaction to the New World, whose utter strangeness encouraged not curiosity but indifference. For the most part, Europeans simply ignored its cultural implications, which might otherwise have caused a conceptual overload. Those who attempted to describe the New World generally employed commonplaces about the old one, mitigating the impact of cultural relativism.[13] Indeed, the assumption that such contact naturally induced relativism is a modern anachronism. Those few who actually attempted to confront the New World on its own terms gave voice to a relativism that derived largely from other sources, especially humanist philology, which revealed the distinctiveness of an ancient culture that Europeans could not but take seriously. The project of restoring ancient culture through the reconstruction of classical texts only served to underscore the historical distance between the ancient and modern worlds, thus inserting the thin edge of relativism between the Renaissance mind and the norms it took for granted.

It is a commonplace that the spread of printing gave tremendous impetus to philology. Although the Renaissance origins of this art essentially predate printing, philological studies did not reach critical mass until the spread of printing made possible the publication of inexpensive editions, in which the scholarly reconstruction of classical texts could be both preserved and extended. Underlying this commonplace, however, is a more subtle and far-reaching development, in which the spoken word gradually became transformed into a visual object. This transformation, combined with the pattern of thinking inculcated by the humanist program of education, greatly intensified the relativizing view of the world fostered by humanist philology. Printing fundamentally altered European consciousness, leaving it more vulnerable to the onslaught of relativism.

Scholars in a range of fields—anthropology, linguistics, literature, and philosophy—have recognized that changes in the technology of communication encourage cognitive changes.[14] They have argued that the introduction of writing—along with the social, political, and economic factors related to this innovation—spurred the development of abstract thinking in previously nonliterate cultures. Writing has the effect of separating language from its living context. Speech exists as a series of transitory utterances, "tied to the movement of life itself in the flow of time."[15] Whereas speech is evanescent, writing has greater permanence; it can be reread, scrutinized, and analyzed into its component parts. "Once speech is 'translated' into writing, language or words cease to be events and become, instead, things."[16]

The transformation of spoken words into visual objects has been described as a process of "decontextualization."[17] Despite its awkwardness, the term concisely depicts the conceptual fragmentation experienced by those undergoing the transition to literacy. One must note, however, that language (be it spoken or written) classifies human experience; the introduction of writing served not simply to fragment reality but also to reorganize it in more elaborate, and generally more abstract ways.[18] In other words, decontextualization entails new forms of classification. Indeed, attempts at classification—especially lists—provide the chief evidence of decontextualization. The introduction of writing in Mesopotamia manifested itself in a profusion of lists—of kings, deities, concepts, and words—representing a new degree of abstract thinking that sought to classify entities now perceived more "objectively." One scholar has remarked of Sumerian lexical lists that, "Every group of names, be it of stones, fields, or officials is complete, perhaps too complete."[19] The compulsive need to order the profusion of entities abstracted from the traditional world is a striking characteristic of decontextualization.

The complexity of pictographic and syllabic writing systems restricted literacy to a scribal elite; whereas the alphabet reduced spoken language to a mere handful of symbols accessible to everyone. By the fifth century B.C., the craft literacy of the scribal elite had begun to give way to scriptorial literacy, characterized by the production of texts for a wider reading public. The spread of alphabetic literacy fostered further decontextualization, manifesting itself in the development of the critical, more "objective" habit of mind that distinguishes Plato from Homer. Rational activity came to be denoted by visual analogy—Plato's term for "idea" or "form" derived from the verb "to see." Platonic and, even more so, Aristotelian metaphysics represent an intellectual accommodation to a growing visual culture by classifying phenomena into essences revealed through their structure. Indeed, the Aristotelian science of classification is evidence of the decontextualization of language, and of the world, fostered by the spread of alphabetic literacy.[20]

The scriptorial literacy of the Hellenistic world reverted to craft literacy after the fall of the Roman empire in the West and then began to revive in the later Middle Ages, along with Greek metaphysics. The advent of typographic literacy, however, marked a stunning advance in the technology of communication. Combined with the availability of cheap paper, printing made possible the broadest diffusion of the alphabet: "Letters at last could escape the bondage of scribal style and whim and could become standardized and legible as never before."[21] Widespread literacy, defined by reading as well as writing ability, now became possible in a culture that had previously been largely oral.

The actual extent of literacy in the early modern period is hard to determine. The ability to write one's name (the traditional benchmark of literacy) does not necessarily indicate the ability to read, an ephemeral activity that cannot be documented for the vast majority of Europeans.[22] In general, though, the Reformation created fertile ground for the growth of literacy. When forced to consider doctrinal questions, Christians ultimately referred to the Bible. The ability to read thus became bound up with the issue of salvation; as one scholar has phrased it, "Luther made necessary what Gutenberg had made possible."[23] Of course, one could receive spiritual guidance by listening to the Bible, and committing passages to memory, rather than reading them. But Protestant and Catholic reformers alike began to stress the importance of primary and secondary education for one's adherence to faith, and such schools appear to have expanded in size and number during the sixteenth century.[24]

This ideological "push" toward literacy was accompanied by the "pull" of social and economic advantages accruing to those in certain professions where reading ability was becoming essential. In particular the growth of royal bureaucracies in this period encouraged the spread of literacy among both the nobility and those aspiring to it. La Popelinière, for example, considered himself a nobleman; and he addressed his first historical narrative, on the beginning of the French Wars of Religion, to his noble compatriots, whom he tried to convince of the efficacy of reading histories. The argumentative tone of his address suggests that some members of the nobility still doubted the value of literacy; but had he been living in the previous century, he probably would not have had any noble readers at all, or, for that matter, any inclination or ability to write.[25]

The utter lack of style and grace in La Popelinière's writing is suggestive of the recent diffusion of literacy. To some extent, of course, he was simply a bad writer, living at a time when the rules of grammar had yet to be formalized. But his frequent failure to make subject and verb, and article and noun, agree in number goes beyond the lack of literary ability and grammatical rules. He formulated sentences according to how they sounded, not how they looked; thus he could write *les chose* instead of *les choses*. This kind of relationship between speech and writing is characteristic of an early phase of literacy, when the imposition of the visual upon the oral manifested itself in the process of decontextualization.

La Popelinière's writings provide many striking examples of this phenomenon. His compulsion to record virtually every historical detail is apparent not only in his proposal for a perfect history but also in his *Histoire de France,* the narrative of the Wars of Religion to which he devoted the bulk of his energy. La Popelinière's biographer has briefly summarized the modern reaction to the excessive detail of this work: "It is precisely such exhaustive detail, methodically presented even for the most trivial encounters, which seems to indicate an awesome lack of perspective on the part of the author and to make the *Histoire de France* excessively dull and unimaginative today. But La Popelinière catalogued each fact, each minute occurrence, precisely because he thought that they were of potential value for future commanders."[26] Indeed, La Popelinière eventually bankrupted himself by visiting every battlefield, no matter how insignificant, in an effort to guarantee the accuracy of his account.[27] This fetish for detail reflects not only his traditional notion of the practical value of history but also his more critical appreciation of the complexity of historical events, themselves composed of myriad details, all crucial to the outcome. The more critical view of history was, as we shall soon see, inspired by humanist philology; but the compulsive form that it took—emphasizing the specificity of *every* historical detail—is indicative of a process of decontextualization. Indeed, the subtle effect of printing conspired with, and compounded, the more apparent one of philology, intensifying a broader process of decontextualization in which the meaning of events became detached from the traditional framework of historical understanding. Implicitly, La Popelinière's more critical view of events began to undermine the very utilitarian notion of history that had ostensibly inspired his interest in historical detail.

We shall see in the next chapter how this critical advance necessitated a new, more abstract ordering of the past. Suffice it to say, though, that La Popelinière and his contemporaries broke with the received tradition of French historiography, as embodied by the ongoing historical project known as the *Grandes chroniques de France,* and substituted in its place a more analytical treatment of the state.[28] The *Grandes chroniques* began with the Trojan origins of the Franks, interwove tales of chivalrous combat and high diplomacy with divine miracles, and followed the plan of providential history. Perfect history, however, would begin with the Gauls, would set forth analyses of diverse topics—religion, law, finance, military discipline, and so forth—and would follow a plan of historical periodization based on the changes in the institutional structure of the state. Instead of recounting tales about the French, perfect history would classify France. The impulse to extend classification to the historical realm can be attributed, at least in part, to the more analytical cast of mind born of typographic literacy.

The effects of decontextualization were everywhere apparent at this time—in the proliferation of "cabinets of curios," in compilations of commonplaces, in lexical, herbal, and zoological lists—but nowhere more so than in systems of "place logic." These were pedagogical schemes for breaking down any given body of knowledge into its component parts. They culminated in the mid sixteenth century with the work of Peter Ramus, a French educational reformer primarily concerned with making logic more accessible to students. Ramus formalized a method of bifurcating analysis that could be applied to any given subject. His aim was to divide and repeatedly subdivide the subject into its *loci,* the "places" or "seats" of knowledge. This dichotomized taxonomy provided a visual representation of the subject that could be taken in at a glance. The vogue of Ramism—and the whole Renaissance fascination with the idea of "method"—reflects the general need to order any given universe of decontextualized objects.[29]

Of the many factors contributing to the new, more abstract view of the world, typographic literacy was the most pervasive. While Europeans could remain immune to the skeptical relativism inherent in Reformation debates, and the cultural relativism implicit in overseas discoveries, they could not escape the cognitive repercussions of newly acquired literacy, which contributed to a compulsion for order. In and of itself, though, the effect of printing need not have been problematic, for the humanist program of education imparted a means of interpreting the world according to universal moral norms that served to order experience. But humanist education linked this normative view of the world to a skeptical habit of mind. As advances in classical scholarship undermined accepted norms, skepticism would become exacerbated, thus increasing the compulsion for order. Let us now turn to the practice of education, which in conjunction with typographic literacy and humanist scholarship, conspired to create the problem of relativism.

The Humanist Program of Education

During the sixteenth century, the humanist curriculum became established in schools extending from London to Cracow. It is a truism that every educational system is outdated at its very inception, being imposed by an older generation on a younger one, whose world is necessarily different. But the humanist program of education was in crucial ways uniquely unsuited to the world in which it flourished. It was based upon the internalization and manipulation of a storehouse of knowledge whose foundation had been laid by a largely oral culture, one chiefly concerned with preserving the traditional stock of wisdom. It inspired a normative frame of mind increasingly disconsonant with a rapidly changing world, characterized by religious strife, overseas discoveries, and scholarly advances—the impact of all of which was redoubled by printing. Of course most students, even in their later years, would never question their education; and humanist schools long remained successful at producing the literate elite demanded by a court society. But those exceptional thinkers who did begin to question their education faced the extraordinary problem of having to restructure the storehouse, which threatened to collapse into decontextualized bits of information. For them, humanist education reacted with the unique cultural forces of the age to heighten the problem of relativism.

The humanist curriculum emphasized the study of classical languages, with primacy placed on Latin.[30] Humanists regarded Latin as the medium of eloquence, and eloquence as the means of applying wisdom to human affairs; indeed, for the humanists (as for their beloved Cicero) true eloquence was wisdom. Theirs was an ideal of practical wisdom for daily life, as opposed to the supposedly useless philosophical abstractions of the scholastics; it emphasized the role of the will in human affairs, rather than that of reason, and the art of persuasion rather than the science of logic.[31] The contention that the study of letters could provide practical wisdom was based on two assumptions, that universal norms, or "commonplaces," underlay the apparent diversity of examples found in humane letters, and that these norms could be illuminated by the skeptical mode of reasoning *in utramque partem,* on both sides of a question. These two assumptions comprised what I shall refer to as the intellectual system of "commonplace thought."

In the Renaissance, commonplaces were known interchangeably as either *loci* or *loci communes;* but in antiquity these two terms had different meanings. *Loci* were universal categories of argumentation by means of which all statements could be analyzed, mental "places" where one searched for knowledge. *Loci communes* were those expressions and ideas acceptable to all listeners, "commonplaces" embodying the traditional wisdom of society. The heavy reliance that the ancients placed on these rhetorical devices is characteristic of a largely oral culture, for they helped preserve a store of knowledge that might simply have been forgotten were it not constantly reiterated.[32]

Classical rhetoricans used *loci* and *loci communes* to construct arguments *in utramque partem.*[33] Aristotle had originated this technique of arguing on both sides of a question in order to establish verisimilitude where truth could not be ascertained, reasoning that the probability of a proposition increased in proportion to the improbability of its opposite. His technique was later adopted by the Academic skeptics, who denied that one could ascertain any truths, thus limiting all human knowledge to verisimilitude revealed by discoursing *in utramque partem.* In his orations, Cicero combined this skeptical mode of reasoning with the judicious use of *loci* and *loci communes.* He used *loci* to generate arguments juxtaposed *in utramque partem;* and he attempted to reduce all debates to *loci communes,* theses acceptable to both sides, which he then explored *in utramque partem.*[34] Whereas Cicero applied these procedures chiefly to forensic rhetoric, medieval and Renaissance rhetoricians applied them to an oratory that addressed Christian moral concerns. The moral thrust of Christian oratory gradually transformed the *loci* from categories of argumentation to those virtues and vices; they thus tended to become fused with the *loci communes* representing the traditional wisdom of society.[35] Out of this fusion emerged a system of commonplace thought that classified knowledge in mental places embodying the traditional wisdom of society, which could be exploited by arguing *in utramque partem.*

Through its emphasis on Latin eloquence, the humanist program of education inculcated an intellectual system that united a normative view of the world with a skeptical mode of thinking, balancing one against the other. In a largely oral culture, concerned with the preservation of the traditional stock of wisdom, this balance was maintained by anchoring the skeptical habit of mind with commonplace norms. But the spread of typographic literacy made this balance increasingly precarious, first, by expanding the stock of wisdom to the point where commonplaces threatened to burst from within, and, second, by encouraging a more abstract view of the world that threatened to overwhelm commonplaces from without. We shall now see how these threats were forestalled by the use of increasingly elaborate classificatory schemata to accommodate the growing diversity of information. But such techniques for broadening and deepening the traditional normative view of the world enabled the European mind to control the problem of relativism only until commonplaces began to break down, after which the skepticism they had held in check was unleashed.[36]

In humanist schools, commonplace thought was enhanced by the use of notebooks, known as commonplace books, that aided students in the emulation of classical Latin. Petrarch, among other early humanists, had anticipated this practice of note-taking. He recommended annotating and cross-referencing one's readings in order to provide a stock of words, idioms, and ideas for use in one's own compositions. Leonardo Bruni first suggested keeping these references in notebooks, and Guarino da Verona later proposed using two kinds of notebooks—the *methodice* (containing rhetorical forms and idioms) and the *historice* (containing general information). Because the latter could easily become disorganized, Rudolf Agricola recommended classifying its contents under headings (*loci*) paired with their opposites for easy recall—like virtue and vice, love and hate, life and death—in the manner of medieval sermon books. The *historice,* later known as the *liber locorum rerum,* was the largest and most important of the commonplace books.[37]

Erasmus adapted Agricola's plan for a *liber locorum rerum* to the world of typographic literacy, making its categories more elaborate to accommodate a wider range of information. In *De copia* he declared that a learned man is one who has read through the entire corpus of classical literature at least once with pen and notebook at hand—an undertaking made possible by the spread of printing. He outlined a *liber locorum rerum* comprised of three groups of *loci.* The first group consists of paired virtues and vices, such as piety and impiety, which are in turn divided into subheadings, such as piety (or impiety) toward God, the fatherland, the family, and so on. These pairs of *loci* are to be listed alphabetically, or according to some other system of recall. The second group of *loci* consists of *exempla,* categories of unusual examples—extraordinary longevity, vigorous old age, senile youth, and so forth—which are also to be paired with their opposites. The third group are the *loci communes*—maxims or proverbs, like "He gives twice who gives quickly"—which are to be entered with the two previous groups of *loci,* from which they are derived. Erasmus urged students to exercise their ingenuity in deriving as many *loci communes* as possible from the noteworthy examples in their readings.[38]

This form of textual analysis serves to distill enduring moral norms from a diverse and fluctuating world. Erasmus encouraged students to extract moral content from even the most unlikely sources, such as mathematics and geometry: "No learning is so far removed from rhetoric that you may not enrich your classifications from it. . . . For example, a wise man, happy in his wealth, not dependent on anyone else, constant and unmoved in his own virtue whatever way the winds of fortune blow, is compared with a sphere everywhere similar to itself."[39] The sphere is an *exemplum* of wisdom and a symbol of the *locus communis* that the wise man is self-sufficient. The *loci* of a commonplace book thus represent not arbitrary categories but the moral substratum of reality. Melanchthon sums up this attitude when he remarks in one of his own textbooks on rhetoric that the *loci* used in note-taking are elicited from the innermost foundations of nature and thus represent the essential "forms" of all things: *ex intimis naturae sedibus eruti, formae sunt seu regulae omnium rerum.*[40]

The influence of this notebook technique on the theory and practice of education was enormous. Erasmus's *De copia* was one of the most popular textbooks in history; over one hundred editions were published in the sixteenth century alone. Its remarks on note-taking were also excerpted and published separately, together with those of other famous humanists like Agricola and Melanchthon. After mid-century virtually every progressive educational treatise included a discussion of note-taking and recommendations for structuring a *liber locorum rerum.*

Humanist schools favored the compilation of commonplace books. This is apparent not only from the many treatises on educational theory but also from the rare accounts of educational practice. In regard to the latter, two sources are particularly valuable: the *Schola Aquitanica,* which describes the curriculum at the Collège de Guyenne while Montaigne was a student there; and the Jesuit *Ratio studiorum* of 1599, which, in conjunction with part 4 of the *Constitutiones Societatis Jesu,* describes the type of humanistic education that Descartes received at the Collège de La Flèche. Montaigne and Descartes were the foremost graduates of the foremost schools of their day, which inculcated a system of commonplace thought that each man would, in his own particular way, overturn.[41]

Our two sources describe essentially the same pattern of education, despite over seventy years intervening between Montaigne's boyhood and Descartes's. Students would read a passage from a classical text at home and copy it into a notebook, leaving extra space between each line. They carried this notebook to school in lieu of the text itself. In class the teacher would analyze the passage word by word, identifying parts of speech, indicating striking phrases and idioms, and elucidating commonplaces, along with examples in the passage illustrating each commonplace. As the teacher analyzed the passage, his students would gloss it in their notebooks, using the extra space left for this purpose. When they returned home, they would generally copy their notes into three separate commonplace books, a *liber styli* that served as a reference grammar, a *liber sermonis* that served to provide eloquent expressions for their compositions, and a *liber locorum rerum* that served as a storehouse of moral examples.[42]

Students in humanist schools generally worked from notebooks rather than from classical texts themselves, which were usually left at home. This practice indicates that reading was not emphasized; rather, students were drilled in the grammar and rhetoric requisite for effective speaking and writing. Throughout his seven-year course of instruction at the Collège de Guyenne, for example, Montaigne hardly read more than some Cicero, Terence, Ovid, and Horace. In class these texts were minutely analyzed for their grammatical and rhetorical content, in which he was drilled relentlessly. This regimen illuminates his complaint that the Collège instilled a hatred of books.[43] Students were encouraged, not to search for knowledge, but to present it effectively. This emphasis is characteristic of commonplace thought, for the task of presenting knowledge stored in *loci* required more skill than finding it.[44]

Humanist education fostered contentment with the storehouse of knowledge at a time when its foundations were being progressively undermined. As this structure weakened, the balance between the normative and skeptical views of the world was disturbed, engendering a form of skeptical relativism. The humanist program of education inculcated the very skeptical techniques that would eventually bring about the downfall of commonplace thought, thus intensifying the problem of relativism and exciting the need for a new, more comprehensive ordering of reality.

Humanistically trained students used the material in their commonplace books to formulate discourses *in utramque partem*. This pattern of thinking from both sides—already implicit in the organization of notebooks that paired contrasting *loci*—was made explicit through constant exercises in disputation. Unlike the medieval practice of logical disputation, the humanistic practice was specifically rhetorical, concerned with probability rather than certainty, and persuasion rather than proof. In these exercises, students were encouraged to demonstrate their virtuosity in manipulating the common stock of words, idioms, ideas, and examples to form persuasive arguments.

A spirit of rivalry and emulation spurred students to ever greater virtuosity in their disputations. In the Collge de Guyenne, the best students sat on the first bench, the second best on the next bench, and so forth. During class, students on the first bench drilled those on the second, while those on the third tested their opposites on the fourth, and so on. A student's position in the classroom advanced or regressed according to his daily performance; he could even challenge someone ahead of him and win his seat.[45] The Jesuits further refined this arrangement by dividing every class into two camps, each of which was led by a select group of student "officers," hierarchically ordered, with titles drawn from ancient political or military appellations, such as *senator, tribune, praetor,* and *emperor.* Every soldier, down to the lowest private, had his counterpart in the opposing camp, with whom he would engage in constant struggle, challenging and correcting his classroom performance; he was even encouraged to keep a ready eye on the performance of his superiors, whom he could challenge and supplant.[46] The very organization of the humanist classroom thus fostered the spirit of rivalry necessary for vigorous disputation.

The explication of texts formed the primary period of instruction in humanist schools, repeated up to three times a day. As a rule each of these sessions culminated with a disputation. During these exercises, students questioned each other on the previous lesson. In elementary classes, they tested each other on grammatical points; in more advanced classes, they disputed *in utramque partem.* The teacher would customarily assign one group of students the task of defending a proposition and another group that of attacking it—for example, they might dispute whether Brutus was justified in killing Caesar. After the completion of this assignment, they were often made to switch sides. Students thus became skilled in the presentation of knowledge; they learned to think and speak *in utramque partem.*

Daily disputations within each class were supplemented by daily and weekly ones between classes. This practice transformed the humanist school into a competitive arena in which younger students were encouraged to emulate older ones. The intense spirit of rivalry, fostered both within and between classes, honed each student's competitive edge. He learned to be quick-witted and facile with his knowledge, eager and able to defend or attack any proposition from a variety of perspectives. This facility was further encouraged by the practice of having individual students periodically present their own compositions, in prose or verse, before the entire school. Students composed these recitations either in advance, on assigned topics, or extemporaneously on subjects proposed then and there "to discover their readiness." The threat of extemporaneous exercises forced students to internalize the material in their notebooks, thus instilling not only the rules of grammar and rhetoric but also the moral view of the world for which eloquence served as the handmaiden.[47]

The intellectual system inculcated by humanist education is strikingly apparent in the annotations Montaigne made in his copy of Nicole Gilles's *Annales et chroniques de France,* which he read around 1564, about eighteen years after his graduation from the Collège de Guyenne. These annotations—all the more remarkable for being private—reveal the presence of a commonplace reflex that anchored a skeptical habit of mind. In Gilles's chronicle, Montaigne encountered a passage relating how a father had commanded his son to attack a man with whom the son had previously sworn a truce. Montaigne noted that this story might serve as the basis for a discourse on whether a paternal command can supersede a son's other obligations: "It would be possible to draw from here the foundation of such a discourse: if the authority of paternal commandment could release the son from his promise. Our history furnishes us with enough examples of popes, kings, and magistrates who do it; but fathers are subordinate to them. Which leads me to that perfect virtue of the ancient Romans and Greeks—indeed, I know I will find that the magistrate would never undertake it, but to the contrary."[48]

Although Montaigne's argument here is only a sketch, it clearly reveals the balance between normative and skeptical tendencies instilled by his education. He starts with a general question concerning the nature of paternal authority, which he explores with reference to particular examples, like those found in a *liber locorum rerum.* His argument clearly proceeds *in utramque partem.* On the one hand, modern magistrates (taken as father figures) claim the ultimate allegiance of their citizens; on the other, fathers do not have the authority of magistrates in modern society. And again, whereas modern magistrates hardly scruple to compromise their citizens' personal obligations, ancient magistrates—in their "perfect virtue"—would never have assumed such authority. The entire argument devolves upon this observation about the "perfect virtue" of the ancients. Thus, Montaigne anchored his argument *in utramque partem* with an accepted cultural norm that enabled him to arbitrate between contrasting positions.

Montaigne probably noted this passage in Gilles because he sensed an underlying commonplace. Doubtless, the story recalled his love and respect for his own father, to whom Montaigne was especially devoted. Yet he did not sketch a discourse on whether *he* should respect his father's wishes regardless of his own obligations. Rather, he outlined it in terms of paternal authority in general, as if the whole range of examples from ancient and modern history could be distilled into a single moral statement—a commonplace that could serve as a universal rule of conduct.

Commonplaces of this sort eventually became undermined by the very classical revival that had spurred their use. To some extent, this degenerative process was inherent in the humanistic ideal of *imitatio*. The imitation of ancient literary models led either to the slavish following of classical style—which Erasmus derided as "Ciceronianism"—or to the creative emulation of its spirit. The latter course entailed "digesting" an ancient model, which could then be transformed for modern use. In effect, the practice of *emulatio* heightened the awareness of anachronism, for the differences between antiquity and modernity became the area in which the modern author attempted to transcend his classical model and establish his own originality. The growing sense of anachronism inherent in the ideal of *imitatio* helped pave the way for a historical and cultural relativism that made commonplace norms increasingly difficult to establish.[49]

Yet the rudest shock to the normative view of the world came not from literary theory and practice—which, despite the sense of anachronism, were still patterned on classical models—but from advances in legal scholarship, which called the very authority of classical precedents into question. The application of humanist philological techniques to the study of Roman law demonstrated the relativity of laws and institutions, undercutting the notion of any normative standard derived from antiquity. The popularity of legal education in France grew apace with the royal bureaucracy, increasing the general awareness of the problem of relativism. Indeed, the education of virtually every one of the figures we shall examine culminated with the study of law. It is to the "French historical school of law" that we shall now turn, for legal scholarship was perhaps the initial corrosive of commonplace thought. Once this intellectual system was sufficiently weakened, it began to self-destruct, engendering skeptical relativism and, ultimately, the compulsive need to order reality.

Legal Scholarship and the Rise of Historical Relativism

Modern philology originated in fifteenth-century Italy, where humanists began to restore classical language and literature to their original purity, hoping to resurrect the spirit of classical culture. This goal encouraged the development of philological techniques for identifying the errors and anachronisms introduced into classical texts by earlier scribes and for substituting appropriate terminology. Prior to the end of the fifteenth century, humanists like Lorenzo Valla and Angelo Poliziano had argued that their philological techniques should be applied to a study of the text of Roman law, Justinian's *Corpus juris civilis.* The reigning tradition of medieval jurisprudence, derived from Bartolus of Sassoferrato, treated Roman law as an internally consistent body of universal law, to be freely interpreted for application to the modern world. The humanists, however, called for a philological analysis of the text in order to establish its true meaning before applying it to contemporary legal problems.[50]

The French implemented the program of "legal humanism" recommended by the Italians. In 1508 Guillaume Budé published his annotations on the first twenty-four books of the Pandects, the most important part of the *Corpus juris.* His philological studies undermined medieval jurisprudence by demonstrating that the Bartolists had worked from defective manuscripts that obscured the meaning of Roman law. Even where their texts were accurate, Budé showed, they had nonetheless misinterpreted the law through ignorance of Roman history and culture. In effect, his research implied that Roman law was not universal law but rather the law of a past society, promulgated in response to that society's own particular needs.[51]

Although Budé had studied law in his youth, he was not a lawyer; it remained for an Italian professor of law sojourning in France, Andrea Alciato, to incorporate Budé's philological approach to Roman law into the French legal curriculum. By the time Alciato returned to Italy in 1532, he had helped establish the University of Bourges as the chief center for the new, humanistic study of law, which became known as the *mos gallicus docendi*—or "French manner of teaching" Roman law—as opposed to the *mos italicus* of the Bartolists. For Alciato, philology remained the handmaiden of law, helping illuminate the universal legal principles of the *Corpus juris;* his most famous successor at Bourges, Jacques Cujas, subsequently elevated it to the reigning principle of all legal scholarship. Instead of focusing on the *Corpus juris* as the chief expression of Roman law, Cujas used it to illuminate the sources from which it derived; he was less concerned with the modern application of Roman law than with its historical reconstruction. Cujas's historical study of law made the legal relativism implicit in Budé's research more explicit.[52]

Historical scholarship introduced a "discontinuity" between past and present by placing Roman law in the context of an ancient world that was very different from the modern one.[53] This discontinuity represents the thin edge of relativism. The historical view of Roman law, for example, implicitly called into question the very notion of history as the *magistra vitae,* the mistress of life—how could one derive practical lessons from a past whose circumstances were radically different from those of the present? And this question, in turn, began to undermine the very foundations of commonplace thought, for how could one find underlying moral norms when human behavior was contingent upon circumstances?

French legal scholarship in particular, and the classical revival in general, raised the problem of relativism for the European mind at a time when it was still grappling with the effects of typographic literacy. The result was the decontextualization not only of words but also of ideas, putting great strain on the normative view of the world that held the humanist intellectual system together. And as these norms weakened, the skeptical mode of reasoning they held in check was exacerbated. Sixteenth-century thinkers need not have worked out this equation in self-conscious detail to have instinctively felt themselves threatened by relativism.[54]

Cujas's successor at Bourges, François Hotman, exemplifies the ambivalence of sixteenth-century Frenchmen toward a legal and historical relativism that potentially undermined accepted norms. Hotman wrote his *Antitribonian* in response to the growing vogue of legal education, which was producing a crowd of lawyers more familiar with Roman than with French law. The *Antitribonian* combines a critique of the study of Roman law with a critique of the work of Tribonian, the editor selected by Justinian to compile the digest of Roman law. Hotman's polemic makes explicit the legal and historical relativism implicit in the *mos gallicus,* for which he would propose a metanormative solution.[55]

Hotman begins by asserting that public law is relative to the historical circumstances of a state. Each of the three types of government—monarchy, aristocracy, and democracy—has a different form of law; and within each type, every state is itself unique. Indeed, according to Hotman, the laws of each state are themselves in flux, "often changing according to the seasons, and the mutation of the manners and condition of a people."[56] In other words, the public law of Rome, governing the form of its civil institutions, reflected the changing historical circumstances of that state and thus cannot be applied to France.

Hotman then proceeds to demonstrate that not only the public but also the private law of Rome is inapplicable to France. Through a detailed analysis of the categories of private law, Hotman shows that Roman terminology and practice reflected the changing historical circumstances of the Roman state, and thus are inapplicable to France. For example, the Roman distinction between property acquired by special and ordinary procedures reflected the original distinction between the citizens of the Roman republic and those of neighboring, allied states, a distinction rendered meaningless when Roman citizenship became universal throughout the empire. Surely, argues Hotman, this distinction is even more meaningless to a modern Frenchman than to a Roman of the later empire. He maintains that French law students should study the chief administrative, judicial, and financial institutions of their own realm, rather than the laws and institutions of Rome and Constantinople.[57]

Whereas his predecessor Cujas pursued the philological analysis of the *Corpus juris* purely as a matter of historical interest, Hotman concludes his critique by showing that the *Corpus juris* is virtually worthless even for the historical study of Roman law in view of the improbity of Tribonian and the incompetence of his assistants. Charged by Justinian with the task of codifying Roman law, Tribonian had faced the enormous problem of sorting through a myriad of sometimes contradictory laws extending all the way back to the period of the kingship. He and his sixteen assistants tackled this job with perhaps too much energy, reducing over two thousand volumes of jurisprudence to fifty in barely six years. Hotman argues that neither Tribonian nor his assistants were really up to this task. The latter were not even native speakers of Latin but rather Greeks confronted with the task of interpreting very obscure and difficult Latin texts. And Tribonian himself was morally unfit to understand the civic virtue that had animated Roman law. Thus the *Corpus juris*—compiled in haste by editors devoid of Roman virtue, unfamiliar with the Latin language, and ignorant of Roman law—is a document unworthy of historical interest; it embodies not the grandeur of Roman civilization but the decadence of its own age. Indeed, Hotman even implies that it is useless for understanding Byzantine law and history.[58]

No sooner does he demolish the *Corpus juris* than Hotman paradoxically gives it pride of place in the proposal for legal reform that concludes the *Antitribonian*. Under the "new Solon," Michel de l'Hôpital, the time is ripe to assemble a commission of jurisconsults and statesmen to distill from the laws of the most noteworthy peoples a new body of universal law. For example, Hotman recommends that the commission examine the laws of Moses in order to draw from them not the specific regulations governing the Jewish kingdom but rather those general ones, "founded on a natural justice, reason, and equity." The universal law abstracted from the "natural equity" inherent in each body of law can, with slight modifications, be adjusted to the needs and circumstances of any state. In this undertaking the *Corpus juris* will be like a "priceless treasury," where one can find "all the best and most admirable things." Indeed, it will provide not only some of the best examples of "natural equity" but also the principle for the organization of the new legal code. Hotman thus transcended historical relativism with a metanormative program of "neo-Bartolism" that preserved the primacy of the *Corpus juris*.[59]

The paradoxical, "Pro-Tribonian" conclusion of the *Antitribonian* underscores Hotman's profound ambivalence toward the weapon of historical and cultural relativism that he wielded. Some scholars have interpreted this paradox in terms of the distinction between public and private law introduced at the beginning of the work. Public law necessarily reflected historical circumstances, whereas private law could still be analyzed according to the universal principles evident in the *Corpus juris*. Seen from this perspective, Hotman's detailed analysis of the differences between Roman and French private law serves not to demonstrate the relativity of all private law in general but rather the need for a codification of French private law in particular. He had criticized Cujas's purely philological study of Roman law because it obscured the need for the proposed reform of private law.[60]

The only problem with this interpretation is that Hotman does not rigorously maintain the distinction between public and private law. In one crucial passage, he includes both in his new code: "These commissioners may produce one or two good books written in the vernacular and in intelligible language, as much as of public law, which deals with matters of the state and the crown, as of all parts of private law."[61] This passage has led one scholar to conclude that Hotman did not conceive of an absolute dichotomy between the historical nature of public law and the universal nature of private law; rather, "both public law and private law were amenable to both universal and historical principles, but each to a differing degree."[62]

This conclusion highlights Hotman's ambivalence. Were he to have asserted the fully historical nature of public law, he would have undermined the possibility of codifying private law on the basis of universal principles. If public law were solely a function of the historical circumstance of a state, what would have kept Hotman from ultimately concluding that private law, too, was solely a function of the circumstances of individuals in a state? Indeed, he had already come dangerously close to this conclusion by showing that French private law reflected feudal social relationships that had no parallel in Roman law.[63] Although he may have undertaken this comparison to highlight the need for a new codification of private law of more universal value than the Roman one, he pursued this normative end by way of intensely relativistic means. The very acuteness of his sense of relativity compelled him to assert, if only as an afterthought, that public law, too, had normative characteristics, lest he undermine his whole enterprise.

Perhaps Hotman's ambivalence toward relativism is only to be expected in a work primarily concerned with the codification of private law, but it is also apparent in his subsequent inquiry into the origins of French public law. As an examination of the "ancient constitution" of France, the *Francogallia* complements the treatment of private law in the *Antitribonian*. The two works, however, are radically different in style. Whereas the *Antitribonian* is a polemical treatise, the *Francogallia* is an antiquarian one, purporting to be a dispassionate examination of the fundamental law of France that originated when the Frankish and Gallic peoples were united by the Merovingians.[64] The ancient constitution Hotman describes is ultimately based on the classical ideal of mixed government, combining monarchic, aristocratic, and democratic elements. Hotman extols this mixed constitution as the most perfect form of government, citing the authority of Plato, Aristotle, Polybius, and especially Cicero; and he establishes its universality as a political norm by referring to examples of noteworthy states both ancient and modern. So universal is this norm that long before their union both the ancient Gauls and the Franks had adopted it as the basis for their separate constitutions. Hotman thus subsumed the historical nature of public law under a political ideal, which provided him with the means of ordering a historical reality that threatened to become too complex.[65]

Human beings naturally tend to order and classify their experience of the world; but in the sixteenth century, various factors conspired to transform this natural tendency into a compulsion. Typographic literacy entailed the decontextualization of words and ideas, giving impetus to more abstract forms of classification. In the very process of responding to this stimulus, the humanist program of education intensified it by linking commonplace norms to a skeptical mode of thinking. The more complex view of the world afforded by advances in classical scholarship weakened established commonplaces, hence strengthening the tendency toward skeptical relativism and redoubling the initial impetus toward new forms of classification. The compulsion for order thus became one of the distinctive characteristics of the sixteenth-century mind.

As old norms began to lose their force, the simplest and most immediate recourse was to ascend to a metanormative level. Hotman, for example, adopted a "neo-Bartolist" project that aimed at supplanting Roman law with a new form of universal law. He assumed that the comparative study of legal history would reveal the principles of "natural equity" underlying the apparent diversity of laws and institutions.[66] Although Hotman only mentioned the project in passing, his contemporary, Jean Bodin, described it in greater detail. In the *Methodus ad facilem historiarum cognitionem,* Bodin elaborated a system of commonplaces for the organization of history, in which "the best part of universal law lies hidden":

> Such is the multiplicity and disorder of human activities, such the abundant supply of histories, that unless the actions and affairs of men are confined to certain definite types, historical works obviously cannot be understood, or their precepts long retained in mind. What scholars, then, are accustomed to do to assist memory in other arts should, I think, be done for history also. That is, similar instances of memorable matters should be placed in a certain definite order, so that from these, as from a treasure chest, we may bring forth a variety of examples to direct our acts.

He argued that of the plans, words, and deeds that comprise human activity, only the words had previously been collected. He now wanted to extend humanist notebook technique to encompass plans and deeds, creating a would-be *liber locorum historiarum* that would help reveal the principles of universal law.[67]

Bodin's commonplace book would be organized according to the nature and purpose of human activity in general, starting with self-preservation and culminating with contemplation. This abstract, hierarchical arrangement would be further subdivided into pairs of contrasting *loci*, such as life and death, riches and poverty, pleasure and pain, beauty and deformity, and ignorance and knowledge. Furthermore, the contents of each *locus* would be glossed with marginal notations indicating the kinds of moral norms illustrated. The metanormative impulse of the neo-Bartolists thus derived its chief support from the system of commonplace thought that was most threatened by relativism.[68]

It was difficult for Europeans to break the deeply engrained commonplace reflex—and we shall encounter it again and again, even among those who consciously tried to transcend it. Yet, as the diversity of the world became more problematic, and the schemes for classifying it became more complex, a countervailing tendency emerged from within this very habit of mind. The urge to put each "bit" of historical information in its appropriate place necessarily encouraged an individualizing view of entities, thus heightening the awareness of their relativity. For example, La Popelinière's list in the *Dessein* might appear to be little more than the outline for a historical commonplace book divided into topics, such as social structure, civil administration, ecclesiastical institutions, and military organization. But the obsessive detail of the work overwhelms the topical organization. This detail reflects La Popelinière's profound concern for the uniqueness of the historical entities that comprised France, each one of which contributed ineffably to the whole. The desire to understand the role of these unique entities in the formation of France led La Popelinière to illuminate the interconnections between them, thus transforming his proposed history into a list. We shall now turn to the new view of historical reality that began to emerge from French legal humanism, our chief concern being to explore the relationship between the compulsion for order and early modern historical consciousness.

CHAPTER 2

THE ORDER OF HISTORY

The Traditional Way of Thinking

Scholars influenced by the *mos gallicus* branched off in two directions. We have already seen how one group followed a metanormative approach to historical and cultural relativism, seeking to identify the similarities underlying apparently diverse entities. Now we shall see how another group took a more historical approach by attempting to understand such entities in their own terms. We should be careful, though, not to distinguish too sharply between these two approaches, for they diverged from a common philosophical path. In the sixteenth century, the techniques both for classifying entities and for analyzing their distinctiveness derived from the traditional Aristotelian way of thinking.

Aristotle had articulated a logical means of classifying diverse entities according to their common properties. He assumed that the mind had direct access to the extra-mental world by means of the senses, which conveyed to the mind a faithful image of the external object. The mind then transformed this image into a "mental extract" by focusing on one aspect of the image to the exclusion of others. By differentiating the specific properties of the "mental extract" from the surrounding sensory information, the mind was able produce concepts delimiting the nature of the external object. It could then group the concepts it apprehended according to their shared properties, establishing subspecies, whose commonalities themselves comprised species, which, in turn, comprised genera. The metanormative project of the neo-Bartolists and, indeed, the whole system of commonplace thought derived from the transposition of Aristotelian logical analysis to the historical and moral realms.[1]

An idea of "substance" underlay Aristotelian logic, assuring that one's classifications were not arbitrary but reflected the nature of reality. According to Aristotle, substance was a composite of matter and form, which were less physical than metaphysical attributes of an entity. All temporal or worldly substances were subject to change, conceived of as not an arbitrary but a determined process. A thing could become only what it had the potential to become; matter continuously "strove," as it were, to achieve its inherent form. This process was understood in four ways explaining the "reasons why" a thing had those qualities that characterized it as a particular kind of thing. Aristotle enumerated four "reasons why," the Greek term for which Cicero subsequently translated as *causae,* hence popularizing the notion of the four causes: the material (from what a thing derived), the efficient (by what agent it was made), the formal (with what conception it was made), and the final (for what end it was made). In the traditional way of thinking, all exact knowledge—*scientia*—was knowledge of causes, which enabled one to distinguish the essence of a substance from its accidents.[2]

Whereas the neo-Bartolists relied on the logic of classification to establish the similarities underlying diversity, others seeking to understand the uniqueness of historical entities relied on the "science" of causation. For example, in the preface to his first history of France, La Popelinière wrote, "The most true and certain knowledge of a thing is to know and comprehend it by its cause and origin"; and in his chief theoretical work, the *Idée de l'histoire accomplie,* he stated, "Of the sciences, those are perfect which are acquired through the knowledge of causes; and those are imperfect, in which causes are ignored."[3] By definition, "perfect" history entailed a knowledge of causes that clarified the unique essence of historical entities. Following common usage, La Popelinière termed the essential nature of these entities their "substance."

The "science" of history emerged largely in response to historical Pyrrhonism, a skeptical attitude toward knowledge of the past that blossomed in the Renaissance. One effect of the growing critical interest in history was to encourage doubts about the veracity of historical acccounts. For example, Cornelius Agrippa and Charles de la Ruelle contended that the numerous instances of error and outright mendacity in histories were sufficient grounds to impugn all historians. Francesco Patrizi supplied such hypercritical arguments with a convincing theoretical dimension. He reasoned that the best historians had witnessed the events they described, either as participants or as neutral observers; but participants always wrote biased accounts, while neutral observers—ignorant of either side's secrets—always wrote superficial ones. Patrizi hoped by this line of argument to encourage a more critical understanding of the past, which could be achieved by focusing less on the partisan account of events than on the impartial description of institutions.[4]

It remained for French scholars, influenced by the *mos gallicus* and impelled by the Wars of Religion, to elaborate upon the program of institutional history suggested by Patrizi. In so doing they relied on the Aristotelian notion of causation to provide them with an "exact" knowledge of the origins and mutations of the kingdom of France. As we shall see, the traditional way of thinking was transformed when applied to this historical task. Of the four causes, the material one received the most emphasis, leading to a fascination with the origins, or "first cause," of a people or state, from which all of its manifestations derived. This emphasis on material causation itself transformed the related activity of classification. In place of the neo-Bartolist attempt to transcend diversity, historians began to construct cultural taxonomies that served to explain it. The traditional way of thinking offered them a means of ordering decontextualized entities in a hierarchy that charted the unfolding of each unique people from its origins in the remote past. This notion of an entity's unfolding from its genus into its species and subspecies provided the ultimate explanation of historical change.

We shall explore this form of historical consciousness with reference to three figures, whose responses to the problem of relativism embody complementary aspects of the "science" of history. La Popelinière's theory of "perfect history" reveals the philosophical assumptions underlying sixteenth-century French historical thought, assumptions highlighted by his compulsive list-making. Nicolas Vignier's "historical library" exemplifies the practical application of La Popelinière's theory, fully displaying its inherent encyclopedic aspect. And Estienne Pasquier's project of "researches" provides an alternative to this encyclopedism, but one that further underscores the taxonomic nature of historical understanding. Confronted with the problem of relativism, historians had natural recourse to the traditional Aristotelian way of thinking, which accounts for the distinctive shape and texture of historical thought on the threshold of modernity.

The Challenge of Historical Pyrrhonism

La Popelinière's initial exposure to historical and cultural relativity probably derived from a legal education. He was born into a family of new or aspiring nobility—his mother was the daughter of a merchant and his father a man-at-arms who had retired to his country estate. Like many of his social status, La Popelinière seems to have been destined for a career in the royal bureaucracy. Judging from the classical allusions in his works, and from his remark that he studied Greek with Adrien Turnèbe, one of the great classical scholars of the day, we may assume that La Popelinière received a humanist education. He subsequently enrolled at the University of

Toulouse, where he presumably studied law, as did most of those intending to enter the magistracy.[5]

In the mid sixteenth century, Toulouse was an important center for the *mos gallicus,* despite the university's occasional hostility to this method of teaching.[6] Many of the great figures of the historical school of law were affiliated with the university during this period, among them Jacques Cujas, Jean Bodin, and Jean de Coras. La Popelinière studied there until 1562, when the Protestants were driven from the city at the outbreak of the Wars of Religion. He then abandoned his studies for a military career, serving with distinction as an officer in the Huguenot armies. In 1571, after the peace of Saint-Germain, he published *La Vraye Entiere Histoire des troubles et chose memorables . . . depuis l'an 1562,* his account of the first phase of the Wars of Religion and the nucleus of his *Histoire de France.* The prefatory letter to this work contains the earliest expression of his theory of perfect history, which he articulated in response to the problem of relativism engendered by scholarly developments.

In this "Epistre à la noblesse," La Popelinière tried to convince the French nobility of the efficacy of reading histories. Traditionally history had been regarded as philosophy teaching by examples; its lessons were considered directly relevant to the present, providing guidance in political, military, and moral life. La Popelinière's readers might have expected him to demonstrate the utility of history in the traditional manner, expatiating on the Ciceronian praise of history as the witness of the past, the light of truth, the life of memory, the mistress of life, and the herald of ancient days. Instead, he declared most histories unworthy of this praise.

According to La Popelinière, most historians are either too ignorant to render events accurately or too biased by obligations to party and patron. Even if one can find an impartial historian, his account usually derives from third-hand sources. And even if he relied on eyewitnesses, they were rarely privy to the underlying causes of events, the secret plans and motives known only by the principal historical actors. How can one profit from an inaccurate description of events, or from an accurate one lacking an account of underlying causes? Those who try to apply the lessons learned from such imperfect accounts usually come to grief, thus discrediting the utility of history in general.

This preface basically marshals Francesco Patrizi's arguments for historical Pyrrhonism in an attack on humanist historiography, which sacrificed accuracy for eloquence and honesty for flattery. La Popelinière had nothing but disdain for humanist historians, dismissing them as "fly-by-nights who were not called to so honorable a vocation"; their distortions had cast the great deeds of the French into "the most profound shadows of a base oblivion." He used the arguments of historical Pyrrhonism, however, to question not only humanist historiography, which chiefly recounted recent events, but also the possibility of any knowledge about the distant French past. Information about the ancient Gauls, he lamented, is necessarily both inadequate and inaccurate. One cannot know anything about them other than what the Romans have deigned to record—they who have only "touched with their little finger the condition and affairs of our ancestors." Worse yet, the Romans grudgingly recorded only the greatest exploits and achievements of the Gauls, "making us presume the state of these peoples greater, more excellent, and more virtuous than perhaps it was." La Popelinière's observations demonstrate how advances in humanist scholarship had increased, rather than decreased, the challenge of historical Pyrrhonism by revealing fundamental differences, not only between past and present but also between the contemporary cultures of antiquity. The new, more critical view of sources called the very possibility of historical knowledge into question.

In responding to this challenge, La Popelinière offered his first, tentative conception of perfect history. Much of what he said was commonplace to the popular genre of the *ars historica,* handbooks concerning the methods and attributes of a good historian: that he should have made a "profession of arms," that he should be experienced in affairs of state, and that he should have a thorough knowledge of letters. But La Popelinière also wanted the historian to be able to profit from accounts of the "establishment, progress, changes, and ruin of commonwealths, or from the police, laws, ordinances, magistrates, officers and other such political matters." In other words, the perfect historian should combine a soldier's knowledge of war and a statesman's knowledge of high politics with a magistrate's knowledge of laws and institutions: "That is to say, a personage worthy of so serious a project [*dessein*] as a historical account of the whole state of affairs of France." And who had the breadth of vision equal to this undertaking? Clearly, La Popelinière was thinking of his compatriots, the new nobility, or those aspiring to it, who had been trained in the French historical school of law. "Among this very rare troop, a number have fashioned themselves to the model of the true historiographer." Indeed, he was confident that such men would soon provide a perfect history of France that would surpass in merit and renown all the historiographical efforts of the ancients.

In the preface, La Popelinière never fully explained what he meant by perfect history, perhaps because he was not writing one. He excluded himself from the ranks of the perfect historians, who far exceeded his own abilities. "Nevertheless, creeping patiently after them, I will content myself . . . with crawling for awhile in the noble dust, where these divine spirits gallop with more merit than recompense for their long and painful labors [*courvées*]." The term *courvée* is double-edged, denoting on the one hand the back-breaking labor of these scholars and, on the other, the nature of this labor as unbefitting a man-at-arms. As a soldier, La Popelinière was probably a little ambivalent about the scholarly side of perfect history. Instead, he was content to pursue the "humbler" task of writing traditional military history, giving so honest and thorough an account of events that his fellow noblemen would be able to derive not only pleasure but profit from reading him.

The Science of History

La Popelinière's military career ended in 1577, when he was severely wounded in, of all things, a duel arising from a dispute about his command decisions during a recent siege. Thereafter he devoted himself full-time to the "calling" of history, as he often phrased it, expanding his first historical effort into the *Histoire de France,* his definitive account of the Wars of Religion. We have already noted how his fetish for detail in this work led him to exhaust his financial resources by traveling to widespread battlefields and interviewing innumerable eyewitnesses. One solution to his financial problem was to seek royal patronage, as Bernard Du Haillan had done when he published his *Desseing de l'histoire de France,* a blueprint for a new history of the realm. In 1599 La Popelinière published his own blueprint, the aforementioned *Dessein de l'histoire nouvelle des françois,* the concluding treatise in his volume of three works on historical theory that included the *Histoire des histoires* and the *Idée de l'histoire accomplie.* In these works he fully articulated the idea of perfect history as a means of ordering historical reality.[7]

The *Histoire des histoires,* the *Idée,* and the *Dessein* constitute sequential parts of a sustained argument. First, La Popelinière criticized the inadequacies of all previous historiography; then he formulated a "new" theory of history; and, finally, he suggested how this theory could be applied in practice. La Popelinière's ideas were less novel than he claimed, having been culled from a variety of ancient and modern authors. But with characteristic single-mindedness, he pursued these ideas more systematically than had his predecessors, pushing them to their logical, and sometimes extreme, conclusions. He not only summarized the historical thought of a generation influenced by the *mos gallicus* but also, by virtue of his methodological excesses, revealed the philosophical substructure of the historical response to the problem of relativism.[8]

The *Histoire des histoires* is the first sustained attempt to write a history of historiography. For the most part, its five hundred pages constitute a tiresome list of all known historians; but it is occasionally punctuated by accounts of the genesis of history as a body of literature. Instead of attributing the origin of letters to the genius of an ancient people—the Hebrews,

Egyptians, Greeks, or even the Gauls—he proposed that all peoples had passed through the same stages of literary development, and that within each stage there was a progression from more primitive to more sophisticated forms of expression. Because history was the cradle of all the arts and sciences, he described the rise of letters in terms of the four stages of historiography: the "natural histories," represented by the earliest songs and dances of preliterate peoples; the "poetic histories" of newly literate societies; the "continuous histories" of early annalistic literature; and sustained historical narratives, beginning with the work of Herodotus.[9]

Despite its rich sense of relativism, La Popelinière's historiographical survey served not to recount the development of this body of literature but rather to prove that true history had not yet been written. He analyzed in detail the historiographical efforts from the time of Herodotus onward, criticizing the faults of the major authors, in order to demonstrate that not a single one had understood the "necessary conditions" for true history.[10] In other words, the author of the first real history of historiography was less concerned with describing the evolution of that body of literature than with discovering its eternal, unchanging essence.

Having proclaimed the deficiency of all previous historiography, La Popelinière moved on to consider the true nature of history in the *Idée de l'histoire accomplie.* The often-quoted Ciceronian praise of history as the *magistra vitae* slipped all to easily off the tongue, beguiling one into believing that one understood the nature of history. But before one can praise something, argued La Popelinière, one ought to know what it is, "for one can scarcely know the substance of history from these praises."[11] La Popelinière's concern with the "substance" of history reflects the influence of the traditional Aristotelian way of thinking.

He explored the substance of history in a roundabout fashion, without ever really describing it concisely. He began by declaring that history comprised a "general narration, both eloquent and judicious, of the most notable actions of men, and other happenings, represented according to time, place, cause, progress, and outcome."[12] But then he found himself having to explain what he meant by a "general narration." It denoted both the form and the subject of perfect history: the form, in that it encompassed all states, one or two large ones, or a single city or small state; the subject, in that it embraced everything necessary for understanding the whole state, rather than some small "bit" of it.[13] His chief criticism of all previous historians was that they had failed to describe the state in sufficient detail; a general history must be complete: "Regarding the subject of history, it will be general when the author will have given the entire and complete *substance* of the state that he wants to represent."[14]

The substance of history, therefore, ultimately devolved upon that of the state, which had its own characteristic laws and institutions. But La Popelinière was well aware of what French legal scholarship had demonstrated, that the laws and institutions of each state varied with its historical circumstances. For example, he criticized previous historians of France for their anachronisms, "by which they judge all our estates—royal, noble, ecclesiastic, judicial, financial and others—to have been such at their commencement as they see them today."[15] If laws and institutions reflected changing historical circumstances, how could one know the enduring substance of the state? Hotman had resolved a similar type of question by appealing to universal norms transcending the diversity of laws and institutions; La Popelinière, however, would find his answer in the very notion of historical change.

He understood historical change in the fourfold, Aristotelian manner, inquiring into the material, efficient, formal, and final causes of an event. The material cause, he declared, is the general category of action to which the event belongs, such as war, sedition, or revenge. The efficient cause is the historical actor who perpetrated the deed. The formal cause is the plan that the actor possessed in order to execute his actions. And the final cause proceeds from the desires or passions (*affections*) toward the fulfillment of which he aimed the conduct of his designs. This formulation, whose wording may have derived from Patrizi, was a commonplace mode of explaining historical events.[16]

La Popelinière belabored this commonplace because some people claimed that history should be limited to the simple narration of events, the causes of which would be explained by philosophers. He emphasized the importance of causation in order to distinguish history from annals and *res gestae,* which recorded facts without making known causes and motives. Although the historian need not concern himself with ultimate truths, La Popelinière argued, he needs to know the causes and motives underlying events, "for that which moves someone to say or do something, be it the cause of something else, is nevertheless always a fact and a separate event, certain and already having occurred, and for that reason is a part of history and should be expressed in it."[17] Far from being beyond the historian's purview, causes were the very "stuff" of history.

That history should reveal causes had itself been a commonplace since the time of Polybius; however, this injunction took on new meaning in the sixteenth century. Polybius had explored the spatial dimension of causation, showing how events in one region influenced those in another. In the sixteenth century, thinkers like Jean Bodin and François Baudouin began to explore its temporal dimension, using the Polybian commonplace to justify the need to trace causes back to their beginnings in the very remote past and forward to their ultimate conclusions.[18] This development reflects the influence not only of providential history during the Reformation but also of the *mos gallicus,* which had demonstrated that Roman law was, in reality, a sequence of laws promulgated in response to changing historical circumstances. The study of law thus helped impart a temporal dimension to universal history, one less concerned with the vicissitude of events than with the mutation of institutions.[19]

Temporal change was not conceived of strictly in terms of cause and effect, however, but rather in terms of the four causes, only one of which (the efficient cause) even remotely resembles the modern historian's notion of causation. Indeed, the new concern with institutional change emphasized the role of material causation in particular. Efficient causes came to be seen as historical accidents, while formal and final causes (themselves closely related) were bound up with the material cause, embodying an institution's ability to realize a certain potential. The emphasis on material causation ultimately led to a concern with the origins and primal institutions of a people. La Popelinière's idea of perfect history summarizes this development, which underlies his conception of a history that would unfold step by step, entity by entity, from a point of origin in the very remote past.[20]

In the *Idée,* he applied the traditional notion of the four causes of historical change not only to events but also to institutions. Common sense dictated that he begin analyzing a historical entity by examining its material cause: he maintained that one could not understand "a people in general" without knowing "where they came from and what their original condition was," and he regarded their origin as their "cause and first quality."[21] This notion, reiterated throughout his theoretical writings, is best summarized in the following passage from the *Dessein:* "One cannot imagine being able to fashion a praiseworthy history of any people, city, or event, if one does not start from its natural source, knowing it from the origin and progress of its first condition [*estate*]; for the most astute of the ancients pronounced happy those who knew the causes of human things, and there can be no understanding [*science*] other than through the true knowledge of natural causes."[22] That intellectual certainty proceeded from a knowledge of causes was common sense for La Popelinière. Indeed, it is close enough to our own commonsense view of the world that we might overlook the fact that his was shaped by a broader notion of causation than ours, in which the "origin" of an entity could also be regarded as one of its "causes."

This broader notion of causation is most apparent in the *Dessein,* a polemic on behalf of institutional history that emphasizes the role of formal and, implicitly, material causes. Here he lambasted all previous historians of the realm for having concerned themselves solely with the lives of kings, captains, and saints, rather than with the institutional structure of ancient Gaul, Roman Gaul, and the kingdom of the Franks. He proposed a history that would begin by examining the "form" of the state of the ancient Gauls—namely, their administration, religion, justice, finances, business, and other *façons de vivre.* Next, it would show how the Romans overthrew this "original" state, substituting one with a different "form," whose component parts would also be detailed. Finally, it would recount how the Franks conquered Gaul and established yet another "form" of rule, with its own institutional structure, which served as the foundation for the modern kingdom of France.[23]

In the exhaustive list that summarizes La Popelinière's *Dessein*, the continuum of history appears as a succession of forms. He ignored the role played by historical actors in the origin and subsequent development of the state, emphasizing instead its distinctive structure at each period of its history. In other words, he ignored efficient in favor of formal causation. This emphasis created a perfect history characterized by the sequential overlay of discrete historical strata, each defined by its own particular institutional composition. Given the absence of historical actors, a temporal dynamic was provided by the unfolding of the state from its primal matter, which could only be grasped in terms of its form. The primal matter of the state—embodied by the customs, laws, and institutions of the ancient Gauls—was the basis for the history of France, whose essence unfolded as this matter took on the successive forms inherent to it. Implicitly, then, the formal cause of the state was bound up with its material cause.

In the *Dessein*, La Popelinière's fascination with the matter of history engendered an obsessive need to trace entities back to their origins. One cannot possibly understand the history of France, he argued, without first examining that of the Franks, which itself depended on that of the Gallo-Romans, which, in turn, devolved upon that of the ancient Gauls. This need to know the primal matter of historical change inspired a potentially ever-regressive quest. La Popelinière envisioned the new history of France as but a small contribution to a vast project, a perfect history of mankind that would ultimately extend all the way back to the beginning of recorded time. Writing J. J. Scaliger soon after the publication of the *Dessein*, he proposed to study the "primitive" peoples of the New World in order to discover the very origins of human society.[24] This proposal derived from La Popelinière's obsessive need to discover the primal matter embodying all the potential of historical change. Although the polemical tone and excessive detail of his writing may bear witness to a compulsive nature, perhaps exacerbated by literal-mindedness, La Popelinière's virtual mania for origins is symptomatic of the structure imposed upon historical consciousness by the traditional way of thinking.

Unlike Hotman, who attempted to transcend the diversity of laws and institutions with a normative view of the state, La Popelinière articulated a historical view in which the substance of the state was embodied by its own distinctive origins. The substance of *history*, which devolved upon that of the state, resided in an account of its "origins and progress."[25] "Progress" referred neither to improvement nor to development through time, but to change viewed from a point of origin. The substance of history was represented by a line of continuous inquiry extending from the very remote past to the present, embodying all the mutations of the state. Since each successive stage of "formed matter" was itself a link in a complex chain of causation, serving as the material cause of the next stage, true history had to be "perfect," in the sense of "complete." If there were any gaps in the representation of the state, be it in a stage of its history or in some portion of its institutional make-up, one could not know its subsequent history with any assurance.

This notion of history as "an empirical totality in space and time" appears strikingly modern, but its underpinnings were strictly traditional.[26] They constrained La Popelinière, who was more prosaic than Bodin or Baudouin, to conceive of history as an exhaustive list in the *Dessein*. Here he overwhelmed the reader with detail in order to avoid omitting any significant institution or stage in the history of France. The impulse to divide and subdivide his subject into ever-smaller pieces derived from the need to have the fullest possible account of a state's "origins and progress," a need reflecting the conceptual underpinnings of his "science" of history.

Given the need for "perfection," La Popelinière's list represents history less as a continuum than as a form of classification. To ensure the completeness of his proposed history, he organized the list of subjects topically, according to the general kinds of institutions all states possessed, and chronologically, according to the mutations of these institutions. He frequently likened this plan to a blueprint for a building divided into rooms.[27] These "rooms" resemble *loci*—topics such as religion, administration, justice, military discipline, finances, and business—that are, in turn, subdivided into the units appropriate for the state and period under consideration. His new history thus served to order decontextualized bits of information spatially, in the manner of contemporary place logic and the classificatory view of the world that it codified.

La Popelinière's system of classification is in one subtle yet crucial way different from that of the neo-Bartolists. Bodin's arrangement of historical material, for example, is based on a normative view of the nature and purpose of human existence, to which the history of each particular state is subordinated. Although many of La Popelinière's institutional topics resemble Bodin's classifications of human activity, they nonetheless serve to explain the distinctive nature of France. Whereas Bodin's system of classification establishes similarities in a vast body of literature that seemed to admit only of differences, La Popelinière's explains difference itself, "scientifically." And since science for La Popelinière depends on the knowledge of causes, the analysis of any given historical entity necessarily draws in its train that of every related entity, until the web of relations extends all the way back to the primal social urge. Thus, perfect history truly is, by its very nature, "the representation of everything."

Perfect History in Practice: Nicolas Vignier's *Bibliothèque historiale*

According to La Popelinière, the man who came closest to realizing the goal of perfect history was the physician turned historian Nicolas Vignier, whose *Sommaire de l'histoire des françois* is the only French history to receive special praise in the *Dessein*.[28] When Vignier published the *Sommaire* in 1579, he had excerpted it from his yet unpublished universal history, the *Bibliothèque historiale,* which finally appeared in 1587. He regarded this monumental work as the crowning achievement of his scholarly career. A comprehensive summary of history, the *Bibliothèque* is universal in both space and time. It encompasses eastern as well as western Europe, and the known peoples of Asia and Africa; and it extends from the creation of Adam to the sixteenth century. Vignier considered the chronological scope of his work as especially important, for "those who extend their narrative from the beginning to the end represent things in their perfection."[29] Given La Popelinière's praise for the *Sommaire,* we might well regard the *Bibliothèque* as the fullest contemporary realization of his concept of perfect history, revealing the extent of its encyclopedic impulse.

The work is not limited to political affairs, but also includes religious ones, as well as touching on cultural developments. Vignier summarized all this material in a bare, unadorned style, reporting the facts of history to those who had neither the time nor the inclination to read hundreds of authors. For those who required more than a bare summary of facts, he intended his *Bibliothèque* as a guide to historical sources, leading one through the "labyrinth" of diverse and often contradictory authors, whose accounts he attempted to reconcile. To this end Vignier combined the study of history with that of chronology. Since the improper dating and ordering of events was the chief source of confusion and error in history, he correlated an event with as many different dating systems as possible. For example, he dated biblical events with reference to Creation, the Flood, Noah, Abraham, and the Pharaohs. And he dated more recent events with reference not only to the Christian but also to the Moslem calendar. He regarded chronology as a new principle of order for universal history, supplanting that of Divine Providence. Like La Popelinière, he articulated a "scientific" response to the challenge of historical Pyrrhonism.

In three massive volumes, he marched forward year by year, covering the four-thousand-year period extending from Adam to the accession of François I. He began by delineating the years in vertical columns running along the left- and right-hand margins of the page, subdividing each column into as many as five parallel dating systems. Historical facts were recorded in a wide column running down the center of the page, which was divided by horizontal lines separating one year's entries from the next. After Vignier had moved from prehistory to the early history of Rome, he switched from a vertical to a horizontal page layout. Each year was delineated by a long, narrow rectangle extending to the margins of the page and divided into as many as two dozen cells, each expressing the year according to a different chronological scheme. This arrangement gave him more room in which to report an increasing number of events. He boasted that his *Bibliothèque* presented the "substance" of history, bare of any rhetorical embellishment, "placed before the eyes like a picture."

In this work, perhaps the world's longest time line, the relationship between events is subordinated to their spatial arrangement on the page. The visual effect is even more striking in the *Sommaire,* whose narrower scope permitted a degree of compartmentalization that would only have been confusing in the larger work. The *Sommaire* is characterized by the use of parallel columns to describe separate but concurrent events. The text may extend to the full margins of any given page; or it may extend only part of the way, the other part forming a truncated column separated from the main body of text by a double line; or the page might be divided into two carefully delineated columns, generally of unequal length, boxed off from the main body of the text flowing around them. As in the *Bibliothèque,* the years are delineated by horizontal lines cutting across the page. Like La Popelinière, Vignier thus organized knowledge spatially, dividing the page into compartments reminiscent of *loci.*

Although Vignier did not articulate a theory of history, the imperatives underlying his work become clear upon comparison with Eusebius's chronological tables, which served him as a model.[30] The *Bibliothèque* uses the Eusebian arrangement of dates in parallel columns, an arrangement that, as in the Eusebian model, becomes simplified from the Roman period onward; and the *Sommaire* measures time according to the length of the reign of each king, as did Eusebius. The latter had used chronology as a polemical device to prove that Christianity was not a new religion but the primitive faith of humanity, extending all the way back to Abraham, and that the church of the fourth century had inherited the true, apostolic faith via an unbroken succession of bishops. In this providential interpretation of history, the birth of Christ was the obvious watershed.

The Eusebian religious imperative is entirely absent from Vignier's chronology, which does not even treat the birth of Christ as an epochal event. In lieu of the traditional providential interpretation of history, chronology serves to order the now-decontextualized bits of information about the past. The chronologically arranged compartments of the *Bibliothèque* and *Sommaire* not only record events but also summarize collections of historical source materials, identified by author, cleansed of errors, and ranked by their temporal proximity to the events they describe. Unlike the more abstract neo-Bartolist schemes for subsuming history under universal norms, Vignier's chronology makes sense out of the past by correlating contemporaneous historical events and entities, locating them in a continuum that provides a "natural" explanation of their mutations through a "perfect" knowledge of their causes.

In both theory and practice, perfect history served to classify the multitude of historical entities revealed by legal and historical scholarship. Before coming to terms with each of these entities in particular, one had to find some way of ordering their general profusion. La Popelinière and Vignier sought this order in a notion of universal history, the account of which would begin in the very remote past and move forward to the present, step by excruciating step. Their conviction that a "complete" record of the past would reveal the essential structure of historical knowledge reflects the persistence of the traditional way of thinking, which shaped their notion of historical change and underlay their classificatory view of the world.

From Perfect History to Historical Genealogy

Whereas La Popelinière and Vignier subordinated the uniqueness of historical entities to the totality of universal history, their contemporary Estienne Pasquier focused on selected entities without integrating them into a grand historical scheme. He explicitly distinguished his undertaking from that of perfect history: "Any man of understanding, without seeing a perfect history [*une histoire accomplie*], can almost imagine the overall temper of a people when he studies its ancient statutes and ordinances; and by the same token can make a sound conjecture about what its laws must have been, by looking at its manner of life."[31] To know a people, one should principally study its customs, laws, and institutions, which embody its distinctive essence. This attitude enabled him to circumvent the encyclopedic impulse underlying perfect history. In his monumental *Recherches de la France,* he devoted himself to the analysis of specific historical problems and questions. Pasquier used the term *recherches* to epitomize a program of historical inquiry into neglected aspects of the French past that would help reveal the uniqueness of France's culture.

His notion of *recherches,* however, emphasized the concept of material causation even more than did La Popelinière's idea of perfect history. La Popelinière conceived of France as a sequence of forms in time: ancient

Gaul was transformed by the Romans, Roman Gaul by the Germans, German Gaul by the Franks, and so on. Although one could not understand this sequence without first examining the ancient Gauls—the original "stuff" of French history—La Popelinière did not go so far as to say that one could understand the modern French simply by studying the ancient Gauls. His concern with origins was counterbalanced by a notion of historical change that required the whole story of a state to be told, from its beginning through all of its mutations. Pasquier, too, was very conscious of historical change, but his program of *recherches* was more fully shaped by a notion of material causation that led him to attribute the distinctive features of modern French culture directly to the "genetic" material of ancient Gaul. In this sense, his undertaking was less historical than genealogical.

Pasquier received a humanist education at the Collège de Presles while Peter Ramus was headmaster there. After graduating from the Collège around 1546, he studied law at the Ecole des Décrets in Paris under Hotman and Baudouin. He continued his legal education at Toulouse with Cujas and completed it in Italy, studying with, among others, Alciato at Pavia. From these renowned legal scholars, he acquired an acute sense of the relativity of laws and institutions.[32]

This sense of relativity took a militant turn during his brief sojourn in Italy, where he encountered Italian disdain for the "barbarian" French. He consequently resolved that, upon his return to France, he would introduce the letter as a genre of vernacular French literature, so that his countrymen could rival the cultural achievements of the Italians. Unfortunately, Pasquier's literary ability was not equal to his ambition, so he soon began to cast about for another way to enhance the reputation of French culture, as well as his own. Friends suggested that he translate classics like Cicero's orations into French, but Pasquier rejected this idea, because "our translations do not bequeath themselves to posterity, but die with our vernacular, which transforms itself from one century to the next."[33] Rather than undertake translation, he decided to make his reputation in historical scholarship, for which his legal education had well prepared him. In a letter to Cujas, he confided his plans: "As for me, I have set myself to the study [*recherche*] of the antiquities of France; and for this reason I have called my work *Recherches*."[34]

He intended this work to fill the gaps left by the chroniclers and humanist historians. The chroniclers, he complained, were monks ignorant of civil affairs; and their accounts were, in a word, "musty." Subsequent attempts to bring eloquence to the writing of history, however, had only raised the specter of historical Pyrrhonism by calling into doubt the motivation of humanist historians, who too often distorted the truth to please their royal patrons. In order to preserve his reputation, Pasquier eschewed modern history in favor of "antiquities," to which he would bring less "artifice" and more "robustness" by expanding the range of sources. They would encompass not only chronicles but also classical texts and archival records, like the registers of the parlement of Paris. Whatever his sources, he intended to quote them at length, having resolved "to say nothing of importance without proving it." He would even quote at length well-known passages from famous classical texts, because they had been "seen without being seen"—their significance for the study of French antiquities had not been previously recognized. He intended to transcribe these as well as more obscure documents so that his readers could, as it were, "touch" ancient France "with their fingers."[35]

He embarked upon this program of historical research in the mid 1550s, while pursuing his legal career in parlement. This profession nicely complemented his avocation, for in parlement he undoubtedly handled documents of historical importance. Although he was ultimately to rise to the position of advocate general of the *chambre des comptes,* his promising legal career was interrupted in 1558 by a near-fatal illness (brought on by mushroom poisoning), which left him incapacitated for more than two years. The *Recherches* owe their publication to this period of professional inactivity. Book 1, on the ancient Gauls, appeared in 1560, and book 2, on the chief political institutions of the kingdom, in 1565. By the time of his death in 1615, the *Recherches* had grown by five additional books on the ecclesiastical institutions of France, her notable customs and laws, her neglected historical figures, and her language and literature. Posthumous editions contain three more books, notably one on French learning. Taken together, the varied books of the *Recherches* celebrate the unique achievements of French culture.

Druids and Gauls

From the very first book, the *Recherches* represent a striking departure from previous French historiography. Traditionally, histories of France had begun with the legend of the first Frenchman, Francio, the fugitive from the destruction of Troy who founded the Frankish monarchy. Although he refused to pronounce final judgment on this myth, Pasquier in effect dismissed it as a product of misguided national pride. The question, "Who was the first Frenchman?" was trivial—a mere matter of historical accident and impossible to ascertain. The really important questions were, "From which *people* did the French arise, and what were their habits, customs, laws, and institutions?"

Pasquier found his answers in Julius Caesar's account of the Gallic War. At one stroke, the whole question of origins was removed from the realm of myth and placed in that of historical fact. Caesar was an eyewitness to the ways of life of a people who long preceded the Franks. He was, furthermore, a reliable observer, having been impressed by the Gauls despite his traditional Roman disdain for the "barbarian" tribes of the West.[36] On the basis of Caesar's observations, Pasquier formulated an interpretation of ancient Gaul that served as the touchstone for his understanding of modern France.

Just as modern French society was divided into three estates, so too the Gauls had their priests, nobles, and commoners.[37] Pasquier paid special attention to the priestly class of Druids, to whom he attributed the civil government, or *police,* which distinguished the Gauls from their barbarian neighbors. Although they were divided into independent tribes, all Gauls nonetheless submitted to the decisions of the Druids, who assembled yearly at Chartres to arbitrate disputes among their people. Whoever ignored the judgments of these assemblies risked "excommunication."[38] The Gauls flourished under this combined civil and ecclesiastical administration; without any foreign assistance, they raised huge armies of up to 200,000 men, with which they sacked Rome and conquered the bulk of Europe. Indeed, the Gauls ruled a powerful empire long before the Romans, and Caesar would not have conquered them had they not been weakened by civil war.

About the Franks, Pasquier had relatively little to say, except that they originated not from Troy but from German tribes along the upper Rhine. When they conquered Gaul, the Franks simply adopted the existing Gallic institutions. Pasquier was concerned to show that the Frankish conquest of Gaul was proof, not of the superiority of the Franks, but of the vicissitude of events whereby the Franks avenged their previous defeat by the Gauls. Indeed, fortune came full circle when Clovis, the Frankish king who conquered Gaul, marched eastward to subdue Germany, "induced by a Gallic destiny." Pasquier had a very ambivalent attitude toward the Franks because he regarded the Gauls, and especially the Druids, as the nucleus of French culture.[39]

In the chief books of the *Recherches,* Pasquier systematically traced the distinctive features of modern France back to the "genetic" matter of ancient Gaul. We shall analyze his view of the "origins and progress" of parlement in book 2, of the Gallican church in book 3, of French poetry in book 6, and of the French language in book 7.[40] Excluded from this inquiry will be the posthumous books, as well as books 4 and 5. The former group of books may well be incomplete; and the latter, concerning obscure customs and neglected historical figures, are random collections of disparate research. When Pasquier set himself the task of depicting the principal features of the kingdom and culture of France, he framed his historical research with a view of the past that attributed the uniqueness of all things French to their seeds in ancient Gaul.

Pasquier begins book 2 of the *Recherches,* on civil institutions, with a prefatory chapter on whether fortune or *conseil* has contributed more to the welfare of the kingdom. How, he asks, has France survived for 1,200 years after Clovis, while so many other states have succumbed to the ravages of time? Although fortune has undoubtedly contributed to this longevity by providing the realm with good kings and captains at crucial moments in her history, he concludes that sound administration (*la police, & bonne conduicte de nos Roys*) has nonetheless played an equal role.[41] Parlement, according to Pasquier, accounts for the durability of the kingdom, by ensuring both the "good conduct" of kings and the obedience of their subjects.

This institution originated from the tradition of royal restraint inaugurated by Clovis. After conquering Gaul, Clovis willingly accommodated himself to the prevailing civil and religious observances, "which . . . was one of the principal means by which he induced the common people of Gaul to bear him affection." Under his successors, the mayors of the palace upheld the appearance of royal restraint by introducing "a form of annual parlement," composed of the great barons of the realm. These assemblies were in effect sham parlements, carefully staged by the mayors to disguise the reality of their political power. When Pepin usurped the monarchy and established the Carolingian dynasty, he invested these assemblies with real authority in order to gain the support of the nobility. In Pasquier's assessment, these early Carolingian assemblies mark "one of the first beginnings of the parlements we have in France."[42]

Pasquier subsequently shows how these early parlements steadily increased in importance during the Carolingian and Capetian dynasties. Charlemagne continued Pepin's practice of calling such assemblies, doing so even more frequently than his father; and Charlemagne's son, Louis Debonnaire, further increased his reliance on parlements, which started meeting twice yearly. Under Hugues Capet and his successors, parlements had even greater authority and grandeur, in part because of the weakness of the early Capetians. Pasquier notes that the Capetian parlements arbitrated disputes between the king and his magnates in almost the same way that the druidical assemblies of ancient Gaul had dispensed justice.[43]

After sketching this early history of parlement in the second chapter of book 2, Pasquier goes on in the third chapter to detail the royal ordinances of the fourteenth and fifteenth centuries that established parlement in its modern form. This chapter, more than twice the length of the previous one, contains lengthy quotations from the edicts and ordinances decreeing, among other things, the establishment of the parlement of Paris, its division into separate chambers, their composition, and even the salaries of their officers. In this collection of documents, crucial for understanding the formation of parlement, Pasquier's program of research bore one of its greatest fruits. Indeed, it is with these documents that modern histories of parlement begin.

Unlike a modern historian, however, Pasquier viewed parlement as originating during the Carolingian period rather than the fourteenth and fifteenth centuries. Clovis planted the seed for this institution in a soil that, by implication, had previously been cultivated by the Druids, whose assemblies had moderated the power of their kings. This seed gradually matured into an entity whose form varied with "the diversity of the seasons" but whose function became ever more sharply defined.[44] Eventually it emerged as the chief restraint on the monarchy and, hence, as the guarantor of political stability in the kingdom. The roots of parlement thus extended all the way back to ancient Gaul.

In book 3 of the *Recherches*, Pasquier examines what he repeatedly refers to as, "the ancient liberties of the Gallican church." The phrase was a common one, born of several generations of polemics asserting the independence of the French king and his prelates from papal authority. Many of Pasquier's contemporaries contributed to the literature on this subject: Claude Fauchet, for example, studied the ancient origins of the Gallican church, and Pierre Pithou discoursed on its doctrinal basis. Pasquier, however, was one of the first to distill from the mass of Gallican writings a history of the French church from its origins to the present.

He defines Gallicanism in terms of three fundamental propositions: that the king of France cannot be excommunicated by the pope, that the pope has no authority over the king in temporal matters, and that ultimate authority in the Catholic church as a whole resides with the general council of Christian prelates.[45] Taken together, these propositions constitute an accord between the king and his clergy to achieve both religious and secular autonomy from the pope. Modern historians have regarded this accord as arising in response to the crisis of the Great Schism in the early fifteenth century.[46] Pasquier, however, not only traced it back to the founding of the French monarchy in Merovingian times, but also extended the autonomy of the Gallican church back to the very earliest period of Christian Gaul.

According to him, the Gallican church had been "built up over a long period of time," by which he meant the period from the second to the sixth centuries. Under the leadership of its earliest saints—Irenaeus, Hilary, and Martin—the Gallican church developed its own customs, distinct from those of the Roman church. Chief among these was obedience to local church councils rather than the pope, a custom "borrowed from the primitive church and passed on from father to son."[47] With the conversion of Clovis in the early sixth century, the interests of the clergy were conjoined with those of the king, who took upon himself the right to assemble church councils. Pasquier is careful to point out that the Merovingian kings held their temporal authority entirely apart from the pope, with whom they had hardly any contact. When Pepin usurped the throne and established the Carolingian line, he asked the pope to proclaim him king out of respect and veneration for the Holy See. Neither Pepin nor his successors, however, acknowledged the temporal or spiritual superiority of the pope; rather, they continued the "ancient practice" of assembling general councils to preside over matters of faith. The "liberties of the Gallican church" were preserved unchanged until the political collapse of the Carolingian monarchy finally opened the way for papal encroachments.

Pasquier offers a sophisticated historical analysis of the rise of papal authority during the Crusades. These were expeditions instigated by the pope, thus enhancing his prestige; and they led to the formation of new, powerful religious orders, such as the Knights of Rhodes and the Templars, which were beholden solely to him. During this time, the papacy also gained added respect by undertaking programs of monastic reform. All these innovations, combined with the weakness of the French king and divisions within the Gallican church, enabled the papacy to gain control of ecclesiastical administration in the kingdom and to abrogate the authority of the councils, which were reduced to deciding questions of cannonization.

The bulk of Pasquier's account concerns the revival of Gallican liberties. He describes the "Pragmatic Sanction of Saint Louis" (a forged precedent for the Pragmatic Sanction of Bourges) as the "first stone . . . cast for the reestablishment of the ancient dignity of our Gallican church."[48] The most important phase in the revitalization of Gallican liberties occurred during the Great Schism of the late fourteenth and early fifteenth centuries, when king and clergy allied with parlement and the Sorbonne to articulate the doctrine that we now associate with Gallicanism. Pasquier discusses the events leading up to the Council of Constance in great detail, providing as usual extensive documentation. He concludes his account with discussions of the Pragmatic Sanction of Bourges, which "brought some repose to our Gallican church," and the Concordat of Bologna, which he interprets as yet a further confirmation of Gallican liberties.[49]

Despite Pasquier's very thorough account of the events surrounding the Great Schism, he did not view it as the catalyst in the formation of Gallican doctrine—nor, for that matter, did his contemporaries. Instead, they all asserted the antiquity of Gallicanism. Pasquier's innovation, though, was to treat that doctrine as a distinctive characteristic of French culture, to be considered alongside France's political institutions, literature, and language. Although he believed that the earliest Christians in Gaul derived their "conciliarism" from the primitive church, he nonetheless proclaimed that only the French were blessed with ecclesiastical independence from the pope. Why did France, alone among the Christian realms, have this distinction, which supposedly derived from the common inheritance of all Christians? Pasquier never addressed this question. But we should recall that the doctrine took strong and early root among a people who had once been ruled by druidical assemblies that, like the Church councils, were composed of "priests" endowed with the power to "excommunicate."

In the books on literature and language, Pasquier once again traces the distinctive aspects of French culture back to the Gauls. Book 6 is devoted to the "origins, antiquity, and progress" of French poetry. Pasquier begins by defining the feature distinguishing French poetry from that of the ancient Greeks and Romans: theirs were measured verses whereas French ones are rhymed. Despite noting that all modern European poetry is characterized by rhymed verse, Pasquier attributes this innovation specifically to the Gauls. He claims that, after being conquered by Rome, the Gauls adopted for poetry the rhyming scheme that the Romans had previously reserved for oratory.[50] Surprisingly, he offers no proof for this assertion. Instead, he provides a history of rhyme—from Leonine verse to Provençal poetry to the glories of the Pléiade—which demonstrates the special aptitude of the French for composing rhymed verse. He lavishes his greatest attention on the Pléiade (whose theoretical works stress the importance of rhyme), and especially on Ronsard (who had recently popularized the sonnet in France). Book 6 offers not so much a history of the development of French poetry as an account of the unfolding of its distinctive feature, from its humble Gallic origins to its present eminence.

The next book, on the French language, follows a similar pattern of interpretation. Pasquier's previously mentioned reluctance to become a translator demonstrates his acute awareness of the mutation of language. In book 7 he describes two principles governing linguistic mutation: first, there is the variation in fashion and taste common to all peoples, whereby some words become popular and others unpopular; and second, there is change resulting from conquest, whereby the language of the vanquished becomes "corrupted" by that of the victors. French is chiefly a product of the latter process, as the original Celtic tongue of the ancient Gauls (which Pasquier mistakenly labeled "Walloon") was modified first by the infusion of Latin and then by the Teutonic language of the Franks.[51]

Pasquier devotes most of his attention to the imposition of Latin on the ancient Gauls, rightly judging that "our vernacular is infinitely indebted to the Romans." After their conquest by Rome, the Gauls were forced to use Latin as their official language. This linguistic imperialism eventually led them to supplant "Walloon" with a "kind of vulgar Latin," incorporating Latin vocabulary with the grammatical structure of their original language. Given the laconic nature of the ancient Gauls, they shortened polysyllabic Latin words, like *corpus, tempus,* and *asperum,* into their monosyllabic equivalents—*corps, temps,* and *aspre*—while monosyllabic Latin words were borrowed intact and later mutated with changing tastes. The resulting language, *Roman,* was for all practical purposes "French"; it was only slightly modified after the Frankish conquest of Gaul. Thus, French is basically a composite of Latin vocabulary and Celtic grammar, reflecting the national characteristics of the ancient Gauls.

Although others, like Herni Estienne and Claude Fauchet, had studied various aspects of the origins of French, Pasquier was the first to provide a comprehensive view of the formation of the language. His analysis is not too far off the mark, especially considering that many of his contemporaries believed in the Greek origins of French. But his insistence that Latin had been grafted onto "Walloon," and that French had thus resulted from a process of "corruption," reflects the "genetic" view of France, which traced each aspect of modern culture back to its origins in ancient Gaul.

The *Recherches* as Cultural Taxonomy

Pasquier's "genealogy" of France takes the form of a tree-diagram, reflecting the influence of Aristotelian taxonomic principles. At first glance the work appears to be a ramshackle collection of books, assembled over a sixty-year period without regard for its overall organization. But closer inspection reveals a definite plan that Pasquier had in mind from the very beginning of the project. He referred to this plan in the first chapter of the 1560 edition, comprising book 1 on the origins of France. Here he announced his intention to study French "antiquities." Although others had attempted this undertaking, they had done so neither in a sustained fashion nor "with such order [*tel fil*] as I myself deliberate." Pasquier described his undertaking as a "double research" concerned with "things" and "words," adopting for historical purposes the commonplace rhetorical distinction between *res* and *verba.* He then proceeded to outline a work consisting of five books, four on "things" and one on "words." Book 1 on the Gauls, Franks, and other early peoples of France would be followed by a second book on administration (*la commune police*), both civil and ecclesiastic. Book 3 would concern ancient customs affecting not only public but also private life. Book 4 would concern the noteworthy deeds of those historical figures who had been ignored by the chroniclers. And book 5 would be devoted to current words and idioms of ancient origin.[52]

In subsequent editions published during his lifetime, Pasquier remained remarkably faithful to this plan. The proposed book on *police* was divided in two, one on civil and the other on ecclesiastical administration, and a book on French poetry was added, giving more substance to his treatment of "words." Posthumous editions further expanded this category with a book on French learning, in addition to two other books on noteworthy historical figures.[53]

Distinctions between "things" and "words," civil and religious life, and public and private affairs were commonplace in the Renaissance; nonetheless, they serve to delineate a taxonomy ordered according to genus and species. In this traditional mode of thinking, the taxonomy is not an arbitrary classification of entities; rather, it is predicated on the existence of an essence or "substance" shared by all the species of the same genus. Gaul, therefore, stands at the apex of the hierarchy; it embodies the distinctive essence of France, which becomes differentiated in the constituent elements of her culture. The distinction between "things" and "words" marks the principle of difference, separating the genus into its species. The category of "things," for example, is divided into administration, customs, and deeds; and administration is further subdivided into secular and religious, while customs are subdivided into those of public and private life. At the base of the taxonomy are individual entities that cannot be further differentiated; secular administration, for instance, is divided into parlement, the grand council, the Twelve Peers, the constable, the dukes, counts, viscounts, and so on.

When he traced the origins of France back to the Gauls rather than the Trojans, Pasquier was not "beginning at the beginning," in the manner of a modern historian, for Gaul is not simply a chronological but also a taxonomical beginning. Wherever possible, he tried to trace the origins of French institutions, customs, literature, and language back to Gaul. He wanted to describe the uniqueness of French culture not by telling its story but by relating its component parts to its distinctive essence. The druidical assemblies lay at the very heart of this essence, providing the combined religious and secular administration that had unified the Gauls and made them great. These assemblies were the precursors of parlement because they restrained the will of tribal kings and thus furthered the interests of justice. They were also, however, composed of "priests," who were invested collectively with the power to "excommunicate," suggesting the organization of the Gallican church, with its emphasis on councils. Pasquier reinforced this suggestion by equating the social position of the Druids with that of the modern French clergy. Thus, in effect, he treated civil administration in book 2 and ecclesiastical administration in book 3 as differentia of the essence of France presented in book 1.

The sequence of books moves from general to particular in the manner of a taxonomy. The undifferentiated "stuff" of French history treated in book 1 is analyzed into its civil and ecclesiastical components in books 2 and 3. From this treatment of broad institutional matters, Pasquier moved on to a more specific consideration of customs and laws affecting not only public but, even more important, private life. This then led to the even more specific analysis of actual historical individuals in book 5, which concludes the discussion of "things." The discussion of "words" in books 6 and 7, although less extensive than that of "things," also apparently moves from general to particular, starting with literature and ending with an examination of specific words.

This pattern of analysis resembles that of a typical Aristotelian tree diagram. Indeed, one can even see in it the tendency toward the bifurcating logic characteristic of Ramist method, which also proceeds deductively from general to particular.[54] The first step in Ramist logic is to clarify the essence of the thing under examination (Gaul), which is then divided into its principal compartments ("things" and "words"). Wherever possible, dichotomized analysis is the aim of this method, with each successive topic being split in two, until all the topics appropriate to the inquiry are examined. In the original plan of the *Recherches*, "things" are subdivided into secular and religious matters, and secular matters are further subdivided into public and private ones. Of course, the plan of the *Recherches* became obscured in its execution, and rigidly dichotomized analysis was impossible given the antiquarian rather than logical nature of Pasquier's interests. Nonetheless, his tendency to describe his project in terms of dichotomies suggests the influence, if not of his former headmaster at the Collège de Presles, at least of the contemporary place logic that Ramus had tried to systematize.

The taxonomic view of France enabled Pasquier to understand her institutions apart from the events of French history. Events primarily had the catalytic effect of "releasing" the motion inherent in France's institutions. For example, the fortuitous appearance and success of a man of restraint like Clovis could only be ascribed to Divine Providence. The wise actions of this man, however, set in motion a tendency toward the institutionalization of restraint that was already inherent in the druidical assemblies of ancient Gaul and that led eventually to the formation of the early parlements. In this view of history, events are "accidents" in the Aristotelian sense of the word; they are peripheral to the essence of an institution. The way to understand that essence is to establish the relationship of the institution to other entities of the same genus and, in so doing, to grasp the enduring quality that characterizes it as a member of that genus.

One of Pasquier's most distinctive contributions to historiography lies in his vision of culture. He was the first to undertake a systematic description of the uniqueness of France. In thinking about how to approach this enormous undertaking, he made the crucial distinction between "things" and "words." This distinction is important not because it foreshadows the content of modern cultural history but because it represents a solution to the tremendous problem of classification that he faced. In any system of classification, there must be a criterion for dividing the genus into its species. Only after finding the requisite criterion in the commonplace rhetorical distinction between *res* and *verba* was Pasquier able to achieve a systematic vision of French culture. He was justifiably proud of the "double research" characterizing his work. This innovation served as the basis for a new field of study, one more akin to cultural taxonomy than to cultural history.

One must remember that Pasquier was an *érudit,* not a logician or philosopher; he did not self-consciously apply the principles of Aristotelian taxonomy or Ramist method to his study of the past. Indeed, his taxonomic vision becomes apparent only when one examines the overall structure of the *Recherches.* In the actual practice of historical research, he exhibited a fine eye for documents and an intuitive grasp of historical issues. He correctly judged the importance of the fourteenth- and fifteenth-century royal ordinances that established a standing parlement and prescribed its form; he clearly recognized the crucial influence of the Great Schism on Gallican doctrine; he skillfully interpreted the history of French poetry on the basis of its principal characteristic; and when most of his contemporaries were tracing the roots of the French language back to Greek, he offered a much more sophisticated analysis of its origins. Despite his impressive scholarly achievements, however, Pasquier organized the *Recherches* as a taxonomy, differentiating the genetic material of ancient Gaul into the constituent elements of French culture. As a good humanist, he would probably have been offended had one labeled his vision of the past "Aristotelian"; no doubt he would have claimed that he was simply following common sense in ordering his historical materials hierarchically.

Toward a New Vision of History

In response to the problem of relativism, La Popelinière, Vignier, and Pasquier naturally began to apply the traditional way of thinking to the analysis of historical entities, which they understood as unfolding from their origins. Although this concept of unfolding was implicit in the theory and practice of perfect history, La Popelinière and Vignier subordinated it to the exigency of ordering historical material in a vast catalogue extending from the very remote past to the present. Pasquier, however, used it explicitly in his analysis of the constituent elements of French culture. By contrasting Pasquier's attitude toward the past with François Hotman's in the *Francogallia,* we can see how the notion of unfolding served to explain a more complex historical reality.

Hotman attributed the uniqueness of French public law to an "ancient constitution" that originated from the union of the Frankish and Gallic peoples to form the Frankish kingdom in Gaul. This constitution gave primacy to a public council of notables charged with electing and, if necessary, deposing the Frankish kings. Hotman attributed the distinctive features of France to the enduring influence of the ancient constitution. It not only shaped the chief civil institutions of the kingdom, most notably the Estates General, but also accounted for the conciliar emphasis of the Gallican church. He claimed that this constitution survived intact and virtually unchanged throughout the Merovingian, Carolingian, and Capetian dynasties. He implied that when Louis XI undermined the Estates General in the fifteenth century, the ancient constitution was subverted, hence laying the foundation for the civil strife of Hotman's own day. His view of historical change is thus one of "corruption," to be rectified by restoring the ancient constitution to its original purity.[55] This notion of historical change was common to the sixteenth century, a time when Luther, for example, attempted to reform Christianity by "restoring" the church to its original apostolic purity. Analogous programs of *restoratio* characterize the cultural movement associated with humanism.

A notion of corruption ultimately implies a model of perfection. The classical ideal of mixed government underlay Hotman's notion of the ancient constitution. The public council of the Francogallians, later to become the Estates General, was divided into three orders representing the three types of government—"the regal, the aristocratic, and the popular types."[56] Thus, despite his pretense of describing the ancient constitution of France as a unique historical entity, Hotman ultimately portrayed it as but a variation on a universal theme. Although his overriding impulse to anchor historical entities in universal norms may have been natural for a jurist, it also reflects his fundamental ambivalence toward historical and cultural relativism.

In comparison to Hotman, Pasquier was much more tolerant of relativism. Instead of reducing France to the eternal and immutable historical "monad," as it were, of the ancient constitution, he regarded it as a complex nexus of historical entities. For example, although parlement and the Gallican church derived their distinctive essence from their Gallic origins, they were not simply manifestations of the same ideal; rather, they were unique historical entities. France could only be described through an analysis of her constituent parts.

Like Hotman, Pasquier described change in some of these entities as "corruption." The Gallican church, for example, was fully formed by the time of Clovis, corrupted after the decline of the Carolingian monarchy, and restored to its original purity in the fifteenth and sixteenth centuries. And the French language derived largely from a "corruption" of the Gallic tongue. But Pasquier modified this notion of corruption with a greater sense of the waxing and waning of historical entities. Whereas Hotman viewed the ancient constitution as arising almost instantaneously from the union of Franks and Gauls, and declining with equal rapidity due to the actions of one malicious king, Pasquier noted that the Gallican church was "built up over a long period of time," and he charted its decline over several centuries.[57]

In addition to this "gradualist" notion of corruption, Pasquier conceived of another kind of historical change. "Corruption" and "restoration" entail movement away from and back to a norm, a movement perhaps best characterized by the term *vicissitude.* The history of French poetry, however, is one not of corruption but of the gradual refinement of its distinctive feature, rhymed verse. Likewise parlement also derives from the progressive refinement of ancient practices: first it began meeting with increasing frequency; then it acquired a permanent location; and, finally, it divided into chambers. Pasquier thus conceived of historical change not only as the corruption of an ideal but also as the unfolding of inherent potential.

The notion of unfolding suited his fuller appreciation of historical relativism. Pasquier was content to study entities in all their diversity without necessarily anchoring them in universal norms. Of course, he was no more a fully relativistic thinker than Hotman was a fully normative one. Pasquier's analysis of parlement in book 2 begins with reference to a norm of good government: "All those who wanted to establish the liberty of a well-ordered republic have deemed that the opinion of the sovereign magistrate be tempered by the remonstrances of many honorable personages, constituted in an estate for this end."[58] But this normative claim, so tentative and unspecific in comparison to those made by Hotman, is unusual in a work chiefly concerned with analyzing the distinctiveness of historical entities. The notion of unfolding complements this shift from normative to more relativistic thinking, for it enabled Pasquier to account for the diversity and complexity revealed by scholarly developments.

One should be careful here to distinguish the idea of unfolding from that of development. For Pasquier, as for Hotman, historical change did not lead to the generation of novelty. Hotman, for example, explained the appearance of seemingly new institutions, such as the Twelve Peers, as further manifestations of the traditional public council.[59] Pasquier was more sophisticated than this, but he could not conceive of the emergence of an institution that was not somehow inherent in the genetic material of France. An idea of historical development would admit of the emergence of entirely new entities, wholly different from their predecessors and not at all implicit in them. Both Pasquier and Hotman remained under the influence of essentialist thinking, which was incompatible with an idea of historical development. But the notion of unfolding created a more congenial environment for the eventual emergence of an idea of development in the eighteenth century, an idea that subsumed the earlier notion under a more comprehensive explanation of historical change.

One cannot help but be struck by the incredibly detailed nature of the historical vision of these sixteenth-century Frenchmen. Vignier attempted to give a year-by-year account of universal history; La Popelinière and Pasquier each tried to analyze France into the very smallest of her component parts. This fascination with detail reflects a need to discover the causal connections in history, a need that provided the fundamental impetus behind the drive for order. The more detailed the analysis, the more fully revealed the intricate network of causation supporting the detail. Thus, La Popelinière's obsession with the completeness of his enumeration of historical topics complements his mania for extending historical inquiry back farther and farther into the past. The origins of an entity provided the key to understanding that entity in all its complexity—they revealed its material cause, the ultimate source of the causal linkages connecting it to other historical entities. Pasquier emphasized the genetic nature of these causal linkages by showing how the essence of France, embedded in her origins, became differentiated into the component parts of her culture.

In the late sixteenth and early seventeenth centuries, however, this essentialist notion of causation was being called into question by the very experience of relativism that had excited it. For example, Montaigne ridiculed the impulse to search for the causes underlying phenomena: "I see ordinarily that men, when facts are put before them, are more ready to amuse themselves by inquiring into their reasons than by inquiring into their truth. They leave aside the cases and amuse themselves treating the causes. . . . They pass over the facts, but they assiduously examine their consequences. They ordinarily begin thus: 'How does this happen?' What they should say is: 'But does it happen?' "[60] In reaction to his experience of relativism, Montaigne tended to be more concerned with *what* a phenomenon was rather than with *why* it was that way. This substitution of one fundamental question for another had the effect of blurring the Aristotelian distinction between essence and accident. In his self-portrait, for example, Montaigne did not pare away the accidental aspects of his self to arrive at its essence, but rather found that essence revealed in its very accidents. Let us now turn to Montaigne's rejection of Aristotelian classificatory assumptions, and his acceptance of the self as a new point of orientation in a relativistic world.

CHAPTER 3

THE ORDER OF THE SELF

The Breakdown of Commonplace Thought

Montaigne published the first edition of the *Essais,* comprising two books, in 1580. Rather than keep the essays in their chronological order of composition, he introduced book 1 with a late essay, dating from around the time of publication, and book 2 with an early essay, dating from around the time he had begun writing in 1572.[1] He chose this arrangement to highlight the problem of relativism.

The first essay of book 1, "By Diverse Means We Arrive at the Same End," introduces this problem in its conclusion: "Truly man is a marvelously vain, diverse, and undulating object. It is hard to found any constant and uniform judgment on him." The first essay of book 2, "Of the Inconsistency of Our Actions," amplifies it: "There is as much difference between us and ourselves as between us and others." And the last essay of book 2, "Of the Resemblance of Children to Fathers," reiterates it in the concluding lines of the first edition: "There never were in the world two opinions alike, any more than two hairs or two grains. Their most universal quality is diversity."

Whereas the experience of relativism had led his contemporaries to attempt to transcend or classify diversity, Montaigne openly embraced it, using it as the mirror in which to behold the reflection of his self. The acceptance of diversity did not, however, lead him to espouse a doctrine of relativism. The self he beheld was a fixed point, to which all else was referred, a mental object characterized not by its development over time but rather by its own inimitable and immutable structure. In fact, despite his outward rejection of commonplace thought, we shall see how Montaigne's notion of selfhood reflects the same classificatory *episteme* evidenced by La Popelinière.

"How can I save myself if I fall into the hands of my enemies?" Montaigne posed this question in the first essay of book 1. This was a practical question in his age of civil war; indeed, he would have need of an answer on at least three subsequent occasions. But he now posed the question in order to demonstrate that no answer was possible—the diversity of human reality defied systematization. More so than his contemporaries, Montaigne recognized the extent to which the experience of relativism had undermined commonplace thought and the classificatory view of the world.

The title of the essay "By Diverse Means We Arrive at the Same End" is a commonplace, a category or heading classifying various examples of human behavior, and a maxim or proverb serving as a guide to conduct amidst this variety.[2] In the first two sentences, Montaigne stated the problem that, theoretically, would be explicated by the commonplace: popular opinion holds that the vanquished can save himself by submitting to the victor and begging for mercy; however, defiance in the face of defeat sometimes achieves the same end. Citing diverse examples, Montaigne recounted how some victorious princes ruthlessly ignored pleas for mercy but responded favorably to displays of bold and courageous defiance. He concluded that pleas for mercy moved weak hearts—like those of women, children, and the *vulgaire*—whereas acts of bravery moved strong hearts. By this point in the chapter, Montaigne had fulfilled the promise of the commonplace title, for he had demonstrated that by diverse means we arrive at the same end. Whoever found himself at the mercy of an enemy could judge the quality of that man's heart and act accordingly.

But no sooner had he established this conclusion than he overturned it, citing the example of a vulgar Theban mob comprised of weak-hearted men who, disdaining Pelopidas's pleas for mercy, admired Epaminondas's defiant courage. This example heralded Montaigne's real conclusion, that man was such a "marvelously vain, diverse, and undulating object" that it was "hard to found any constant and uniform judgment on him." Then he added, almost as an afterthought, that Pompey had once spared an entire city out of admiration for the courage of one man; whereas Sulla, after witnessing a similar display of virtue, had spared neither the individual nor the city. Montaigne had demonstrated ironically that by the same means we can arrive at diverse ends, thus overturning the commonplace title.[3]

In this composition, Montaigne used the mode of arguing *in utramque partem* to subvert commonplace thought. First he confronted the popular opinion that submission ensured mercy with the opposite opinion—that defiance, too, ensured mercy. Then he contradicted the conclusion that only the strong-hearted admired courage by citing the example of a weak-hearted mob that also admired courage. And finally he juxtaposed the example of the strong-hearted Pompey, who favored a virtuous act, with that of the strong-hearted Sulla, who disregarded a similar act.

We have already noted how this intellectual technique was borrowed from Aristotle by the Academic skeptics, the most influential of whom was Cicero. Unlike Aristotle, Cicero denied that one could ever attain truth or certainty, thus limiting all knowledge to probability or verisimilitude revealed by discoursing *in utramque partem*. This Ciceronian attitude, eclipsed during the Middle Ages, was subsequently revived in the Renaissance. Yet Montaigne used the discourse *in utramque partem* to demonstrate that one could not even establish verisimilitude in human affairs; for any given question, the diversity of human reality provided too many contradictory answers. In other words, Montaigne transformed the instrument of Academic skepticism into that of an even more radical skepticism.

This transformation resulted from the gradual breakdown of commonplace thought. In school Montaigne had been trained to anchor the discourse *in utramque partem* with commonplace norms that enabled him to arbitrate between contrasting positions and derive the more reasonable solution. This mode of thinking began to fail him years after his formal schooling, when he retired from public life in search of sagelike tranquility and wisdom. Frustration at his inability to find what he was seeking led him to begin writing the *Essais* in 1572. Even at this early date, a skeptical crisis is apparent in Montaigne's thought, as commonplaces began to lose their normative value, detaching the discourse *in utramque partem* from its anchor in "truth" and unleashing a more radical form of skepticism. The crisis intensified until 1576, when he finally resolved it in the longest of his essays, the "Apology for Raymond Sebond," where he attacked the assumptions underlying Aristotelian essentialism. In the evolution of the *Essais*, therefore, the breakdown of commonplace thought ultimately undermined the basis for the classificatory view of the world.[4]

Following the standard advice of progressive humanist pedagogues, Montaigne's father first had his son learn Latin as his mother tongue and then enrolled him in the Collège de Guyenne in 1539, at the recommended age of six. Only five years earlier, the noted humanist educator Andre Gouvéa had reorganized the school's curriculum, dedicating it in typical humanist fashion to the task of teaching Latin eloquence. Here Montaigne learned how to emulate the best classical authors, a goal facilitated by the use of several commonplace books, of which the *liber locorum rerum* was the most important. He also learned to manipulate the stylistic and moral content of his commonplace books through constant disputations *in utramque partem*. Seven years of schooling—during which classes met six days a week, eleven months a year—inculcated the intellectual system of commonplace thought. By the time he reached the first form, not even his Sundays were free. This intense experience imparted what he would later portray as his "scar" of irresolution: "I do not want to forget this further scar, very unfit to produce in public: irresolution. . . . I do not know which side to take in doubtful enterprises. . . . I can easily maintain an opinion, but not choose one. Because in human matters, whatever side we lean to, we find many probabilities to confirm us in it . . . so in whatever direction I turn, I can always provide myself with enough causes and probabilities to keep me that way."[5] What would ultimately appear as a "scar" was originally the ornament of a well-trained mind, eager and able to manipulate the common stock of wisdom on both sides, in the manner of the ideal Ciceronian orator.

Hardly anything is known about Montaigne's life from 1546 to 1554, the years between his graduation from the Collège and his debut as a magistrate.[6] He probably remained at the Collège for two years of advanced study; and afterwards he probably went to the University of Toulouse to study law, as was common practice among the new nobility and those aspiring to it.[7] In 1554 he acquired a seat on the newly created *cour des aides* of Périgueux, initiating his fifteen-year career as a magistrate. In 1557 the *cour des aides* and its magistrates were absorbed into the parlement of Bordeaux, where Montaigne met Estienne de La Boétie. The latter had entered parlement several years earlier, embarking on a promising political career; he and Montaigne knew each other by reputation and, upon their initial acquaintance, became fast friends until La Boétie's untimely death in 1563.

His friend's passing was a terrible blow for Montaigne. More than a decade later, he lamented, "Since the day I lost him, I only drag on a weary life."[8] The impact of this death was augmented by those of his father in 1568 and a younger brother soon thereafter. He was also reminded of his own mortality by a near-fatal riding accident around this time. All these factors contributed to his retirement from public life in 1571. An inscription on his library wall, commemorating his retirement on his thirty-eighth birthday, states that "little remains of his life, now more than half run out."[9] He had resolved to retire in order to prepare himself for death; as he later remarked in one of his earliest essays: "I leave it to death to test the fruit of my studies. We shall see then whether my reasonings come from my mouth or from my heart." The words of this resolution recall those of La Boétie on his deathbed, when he begged Montaigne "to show in action that the talks we had had together during our health had been not merely borne in our mouths but deeply engraved on heart and in soul."[10]

The desire to prepare for death led Montaigne to espouse the ancient ideal of the sage. Stoicism provided a doctrine, and Seneca an eloquent spokesman, for this ideal; but Montaigne's interest was not simply Stoic but, more broadly, ancient. Not only Stoics but also Pyrrhonists and Epicurians inspired him as models of the sage. Constancy, for Montaigne, was the virtue common to all sages: "For to comprise all wisdom in a word, says an ancient [Seneca], and to embrace all the rules of our life in one, it is 'always to will the same things, and always to oppose the same things.' I would not deign, he says, to add 'provided the will is just'; for if it is not just, it cannot always be whole."[11] Constancy, wisdom, and virtue were synonymous terms qualifying the actions of a man who guided his life by an immutable moral norm, a man who never strayed from his path, although he might vary his pace. Death was the ultimate test of the sage: if he maintained his path unto death, he proved his wisdom; if he deviated in the throes of death, he belied his life.

Montaigne established a library, on the third floor of a tower isolated from the rest of his château, where he could prepare for death. This library, dedicated to La Boétie's memory, housed the books bequeathed to Montaigne by his dying friend. Adjacent to the library was a small sitting room, and on the second floor was a bedroom. In his tower Montaigne could meditate in solitude, seeking guidance from the books in his library and from the proverbs inscribed on its ceiling. Given seclusion and leisure, he expected that his mind, "weightier and riper with time," would naturally tend to "stay and settle in itself." He thus hoped to achieve a sagelike tranquility that no hardship could disturb.[12]

It has been observed that "the will working for an ideal must accord with existing reality at least to such an extent that it meets it, so that the two interlock and a real conflict arises."[13] Montaigne's pursuit of the ideal of the sage, characterized by its uniformity and simplicity, forced him to confront the diversity and complexity of the world. Under the pressure of this confrontation, the ideal began to crumble, along with the normative view of the world characteristic of commonplace thought. As commonplaces began to lose their normative value, the skeptical mode of thinking *in utramque partem,* which they had previously held in check, was freed from its former constraints, engendering a more radical form of skepticism. Eventually, Montaigne's radical skepticism would undermine the Aristotelian assumption that the mind could directly apprehend reality through the senses, thus calling the whole classificatory view of the world into question.

Montaigne in His Tower

Alone in his tower, surrounded by mementos of his late friend, Montaigne could not but be reminded of his loss. Although La Boétie had been dead for nine years, "a wise man sees his dying friend hardly less vividly after twenty-five years than after the first year"; and even in his old age, Montaigne would still weep for his friend.[14] A soul pained by sorrow cannot "stay and settle in itself." In order to attain the tranquility characteristic of true wisdom, Montaigne probably began to meditate on the means of inuring himself to grief, and in all likelihood, the disturbing consequences of these meditations inspired him to begin writing.

Imagine him perusing one of the books in his library and encountering the story of Psammenitus, the king of Egypt captured by Cambyses, who watched the enslavement of his daughter and the execution of his son impassively but later wept for the fate of a friend. This story no doubt recalled that of Montaigne's contemporary, Charles of Guise, who had steadfastly born the deaths of two brothers in quick succession, only to mourn the loss of a servant soon thereafter. Montaigne surmised that Guise was so "brimful of sadness" that the slightest surcharge caused him to overflow, an inference that may have inspired him to deepen his own soul by means of reason and discipline in order to contain even the greatest shocks. But upon closer consideration, the example of Psammenitus belied such hopes, for this man was so stunned by the fate of his family that he could not even register emotion; whereas he was less moved by the fate of his friend and thus could express his grief with tears. As Montaigne would later conclude, "In truth, the impact of grief, to be extreme, must stun the whole soul and impede its freedom of action." How could any sage hope to free himself from the grip of such emotions?

One can well imagine how disturbing such thoughts would have been for a man who had retired in pursuit of sagelike tranquility. Probably on this account, Montaigne recorded them in "Of Sadness" (1.2), chronologically perhaps the first of his essays.[15] Montaigne's biographers have tended to assume that he had always nurtured literary ambitions, and that he naturally took pen in hand to keep himself occupied in the idleness of retirement. They suggest that, with no definite plan in mind, he began writing simple commonplace compositions, consisting of similar examples gathered around a central theme or moral. He supposedly imitated this popular genre, writing mere "essays at writing essays," until he found the literary form appropriate to himself.[16] But if this essay had been a typical commonplace composition, it would have demonstrated a rule of conduct. Despite their apparent similarity, however, the two chief examples contradict each other and lead to an unexpected and disturbing conclusion. Montaigne began writing in order to resolve an intellectual problem that was likely catalyzed by prolonged grief.

This problem is apparent in every one of the earliest essays, where he consistently failed to find norms underlying the diversity of human reality. For example, in "Whether the Governor of a Besieged Place Should Go Out to Parley" (1.5), he sought to establish a rule of military conduct, for the wisdom of the sage should be apparent in action as well as in contemplation. Montaigne begins with an assertion of historical relativism, that the ancient practice of waging war fairly and honorably cannot be emulated in the modern world, where everyone relies on treachery. On the one hand, he cites recent events confirming the popular opinion that a besieged commander should not negotiate with the enemy in person for fear of betrayal. On the other hand, he mentions the example of a commander who negotiated successfully at a place where he had military superiority. And he concludes with the story of a commander who entrusted himself to his enemies—negotiating with them in their own camp—and thereby saved himself and his men from annihilation. Each successive example in this chapter contradicts rather than confirms its predecessor, thus preventing the establishment of a rule of conduct and encouraging the suspension of judgment characteristic of radical skepticism.

In this essay, Montaigne attempted to employ the intellectual techniques inculcated by his education, which had trained him to use commonplace norms to arbitrate between contrasting examples. The mode of reasoning *in utramque partem* customarily served to exploit the common stock of wisdom for the purpose of persuasion. But in "Whether the Governor . . . Should Go Out to Parley," Montaigne began by rejecting the norm of ancient probity in war and set out to find a new one by arguing *in utramque partem*. He had thus transformed an instrument used to exploit truths into one used to search for them. This attempt to establish new norms ended up emphasizing the diversity of examples rather than their similarity. Instead of building commonplaces, Montaigne unwittingly found himself demolishing them.

This unexpected development must have been genuinely frustrating for a man imbued with the idea that reality could be classified under moral norms. He disparaged his meditations as "chimeras and fantastic monsters," which he put into writing in order to make his mind "ashamed of itself."[17] In other words, he wanted to regain his accustomed manner of thought. But repeated attempts to discipline his mind in the earliest essays only exacerbated its unruliness, confronting him with the difficulty of establishing the norms underlying human diversity.

Montaigne's subsequent attempts to resolve the problem of relativism arising from his retirement provided the dynamic for the evolution of his thought, to which we shall now turn. His persistent inability to establish norms in moral philosophy would eventually undermine the very basis of Aristotelian essentialism, preparing the way for a new orientation amidst complexity. As we explore the development of his thought, however, one should bear in mind that Montaigne ignored and even obscured this dimension of his work. He began writing in 1572, published the first edition in 1580, expanded the first two books and added book 3 in the fifth edition of 1588, and further expanded all three books until his death in 1592. During this twenty-year period of composition, his thought evolved through several stages; yet he made no attempt to distinguish between them. Indeed, he blended them so thoroughly that the evolution of his thought remained unrecognized until the late nineteenth century. We shall later explain this blending of compositional strata in terms of Montaigne's morphological conception of selfhood, rather than a psychological one based on an idea of development; for now, though, let us apply this modern idea to an understanding of the inner workings of his mind.[18]

In response to the impasse apparent in his earliest compositions, he invoked the ideal of the sage in his so-called "Stoical" essays. By enunciating this ideal, Montaigne reaffirmed the goal of his retirement. If he could not attain wisdom by his own means, he could still attain it by following the example of others: "Retire into yourself, but first be prepared to receive yourself there; it would be madness to trust in yourself if you do not know how to govern yourself. . . . Until you have made yourself such that you dare not trip up in your own presence . . . keep ever in your mind Cato, Phocion, and Aristides, in whose presence even fools would hide their faults; make them controllers of all your actions; if these intentions get off the track, your reverence for these men will set them right again."[19] Having "tripped up" in his own presence, Montaigne sought to guide himself with the ideal exemplified by the ancient sages. This ideal would enable him once again to anchor his skeptical habit of mind with a normative idea of wisdom; he would no longer need to find rules of conduct by discoursing on both sides. The titles of these essays, like "That to Philosophize Is to Learn to Die," are commonplaces reinforced by the contents of the essays. Instead of searching for truths, Montaigne now propounded them.

The ideal he proclaimed contrasted sharply with the apparent complexity of the world, especially as it manifested itself in the diversity of customs. All the ancient sages had attained constancy by living according to reason rather than custom. In the essay "Of Custom, and Not Easily Changing an Accepted Law" (1.23), Montaigne inveighed against custom as a "violent and treacherous schoolmistress" who deceives men into believing that their observances are justified by truth rather than mere usage. She alone establishes the bewildering diversity of opinions and beliefs. Of course, some of her effects are beneficial: she can accustom the "common herd" of men to adversity, thus enabling them to live and die like sages. Nevertheless, one is capable of greater accomplishments if one follows reason rather than habit or custom: "I cannot believe that meanness of understanding can do more than vigor, or that the effects of reason cannot match the effects of habit."[20] Montaigne concluded that judgment should be freed from the prejudice of custom: "Whoever wants to get rid of this violent prejudice of custom will find many things accepted with undoubting resolution that have no support but in the hoary beard and the wrinkles of the usage that goes with them; but when this mask is torn off, and he refers things to truth and reason, he will feel his judgment as it were all upset, and nevertheless restored to a much surer status."[21] Beyond the diversity of human reality lay a higher reality of truth and reason. The ideal of the sage thus warded off the specter of relativism conjured up by the skeptical habit of mind gone awry.

For Montaigne, Cato the Younger best exemplifies the sage: "He who has touched one chord of him has touched all; he is a harmony of perfectly concordant sounds, which cannot conflict."[22] In the essay "Of Cato the Younger" (1.37), Montaigne confessed that he could not analyze so rich a soul but only praise it. As he contemplated Cato with awe, however, he began to realize that the ideal of the sage was almost too lofty: "In all antiquity it is hard to pick out a dozen men who set their lives to a certain and constant course, which is the principal goal of wisdom."[23] And the attainment of this ideal, so difficult in antiquity, was even more difficult in Montaigne's own "corrupt" age, which had forgotten the meaning of virtue.[24] Faced with these obstacles, Montaigne sustained himself with the thought that he could at least understand the true meaning of wisdom, even if he could not attain it. Yet a man who so yearned to orient himself in life could not long remain content with the mere contemplation of an unattainable ideal. Instead, he began to modify the ideal with a new appreciation of man's "creatural" nature.[25] This new view of man undermined the ideal of the sage, thus loosening Montaigne's skeptical habit of mind from its anchor in normative truth and inducing the further evolution of his thought.

Montaigne's new awareness of man's creatural nature derived from his reflections on the near-fatal riding accident he suffered just before his retirement.[26] In his tower he undoubtedly contemplated the accident, hoping to familiarize himself with death and thus become indifferent to it. Indeed, he recommended this practice in the essay "That to Philosophize Is to Learn to Die." Such meditations, however, were motivated by the pursuit of an ideal that Montaigne gradually recognized as being unattainable. Amidst this growing realization, the contemplation of his accident yielded an unexpected result that helped undermine the ideal of the sage.

Between 1573 and 1574, Montaigne composed the essay "Of Practice" (2.6), in which he described his mental state after the accident. The trauma had submerged his consciousness in a pleasant limbo, isolated from sense impressions. Although he spoke and gestured, his words and movements bore hardly any relationship to the state of his soul: "What the soul contributed was in a dream, touched very lightly, and merely licked and sprinkled, as it were, by the soft impression of the senses." Thinking himself mortally injured, Montaigne enjoyed the sensation of letting his life slip away: "It would, in truth, have been a very happy death."[27]

In these observations, Montaigne began to acknowledge the extent to which the state of his soul depended on the condition of his body, an observation that he would later amplify in the "Apology for Raymond Sebond." He had overlooked this relationship while pursuing the ideal of the sage because the latter was based on the assumption that reason and discipline could best inure the soul to pain and suffering. Now he realized that his creatural nature obviated the need for such preparations. He did not have to steel himself against the pain he would never feel.

Rather than reject the ideal of the sage entirely, and fall back into the skeptical confusion of his earlier thinking, Montaigne now tried to humanize it: "For all his wisdom, the sage is still a man—what is there more vulnerable, more wretched, and more null."[28] In order to redefine the ideal, he naturally relied on his habit of discoursing *in utramque partem*. The subject of this discourse, however, was the very ideal that Montaigne had previously taken for granted. And as he attempted to redefine the ideal, he progressively undermined its normative value.

For example, he explored the nature of vice in "Of Drunkenness" (2.2), written around 1573–74. This essay begins with an auspicious assertion of relativism: "The world is nothing but variety and dissimilarity." Although the Stoics believed that all vices were equal (because the slightest vice betrayed an inconstant soul), Montaigne could not equate the theft of a cabbage with the desecration of a temple. If he permitted a gradation of vice, however, he had to determine when behavior transgressed acceptability. He examined drunkenness in this context, beginning with the general statement that drunkenness is a "gross and brutish vice" because it overturns the mind. He then investigated this statement from both sides. On the one hand, Josephus plied an enemy ambassador with wine, loosened his tongue, and learned all his secrets. On the other hand, both Augustus and Tiberius had confidants who were heavy drinkers, which neither emperor had reason to regret. Furthermore, German mercenaries, besotted with wine, always remember their quarters, watchwords, and rank. Not content with this simple exposition, Montaigne continued to pile example on example, demonstrating the difficulty of determining whether drunkenness is truly a vice. The ancients did not decry it too strongly; some philosophers even recommended it to relax the soul. Cato, "the true image of Stoic virtue," enjoyed his drink all too well.[29] The ability to hold one's liquor is a prized attribute in some of the most noteworthy states. Montaigne had even heard a famous doctor recommend drunkenness as an aid to digestion. And there is no better remedy for the discomforts of old age. Thus, this apparent vice had many useful attributes. Indeed, the very notion of vice itself—along with the ideal of the sage—began to crumble under the weight of human diversity.

In "Of Drunkenness," Montaigne experienced the same suspension of judgment as in his earliest essays, but he now began to accept the radical skepticism that he had previously rejected. By 1574 he no longer believed that to philosophize was "to learn to die," but rather that it was "to doubt": "If to philosophize is to doubt . . . then to play the fool and follow my fancies as I do, is all the more to doubt."[30] Montaigne's "fancies" were generated by the habit of thinking *in utramque partem* that was now undermining the system of commonplace thought it had traditionally upheld.

In following his fancies, Montaigne claimed "to play the fool," an admission signifying more than mere false modesty, for the doubts of a fool need not be taken seriously. Even if the ideal of the sage was difficult to attain in practice, it remained a theoretical possibility for Montaigne. He believed that the soul, though vulnerable to external accidents, could still regulate itself if left undisturbed: "When straightness and composure are combined with constancy, then the soul attains its ultimate perfection; that is, when nothing jars it, which a thousand accidents can do."[31] In other words, Montaigne was a reluctant skeptic, still yearning for an ideal by which to orient himself, rather than accepting the consequences of doubts that could cast him adrift without any norms for guidance.

He was reluctant to accept his radical skepticism not only because it threatened his traditional orientation but also because it lacked philosophical justification. He was familiar with the limited skepticism of the New Academy, which employed the mode of arguing *in utramque partem* to establish verisimilitude; but he was not yet familiar with the radical skepticism of the Pyrrhonists, which challenged the possibility of attaining verisimilitude. By 1574 he may have read Diogenes Laertius's "Life of Pyrrho," which, along with the works of Sextus Empiricus, provided the principal account of Pyrrhonism; but even if he had, he probably did not equate Pyrrhonism with his own suspension of judgment, for Diogenes did not provide a very forceful or detailed account of Pyrrhonism.[32] Without the justification of a philosophical precedent, Montaigne tended to dismiss his difficulty in reasoning *in utramque partem* as a personal idiosyncrasy.

He did not completely accept his own radical skepticism until reading Sextus Empiricus, probably around 1576. This Greek physician, who had lived around A.D. 200, compiled the only full account of Pyrrhonism. Until Henri Estienne published a Latin translation of Sextus's *Outlines of Pyrrhonism* in 1562, virtually everyone identified skepticism with the moderate position of the New Academy, popularized by Cicero in his *Academica*. After reading Sextus, Montaigne had two medals minted bearing the Pyrrhonist motto "I abstain"; and he had this and sixteen other epigrams from Sextus carved into the beams of his library ceiling. He enshrined these expressions because they legitimized a more radical form of skepticism than that of the New Academy.[33]

Sextus provided him with a detailed, forceful account of Pyrrhonism and its challenge to Academic skepticism. Whereas the latter school had asserted that one could not attain truth or certainty, the former doubted even this assertion. Instead of trying to establish verisimilitude, the Pyrrhonists strove to contradict all assertions about appearances, thereby fostering a suspension of judgment and ultimately inducing *ataraxy,* a state of philosophical stasis. Montaigne's reading of Sextus led him to realize that his own inconclusiveness resembled that of the Pyrrhonists: "Their expressions are: 'I establish nothing; it is no more thus than thus, or than neither way; I do not understand it; the appearances are equal on all sides; it is equally legitimate to speak for and against.' "[34] Pyrrhonism provided philosophical justification for a mode of arguing *in utramque partem* that was no longer anchored by normative truths. Rather than causing a skeptical crisis—as most scholars have assumed—Montaigne's exposure to Pyrrhonism resolved the intellectual problem born of the breakdown of commonplace thought.

In the "Apology for Raymond Sebond," Montaigne forged his doubts into a weapon wielded against the presumption of human reason. Sebond was a fifteenth-century Spanish theologian who had claimed that the truths of Christianity could be found with certainty in the natural world of God's creation instead of in Scripture, which was always subject to misinterpretation. Montaigne had published a translation of Sebond's *Theologia naturalis* in 1568, hoping to provide Frenchmen with a nondogmatic basis for faith acceptable to Huguenots and Catholics alike.[35] He now undertook to defend the theologian, not against those critics who maintained that reason was unable to prove religious truth, but against those who maintained that Sebond's arguments were not good enough. Montaigne's defense of Sebond was really the pretext for a Pyrrhonist attack on all those who presumed to have normative knowledge of the world, an attack that swept from moral to natural philosophy, driving at the very heart of Aristotelian essentialism.

Marshaling a wide array of arguments, borrowed largely from Plutarch and Sextus, Montaigne hammered away at the presumptions of human reason: that it makes man better than other animals, that it makes him happy, that it makes him good. The diversity of philosophical opinions (extravagantly rendered in a discursive list) proves that reason is incapable of discerning any universal truths: "Now trust in your philosophy; boast that you have found the bean in the cake, when you consider the clatter of so many philosophical brains."[36] Normative claims stem merely from opinions authorized by usage. Opinions of this sort usually originated as the playthings of the ancients, who either did not take them seriously or presented them in a competitive intellectual marketplace for critical appraisal. Yet, Montaigne complained, moderns accept such opinions unquestioningly; instead of using reason to criticize them, men use it to bolster them. Indeed, reason itself is responsible for the bewildering diversity of opinions: "I always call reason that semblance of intellect that each man fabricates in himself. That reason, of which, by its condition, there can be a hundred contradictory ones about one and the same subject, is an instrument of lead and wax, stretchable, pliable, and adaptable to all biases and all measures; all that is needed is the ability to mold it."[37] Montaigne had once hoped that reason could transcend diversity; now he declared it to be the very fountainhead of diversity.

The malleability of human reason derived from the soul's relationship to the body. Montaigne had first acknowledged this relationship in the description of his riding accident; but in the "Apology," the insidious effect of the creatural view of man upon the ideal of the sage became fully apparent to him. If a powerful shock like the riding accident can overwhelm the soul, a lesser mishap can disturb it, and even a feeling of slight discomfort has its proportionate effect: "On an empty stomach I feel myself another man than after a meal."[38] Reason cannot attain constancy because the state of the soul fluctuates with the condition of the body, thus spawning the infinite variety of opinions.

In the Pyrrhonistic critique of the senses that concludes the "Apology," Montaigne advanced beyond the realm of moral philosophy to attack the very foundations of rationalism. He argued that the soul is not only buffeted by external forces but also agitated by its own internal instability. Reason depends on senses that are both intrinsically weak, compared with those of certain animals, and extrinsically unreliable, given their fluctuation with the condition of the body. Weak, fluctuating senses cannot grasp the essence of an external object; they convey to the soul only their varying impressions of that object. Furthermore, these impressions are transformed by the state of the soul, which itself is in constant flux. Human reason thus cannot apprehend extra-mental reality.

Montaigne used Pyrrhonism to encourage "fideism," the notion that human reason cannot know God unless aided by divine revelation. By severing faith completely from reason, Montaigne made religious observance a matter of custom, because reason could provide no justification for deviating from the faith of one's forefathers. This might appear to be an ironic conclusion to the "defense" of a natural theologian, but Montaigne remained true to the intention of undercutting religious strife that had originally motivated him to translate Sebond. In the "Apology," however, he went even further. His ultimate aim was not simply to keep Christians loyal to the church but to make them see themselves for what they really were, mere creatures incapable of knowing God's will. This message informs his fideism in the closing lines of the first edition of the essay: "But to make the handful bigger than the hand, the armful bigger than the arm, and to hope to straddle more than the reach of our legs, is impossible and unnatural. Nor can man raise himself above himself and humanity; for he can see only with his own eyes and seize only with his own grasp. He will rise, if God lends him his hand; he will rise by abandoning and renouncing his own means, and letting himself be raised and uplifted by divine grace; but not otherwise." Montaigne's humility here has the intensity of religious feeling, yet it derived not from his awe of God the Creator but from his understanding of man the creature. This understanding would eventually enable Montaigne to reorient himself in a complex world devoid of apparent norms.

In his pioneering history of skepticism, Richard Popkin declared that the "Apology" delivered the coup de grace to an entire intellectual world.[39] The traditional Aristotelian way of thinking classified entities on the basis of shared properties. All such properties were apprehended by means of a process of abstraction operating, ultimately, on the data of sensory impressions. If this foundation was weak, the whole edifice fell. Montaigne's attack on the presumption of human reason had carried the very citadel of Aristotelian essentialism. In the evolution of his thought, the inability to establish moral norms had thus eventually led to the collapse of the whole classificatory view of the world.

The Idea of the Essay

The ultimate answer to the skeptical *Que sais-je?* of the "Apology" was not *Rien* but *Moi-même*. Despite what appears to us as a "subjective" answer, Montaigne did not become a relativist. He conceived of the self as a fixed point of reference in a complex world, a mental object whose outlines became ever clearer as he contemplated the diversity around it. And despite relying on the self as a moral compass, he did not become a proto-romantic, seeking to express his own individuality in the face of traditional morality. Rather, he conceived of himself as "following nature," a benign guide that would never lead anyone astray. Although he characteristically did not push this idea to its logical conclusion, it implied a new social ideal in which individuals could best live together by following their own natures. This conception of selfhood and the morality derived from it were alternatives to a doctrine of relativism.

Montaigne's penchant for self-study originated from his creatural view of man. In the "Apology," he intensified the creatural view through self-observation: "I who spy on myself more closely, who have my eyes increasingly intent on myself, as one who has not much business elsewhere . . . I would hardly dare tell of the vanity and weakness that I find in myself."[40] In this activity he tended to perceive himself as a mere man, a creature typical of his species. As he increasingly contemplated the certainty of his own weakness, however, he began to surmise that he was the only man among his contemporaries to *know* that he was *only* a man. This observation inspired his project of self-portrayal.

In the first essay devoted to self-portrayal, written around 1578, Montaigne noted with ironic modesty, "The only thing which makes me think something of myself is the thing in which no man ever thought himself deficient . . . for who ever thought that he lacked sense?" In this paradox Montaigne confronted the reality of his own judgment. He trusted this faculty because it consistently led him to deprecate himself despite the singular affection he reserved for himself. He reinforced this trust by exercising his judgment on its own conclusions:

> Now I find my opinions infinitely bold and constant in condemning my inadequacy. In truth, this too is a subject on which I exercise my judgment as much as on any other. The world always looks straight ahead; as for me, I turn my gaze inward, I fix it there and keep it busy. Everyone looks in front of him; as for me, I have no business but with myself; I continually observe myself, I take stock of myself, I taste myself. Others always go elsewhere, if they stop to think about it; they always go forward . . . as for me, I roll about in myself.

Judgment was a reflexive faculty; instead of leading him outward to knowledge about the world, it always led him inward to knowledge about himself—judge and judged.[41]

Montaigne derived from the verb *essayer*—to test or assay—the term describing the reflexive movement of his mind. An essay was a test of his judgment, and exercise in which Montaigne measured himself. To a large extent, the idea of the essay derived from the rhetorical theory of "imitation," which prescribed that authors not follow their sources slavishly but rather "emulate" them—that is, contest with them in an attempt to surpass them. This is the procedure that Erasmus followed in the *Adages,* where he tested himself against his sources and thereby defined his authorial identity.[42] Montaigne followed the same procedure, but in a more generalized way, measuring himself not only against classical sources but also against the diversity and variety of the world.

Any subject provided him with the means of essaying himself. In "Of Thumbs" (2.26), for example, Montaigne explored a frivolous topic: barbarian kings customarily pricked their thumbs and sucked each other's blood to seal a pact; doctors call thumbs the master fingers, as reflected in Latin and Greek etymology; Romans signified favor or disfavor with their thumbs; men who had lost their thumbs were exempted from war; a victorious admiral had the thumbs of his vanquished enemies cut off to prevent them from ever again manning a ship. Montaigne listed these diverse examples without any apparent order or purpose; he was simply essaying his judgment on this "vain and nonexistent subject . . . to see if it will find the wherewithal to give it body, prop it up, and support it." His failure to do so with this topic was no less revealing than his success with others—"Every movement reveals us." In other words, the conclusions derived from this activity were less important than the activity itself.[43]

With the idea of the essay, Montaigne resolved the problem of relativism. Instead of taking refuge from the diversity of human reality, by attempting either to order or transcend it, Montaigne immersed himself in it. He rejoiced in exercising his mind upon the manifold complexity of the world. The customs of barbarian kings, the gestures of ancient Romans, and the opinions of modern doctors all mingled in a mind that, in the act of beholding them, beheld itself. The more diverse the examples, the more varied was the reflected image of his mind. Montaigne's skeptical habit of discoursing *in utramque partem,* unrestrained by commonplace norms, now served to generate the many facets of the mirror he held before himself.

There was no need to impose any order on this complexity, but only to contemplate it, and to record one's contemplations. The mind that perceived itself through its own operations fluctuated with the movements of body and soul. Different moods, physical conditions, and positions in time and space engendered different thoughts, even about the same things; all were equally revealing of the thinker. Montaigne affected to record these fluctuations "naturally," as they occurred, as if he were engaged in a rambling conversation with his reader.[44] When he periodically revised the *Essais* for new editions, he attempted to preserve and augment the "natural" appearance of his portrait by inserting new observations into old compositions, often interrupting or even contradicting the original flow of thought. He made no effort to distinguish between the different chronological layers of composition, because he conceived of the *Essais* as a dynamic record of moment-to-moment fluctuations.

Habit and custom buoyed Montaigne in this sea of change. The faculty of judgment that he probed was to a large extent shaped by these factors, which could make even the most bizarre practices appear reasonable and natural. Whereas he had once decried habit as a "violent and treacherous schoolmistress," he now embraced it as life-sustaining. Mere man is first and foremost a creature of habit: "It is for habit to give form to our life, just as it pleases; it is all-powerful in that."[45] Health itself means little more than living in one's accustomed state, which usage varies from person to person and region to region. Habit enables mere man not only to live well but also to die well. During his flight from the terrible plague of 1585–86,

Montaigne witnessed how the peasantry, without the aid of philosophy, confronted the imminence of death with sagelike constancy: "A whole nation was suddenly, by habit alone, placed on a level that concedes nothing in firmness to any studied and premeditated fortitude."[46] The call to "follow nature" that resounds throughout book 3 of the *Essais* entailed acceptance not only of one's primary, creatural nature but also of one's secondary nature of habit and custom: "Habit [*accoustumance*] is a second nature, and no less powerful."[47] Although one might occasionally violate the letter of traditional morality by following his own nature, he would always keep to its spirit, for "nature is a gentle guide, but no more gentle than wise and just."[48]

Habit enabled Montaigne to sustain himself in a reality whose dominant characteristic was flux: "The world is but a perennial movement. All things in it are in constant motion—the earth, the rocks of the Caucasus, the pyramids of Egypt—both with the common motion and with their own. Stability itself is nothing but a more languid motion."[49] Amidst the natural motion of the world, he acquired such knowledge as befitted his condition as a mere man, knowledge not of unchanging essences but of instances of flux. The mind no longer served to transcend the flux of reality but to engage with it. In place of the abstract exercise of reason, which could not accommodate itself to the mobility of existence, Montaigne substituted a form of cognition in which the self-conscious mind interacted spontaneously with reality, registering its own movements within the general flux of the world.

Although the record of each movement of his mind immobilized only a transitory aspect of himself, it was he who moved, he who essayed himself: "So, all in all, I may indeed contradict myself now and then; but truth, as Demades said, I do not contradict."[50] Truth resided not only in the honesty of the portrait but in the reality of the self as a mental object. The "objective" existence of this entity was revealed by the multiple perspectives he took upon himself: "There is no one who, if he listens to himself, does not discover in himself a pattern all his own, a ruling pattern [*une forme sienne, une forme maistresse*], which struggles against education and against the tempest of the passions that oppose it."[51] His *forme maistresse* constituted the shape of his personality, the pattern formed by the many instances of the self, giving unity and substance to a being that could apprehend itself only fleetingly.

Whoever wanted to find his own personal standpoint in existence had only to exercise his mind as honestly and forcefully as possible, without bending to authority or popular opinion. To view the world through someone else's eyes, to feign a point of view, or to restrict unnaturally the operations of the mind was to distort the reflected image of the self. Montaigne sought the companionship of those free and open minds capable of exercising themselves to the fullest. Such men he aptly termed *honnestes hommes,* denoting their intellectual integrity. Although learning could ornament such minds, it did not provide their substance; indeed, it was not even a necessity: "A wellborn mind that is practiced in dealing with men makes itself thoroughly agreeable by itself."[52] The frankness and vigor typical of conversation among such men offered an excellent opportunity for self-knowledge. Although he characteristically did not try to systematize it, Montaigne treated the notion of *honnêteté* as if it were a universal ideal embracing peasants as well as nobles, Brazilian cannibals as well as Frenchmen.[53] An ideal of humanity—albeit one very broadly defined—thus served to encompass the notion of selfhood.

The idea of the essay provided Montaigne with a new cognitive standpoint that enabled him to mediate between the extremes of rationalism and relativism. The rationalist believes that reason has access to normative truths superseding the variety of individual opinions, whereas the relativist believes that such variety invalidates any so-called "truth." The activity of essaying himself complemented Montaigne's sense of relativity without engendering a skeptical denial of truth; it accorded with his awareness of the limitations of his perception, while at the same time serving as a link to the reality he sought to understand. On the one hand, it presented all knowledge as being relative to the observer; on the other, it presented the observer as an entity that could be known objectively. That entity, existing in and of the world, represented the portion of reality accessible to human understanding.[54]

Montaigne's Moral Morphology

Individuality provided Montaigne with his point of orientation amidst relativity. Yet he did not and—as we shall see—could not regard his self as developing in relation to its circumstances. Rather, the intellectual techniques at his disposal constrained him to move in a different direction, one that betrays the residual influence of classificatory thought. Whereas we regard selfhood from a psychological perspective that charts the development of personality over time, he regarded it from a morphological perspective concerned with the spatial rather than temporal ordering of human experience.

We have already noted that Montaigne did not attach any special importance to an idea of personal development. Although the book of his self consists of three chronological strata of composition, he did not make any attempt to distinguish between them. Commenting on the practice of inserting new observations amidst old ones, he remarked, "Myself now and myself a while ago are indeed two; but when better, I simply cannot say."[55]

The substance and sentiment of this remark indicate that he was not concerned with his development through time.

Despite his fascination with selfhood, Montaigne never bothered to ask *why* he was the way he was. This question would have been ripe for an answer that would have explained his personality in terms of its development. To some extent, he conceived of himself as an old man who had long been fully formed, and thus he was not inclined to ask that question. And to some extent, in an explicit rejection of Aristotelian rationalism, he had ceased asking such "causal" questions altogether. But these explanations might imply that he consciously chose not to view himself developmentally, whereas in reality the range of his thought was circumscribed by conceptual boundaries different from our own.

In order to be able to ask why he was the way he was, Montaigne would have had to take a perspective on his life, to see it from a point of view, which then might have enabled him to interpret its development up to that point.[56] The very organization of the *Essais,* however, indicates that he did not view himself from a single perspective, but rather from innumerable ones. This form of multiple perspectivism—the very mode of thinking that enabled him to resolve the problem of relativism—constitutes the chief feature distinguishing his mode of thinking from developmental ones. In his portrayal of the natural flux of his mind, he attempted to capture the distinctiveness of each of its movements, of each moment of his self. Consequently, he focused on the present, writing mostly in the present tense.[57] The present was defined by a nexus of time and space that accounted for its being "this" moment. In other words, each of the multitude of perspectives he took upon himself was characterized by a quality of *haecceitas,* "haecceity" or "thisness," to borrow an expression from scholastic philosophy.[58]

The "thisness" of his perception was intensely relativistic; each moment was separate from the next, characterized by its own nexus of time and space. The individuality of each moment enabled Montaigne to catch a glimpse of his self, as the immediate circumstances of his existence provided a unique perspective on the operations of his mind. He focused, if only for an instant, on one moment to the exclusion of all others; had he not preserved the experience of that moment on paper, it would have been lost when his attention shifted to the next one. He saw his self, not as being *shaped by* his circumstances, but as being *reflected in* them. In other words, that he was a Catholic, a Frenchman, and a Gascon served to reflect who he was, not to explain why he was that way. The "thisness" of his perception mitigated against both his taking a point of view on his life and his seeing it as the outcome of a process of development. Indeed, the notion of development would have obscured the very "thisness" that enabled him to perceive his self.

When one views himself from innumerable perspectives, each with its own special claim to his attention, he can be expected to place the highest premium on a conception of the self that orders its component parts analytically. Without an idea of development, Montaigne had nothing to gain by ordering the moments of his self chronologically, as he clearly indicated in the remark about "myself now and myself a while ago." Instead, it was only natural for him to arrange these moments topically, in part because he had begun his search for meaning in a complex world by emulating the genre of commonplace literature. Indeed, topical organization helped him to discover the true subject of his quest by enabling him to observe the workings of his mind as it focused on a circumscribed subject. The more distinct his sense of self became, the less he needed the artifice of topical organization, which he gradually abandoned. Nonetheless the title of every essay in book 3—his most "personal" book—begins with the preposition *of:* "Of Repentance," "Of Coaches," "Of Experience." Given the rambling nature of these compositions—"Of Coaches" has notoriously little to say about its ostensible subject—it is surprising that Montaigne even bothered to keep up the pretense of topical organization.

The titles of the essays in book 3 reflect the continued influence of classificatory thinking, which received considerable impetus from Montaigne's desire to describe the characteristic shape of his self, its *forme maistresse.* This metaphor reflects the Aristotelian notion of "substance" as a union of "form" and "matter."[59] Montaigne uses the term *forme* frequently in conjuction with notions of self-study and self-portrayal. One might as well study oneself, he argues, because "each man bears the entire form [*la forme entiere*] of the human condition."[60] In the activity of essaying himself, he claims to surrender himself to "doubt and uncertainty, and to my ruling quality [*ma maistresse forme*], which is ignorance."[61] And, he observes, "By long usage, this form of mine has passed into substance [*cette forme m'est passée en substance*], and fortune into nature."[62] From Montaigne's frequent use of the term *forme* in the context of the self, we can conclude that he conceived of his *forme maistresse* as that which distinguished him from others by imparting a unique "form" to his creatural "matter."[63] In other words, he regarded his self not as an entity undergoing a process of development, but as a "substance" in the Aristotelian sense—that is, as "matter" that has received a particular "form."

Of course, he does not actually classify his self in the *Essais.* One would look in vain for any kind of systematic description, much less a taxonomy, of the self; its *forme maistresse* is ineffable. Yet this metaphor nonetheless implies the existence of a pattern or design that orders the instances of his self. In the *Essais,* Montaigne conceives of this order in spatial terms. He describes the act of writing as that of "giving body" to his thoughts by putting them *en registre* and *en rolle,* as if the outlines of his personality can be catalogued and thus rendered visible.[64] In his most striking use of this recurrent imagry, he refers to his self-portrait as a *skeletos* that "displays" himself entire (*je m'estalle entier*)—veins, muscles, and tendons—each part in its appropriate place (*chaque piece en son siege*).[65] The verb *estaller* denotes the spatial arrangement of objects, and the expression *chaque piece en son siege* recalls the terminology of commonplace thought, in which *loci* are the "seats" of arguments, "places" where information is located. Perhaps it was only natural for Montaigne to refer to his self-portrait in physical terms, but he described the *skeletos* as if it were a collection of "places" akin to the contemporary mnemonic device of the "memory theater," filled with the "seats" of knowledge.[66]

Finally, and most important, the separate "pieces" or instances of self encompassed by his *forme maistresse* are homogeneous units, all granted equal consideration. Despite its "thisness," each instant of the self is, in one crucial sense, qualitatively no different from any other: "Every movement reveals us." To the extent that all these instants serve the same function for Montaigne, to the same degree, his morphology of self recalls the arrangement of knowledge characteristic of place logic and commonplace thought, whose *loci* are all qualitatively similar. Of Ramus's dichotomized taxonomies for the organization of knowledge, Walter Ong has remarked that, "In this essentially spatial economy, 'form' is mere grouping of units, all of which are doomed to be pretty much like one another."[67] Although it does not represent an explicitly "spatial economy," Montaigne's *forme maistresse* is embodied by a grouping of homogeneous units, reflecting the pervasive influence of the classificatory way of thinking. Thus, despite having demolished commonplace thought, Montaigne was still unwittingly trapped in its rubble by the very "thisness" of his perception.

The quality of *haecceitas* served to structure the thought of a whole generation of Frenchmen, accounting for the epistemic similarity between figures as diverse as Montaigne and La Popelinière. Both men were responding to the same intellectual stimulus, the need to find order in a relativistic world where words and ideas has been torn from their traditional context by typographic literacy and humanist philology. Decontextualization fostered the "thisness" of their perception and the corresponding drive toward order, both of which are reflected in their extensive use of lists and in their impulse to make these lists as exhaustive as possible. The need for order led them to seek the underlying structure of human reality. Whereas La Popelinière described the "design" of universal history, Montaigne revealed the "pattern" of his self. And just as La Popelinière sought to fix the "substance" of history, so too Montaigne sought to fix the substance of his self: "It is not my deeds that I write down; it is myself, it is my essence."[68] The urge they shared was basically classificatory, concerned with organizing the fundamental "bits" of information about their respective subjects.

Despite these similarities, however, Montaigne succeeded in transforming the classificatory view of the world from a bare catalogue of diversity into a rich stance toward it. He had realized early on that the simple amassing and arranging of information would lead to knowledge neither of the self nor of the world. Instead, he recognized that the mind must engage with this diverse information as a test of its judgment, the faculty with which it reached out toward the world. The experience of relativism became the *sine qua non* of self-discovery, the means by which one liberated oneself from dogmatism and expanded one's mental horizons to their utmost limits. In short, relativism engendered intellectual freedom.

Whereas the "thisness" of his perception formed a conceptual limit of Montaigne's thought, it also provided a window onto a new world, characterized by a different notion of time. "I do not portray being: I portray passing. Not the passing from one age to another, or, as the people say, from seven years to seven years, but from day to day, from minute to minute. My history needs to be adapted to the moment."[69] This famous statement epitomizes Montaigne's departure from previous conceptions of temporal change, which emphasized continuity, toward one of discontinuity. This notion enabled him to describe a world full of novelties, the perception of which was one of the preconditions for the eventual emergence of an idea of historical development.

His contemporaries emphasized the notion of continuity amidst the vicissitude of events by describing change in terms of either the corruption or the unfolding of historical entities. Hotman regarded the "ancient constitution" of France as exerting a powerful and continuous influence on her institutions, which remained strong only as long as the constitution was preserved and were subsequently weakened by its corruption. La Popelinière and Vignier stressed the need for a continuous history from the earliest times to the present, relating institutions to origins that, though remote, still exerted a formative influence on what followed. Pasquier's taxonomy of France made this implicit notion of unfolding explicit by differentiating the genetic material of ancient Gaul into the constituent elements of modern French culture. All these authors comprehended change with reference to essences that endured despite the flux of events.

When Montaigne regarded states, laws, and institutions, he too conformed to the notion of change as corruption: "In all things except those that are simply bad, change is to be feared."[70] In part this attitude derived from his reaction to the Wars of Religion. He repeatedly denounced both Huguenots and Catholic Leaguers alike as "innovators" who had rent the age-old fabric of the monarchy, which he believed should be mended rather than refashioned. But unlike Hotman, for example, whose notion of corruption was based on a metanormative ideal of mixed monarchy, Montaigne's "conservatism" reinforced his acceptance of relativism: "Now laws remain in credit not because they are just, but because they are laws. That is the mystic foundation of their authority; they have no other."[71] Laws are observances of trivial origin authorized by custom, which varies from state to state; their insubstantiality necessitates that one not examine them too closely, for fear of encouraging attempts to replace them with "better" ones, lacking even the authority imparted by prolonged usage: "And no laws are held in their true honor except those to which God has given some ancient duration, so that no one knows their origin or that they were ever different."[72] This conservatism complemented his enthusiastic endorsement of custom as the chief support of life; one should not abandon the way of life that helped constitute his point of orientation in existence.

The positive acceptance of custom freed Montaigne to immerse himself in the moment-to-moment experience of life; and as he increasingly emphasized this aspect of existence, he began to undermine the traditional notion of continuity in time. Instead, he came to experience time as discontinuity; it was the flux of the world, and of the self in the world. He focused on each moment of the self in isolation from previous and successive ones; in effect, he portrayed a multiplicity of selves, each bounded by a separate instant of time: "With the radical discontinuity of a world made of occasions there is mingled the similar discontinuity of successive selves that are created by these occasions."[73]

One of the chief impressions to emerge from this radical discontinuity was a sense of novelty. Each moment, each self, was utterly new; indeed, the selves he beheld from one moment to the next were so unexpectedly new as to appear strange to him: "I have seen no more evident monstrosity and miracle in the world than myself. . . . The more I frequent myself and know myself, the more my deformity astonishes me, and the less I understand myself."[74] This sense of novelty was born of his awareness of the contingency of his existence. At table, on horseback, or in conversation, Montaigne observed different instances of the self embodied by his concrete circumstances. These contingencies of time and space were enfolded within an envelope of habit and custom, themselves contingencies of a broader sort, born of unrepeatable accidents authorized by usage. The contemplation of these novelties—in which Montaigne opened himself to their strangeness—provided him with striking images of his self.

Seen in the context of the traditional notion of change, Montaigne's sense of novelty and its contingency upon circumstances is more compatible with the eventual emergence of an idea of historical development. Traditional notions of change did not admit of the presence of wholly new entities that were not somehow implicit in what had gone before. As we saw in chapter 2, Hotman interpreted the creation of ostensibly new institutions, like the Twelve Peers, as further manifestations of the ancient constitution; and Pasquier regarded every aspect of modern French culture as being inherent in ancient Gaul. Change was characterized not by an entity's development in relation to its circumstances but rather by its unfolding in fulfillment of a predetermined form or essence; events served not to shape the entity in new ways but to impede or impel the realization of its potential. Montaigne's emphasis on time as dicontinuity focused attention not on what endured through change but on what was new and unique. As wonderment at novelty born of change became more widespread and thoroughgoing during the next two centuries, it gradually stimulated a way of thinking that would explain novelty as the product of a process of historical development.

Of all his contemporaries, Montaigne was apparently the only one to delight in the complexity of the world, finding his point of orientation amidst it. His solution to the problem of relativism, however, was destined to remain idiosyncratic. Contemporaries hailed him as the "French Seneca," whose work provided a storehouse of moral wisdom. Yet in the same breath that he praises Montaigne's teachings, a reader no less astute than Estienne Pasquier criticizes him for departing from the model of commonplace literature: "He was a bold person who followed his own advice, and as such he easily let himself be carried away by the beauty of his mind; so much so that in his writings he took pleasure in being pleasantly displeasing. Whence it happens that you will find in him several chapters whose heading bears no relation at all to the rest of the body, except the feet." These chapters are, of course, in book 3, where Montaigne most fully articulated his conception of the self as one's point of orientation in a complex world. Pasquier, though, entirely misunderstands him, dismissing the self-portrait as a product of Montaigne's dotage: "While he gives the appearance of disdaining himself, I never read an author who esteemed himself as much as he. For if anyone had scratched out all the passages he used to talk about himself and his family, his work would be shortened by a good quarter, especially in his third book, which seems to be a story of his ways and actions; a thing that I attribute rather to the freedom of his old age when he composed it."[75] Thus, some of Montaigne's contemporaries simply failed to understand what he was saying. Perhaps the resemblance of the *Essais* to commonplace literature misled them, creating false expectations.

But as we shall see, there were some readers who understood the *Essais* all too well, and did not like what they read. Ultimately they were disturbed by the very feature that most clearly distinguishes Montaigne's thought from our own—namely, his complete acceptance of *who* he was, without any concern for *why* he was that way. The self to which all was referred, and through which all was understood, floated in an amorphous ether. To locate the self in the matrix of habit and custom only begged the question, because these were accidents authorized by mere usage. For Christians enduring a fight to the death over the issue salvation, Montaigne's existential nonchalance must have been unsettling, and all the more so for having been the logical outcome of that struggle. They could find little comfort in a moral philosophy whose anchor was merely the product of chance. Much like Einstein confronted with quantum mechanics, they refused to believe that God played dice with the universe.

CHAPTER 4

THE MORAL ORDER

Pandora's Box

Usbek, Montesquieu's epistolary critic of French culture in the *Lettres persanes,* offers a striking caricature of the religious nonchalance of eighteenth-century Parisians:

> They are no more steadfast in their incredulity than in their faith, but live in an ebb and flow of belief which carries them ceaselessly from one to the other. One of them said to me one day: "I believe in the immortality of the soul periodically. My opinions depend entirely on my physical condition. According to whether I have greater or less vitality, or my digestion is functioning well or badly, or the atmosphere I breathe is thick or thin, or the food I eat is light or heavy, I am a Spinozist, a Socinian or a Catholic, unbelieving or devout."[1]

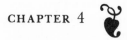

Here we have the reductio of Montaigne's amusing comment, "On an empty stomach I feel myself another man than after a meal." Beneath the self-deprecating charm of this comment lay an abyss of relativism that threatened to swallow up even the certainty of religion, an abyss Montaigne perpetually skirted. "We are Christians by the same title that we are Perigordians or Germans."[2] In Montaigne's skillful hands, this inflammatory observation, bordering on the heretical, becomes an almost innocuous goad to Christians to embrace the true faith out of the sincerity of belief rather than the stupor of habit. Despite the sincerity of his own belief, however, Montaigne's aim was to set God aside in order better to understand the fluctuating world of man, characterized by the diversity of customs, laws, opinions—and beliefs. The distinction between divine and human things circumscribed the role of religion and, in so doing, had the incidental effect of undercutting it. Our sixteenth-century Gascon's ruminations on digestion foreshadowed those of the eighteenth-century Parisian.

Yet Montaigne never allowed himself to be swamped by the abyss. He was too conscious of the intimate relationship between mind and body—between soul and stomach—to pursue the implications of his musings systematically—as if, he feigned, he were even capable of such sustained mental effort. And his powerful sense of self anchored him, even in seemingly bottomless depths. Secured to the stable reality of his own being as a man, Gascon, Frenchman, and Catholic, he could range freely over dangerous waters, buoyed by his cheerful acceptance of an individuality that had been, by definition, spawned in a sea of relativity. Few of Montaigne's readers, either past or present, have had such existential stability; and those among his contemporaries who attempted to follow in his wake must have experienced intense discomfort.

One such man was Pierre Charron, best known for his moral treatise *De la sagesse*. Charron's heavy reliance on his predecessor's work has led even his biographers to characterize him as *l'herbier de Montaigne,* desiccating the fruits of the *Essais* in an attempt to systematize them.[3] But Charron was no slavish admirer, content to tidy up after his master. He had assimilated enough of Montaigne's relativizing insights to know that he could neither ignore nor fully accept them. On the one hand, he recognized that in a complex world, the individual had to use his self as his point of orientation; on the other, he felt compelled to locate the self within a broad intellectual and moral system extending, step by step, from the Creator down through his creation. In effect, he wanted to accommodate Montaigne's insights to a revitalized system of classification, but he only succeeded in demonstrating that the heightened awareness of relativism precluded a return to the traditional way of thinking. It is ironic that the fruits of Montaigne's mind, far from being desiccated by Charron's systematizing, became instead hypertrophied, and that Charron himself—a priest no less—unwittingly disseminated the attitude of religious nonchalance that Montesquieu would later parody.

Charron was born in 1541, the son of a Parisian bookseller, and educated at the University of Paris, where he was influenced by both scholasticism and humanism. He studied not only ethics, logic, physics, and metaphysics, but also Latin and Greek. The exposure to classical languages and literature no doubt contributed to his profound sense of relativism, which must have long predated his familiarity with Montaigne's *Essais*. The university's scholastic curriculum was being challenged at this time by reformers like Peter Ramus, from the likes of whom Charron probably acquired the distaste for metaphysical speculation that would underlie his subsequent interest in moral philosophy. Nonetheless, his systematic approach to moral philosophy reflects the predominate influence of scholasticism at the university. Perhaps the duality of his education at Paris laid the foundation for the characteristic tension in Charron's thought between relativizing insights and normative impulses.

From Paris, Charron went on to study law first at Orléans and then, while Cujas was there, at Bourges. Since Bourges was the chief center of legal humanism in France, we may assume that he was exposed to the *mos gallicus* there, and to the sense of historical and cultural relativity that it inspired. His legal education, interrupted by his ordination to the priesthood, was completed at Montpellier, where he obtained degrees in both civil and canon law in 1571. Thereafter he became a very popular preacher in several dioceses in the Bordeaux area, and eventually attracted the attention of Marguerite de Navarre, who chose him as her *prédicateur ordinaire*. During this time he also got to know Montaigne, who presented him with a copy of Bernardino Ochino's *Catechismo* in July 1586. Perhaps Montaigne intended this gift—a prohibited book by an Italian Lutheran—to aid Charron in his mission of preaching in a area dominated by Huguenots. The immediacy of doctrinal strife, and ultimately of civil war, probably honed both Charron's sense of relativism and his countervailing need for a normative standpoint amidst complexity.

By Charron's own admission, the low point of his career came after the assassinations of the duke and cardinal de Guise, ordered by Henri III in December 1588. Outraged by the king's brazen act, Charron flirted briefly with the Catholic League, the party that the Guises had led in opposition to the Huguenots. Soon, though, he recognized that the league's cure for the body politic was worse than the disease, and he recanted his public behavior in the unfinished "Discours chrestien, qu'il n'est permis au subiet . . . de se liguer . . . contre son roy," begun in April 1589. Here he dismissed his flirtation with the league as folly born of passion: "I was always as it were in anger, in a continual fever and agitation; whence I have learned, at my own expense, that it is impossible to be both moved and wise at the same time."[4]

Charron's brush with the league is crucial for understanding the subsequent development of his thought, which aimed at creating a systematic distinction between religion and politics. On one level, this distinction would enable Charron's countrymen to avoid his own recent pitfall; on a deeper level, however, it would enable him both to express and to resolve a profound sense of relativism. Civil war had catalyzed his need to find a new standpoint in a complex reality where religious truths no longer provided satisfactory answers to political and ethical questions. The catalyst of civil war reacted with the compound of a humanistic and legal education that revealed fundamental differences between the classical pagan world and the modern Christian one. Recognition of these differences underlay Charron's need for orientation. The distinction between religion and politics enabled him to assert that there were two realms of experience—faith and reason—while maintaining that they were both suffused with divine light. This qualified fideism provided a bulwark against the relativism he was forced to acknowledge.

The initial step in Charron's program of reorientation was to secure the realm of religious belief. In *Les Trois Veritez,* first published anonymously in Bordeaux in 1593, he established the fundamental truths of religion, while dispensing with their corresponding errors: the truth of the existence of God (versus atheism), the truth of Christianity (versus the infidels), and the truth of Catholism (versus the Protestants). *De la sagesse* was the secular counterpart to *Les Trois Veritez,* establishing the realm of human reason as distinct from, yet complementary to, that of religious belief. Charron began writing it in 1597, completed it in 1599, and finally had it published—after a delay in the granting of a royal privilege—in 1601. It quickly drew considerable attention and criticism, leading Charron to revise the work extensively for its second edition, which appeared posthumously in 1604. He also composed a companion piece to the second edition, the *Petit Traicté de sagesse,* a clarification and defense of the larger work. Despite being placed on the *Index* in 1605, the *Sagesse* went through about forty editions in the seventeenth century alone, making it one of the most influential products of learned culture in early modern France.

Charron consciously intended the tripartite structure of the *Sagesse* to mirror that of his previous work on religion: "This work, which instructs life and manners on living and dying well is entitled 'wisdom,' just as our previous work, which taught about proper belief, had been called 'truth,' or better yet 'three truths,' there being three books in the latter as in the former."[5] Book 1 of the *Sagesse* describes man in and of himself, his position in the hierarchy of earthly beings, and the characteristics distinguishing one man from another. It calls upon man to know himself, his faults, and the misery of his condition in order better to receive the teaching of wisdom. Book 2 lays out this teaching schematically: its two preliminary requirements, its two essential qualities, the six laws governing its exercise, and the moral benefits ensuing from its practice. Book 3 applies the general lessons of the second book to specific social and political circumstances, which are organized according to the four cardinal virtues—justice, prudence, fortitude, and temperance. Throughout the *Sagesse,* Charron strictly maintained the distinction between religion on the one hand, and ethics and politics on the other, referring the reader to his previous treatise whenever he approached matters of faith.[6]

The *Sagesse* was nothing less than an encyclopedia of moral and political philosophy. A glance at its table of contents easily explains its tremendous popularity: chapters like "Of Hate," "Of Ambition," "Of Marriage," and "Of Flattery, Lying, and Dissimulation" were bound appeal to an audience infatuated with commonplace literature. And in the manner of a compiler of commonplaces, Charron described himself as having culled the flowers of other authors: "I have searched here and there, drawing most of the materials of this work from the best authors, both ancient and modern, who have treated this moral and political matter, which is the true science of man."[7] Aside from the ancients, especially Seneca and Plutarch, he relied heavily on Huarte, Bodin, Lipsius, and Du Vair, among others. Although I shall focus chiefly on Charron's reaction to the relativistic message of the *Essais,* one should note that he was much more than a mere *herbier de Montaigne.*

Charron's claim for the originality of the *Sagesse*—and another reason for its popularity—lay not in its content but in its form: "It is the compilation of a part of my studies; the form and order are my own."[8] It was a heroic attempt to fashion from the accumulation of moral precepts a universal science of ethics that could elucidate the good and apply it to the political world in a systematic fashion. Charron's systematizing impulse is apparent on every page of the treatise, where he analyzes topics into their subtopics—such as the three types of wickedness, the five duties toward parents, the five ways of facing death—each of which he treats in turn, using appropriate examples drawn from his readings. Many in Charron's audience, deluged by the spread of printing with two millennia of moral thought, must have welcomed this imposition of "scientific" order upon the chaos of humane letters.

The imposition of order in the realm of reason was, however, inherently more difficult than in that of faith. Revelation provided the touchstone for the latter, with scriptural ambiguities being resolved through natural theology. But where amidst the diversity of customs, laws, and opinions could one find the touchstone for human understanding? Charron found it in the natural law of reason, the "first and universal law and light inspired by God."[9] The only problem was in distinguishing the natural law of reason from the variety of human reasonings.

Charron betrays his greatest debt to Montaigne in his solution to this problem, a debt incurred less through his numerous borrowings from the *Essais* than through his assimilation of some of Montaigne's most fundamental insights. Of all Montaigne's contemporaries, Charron was probably his most astute reader. Unlike Pasquier, for example, who dismissed Montaigne's self-portrait as an indiscretion of old age, Charron recognized that in a world characterized by diversity, Montaigne had no choice but to seek the universal in the individual. Consequently Charron, too, acknowledged that moral philosophy must accommodate itself to the circumstances of the individual's life. Hence in book 1 of the *Sagesse,* he describes self-knowledge as the prerequisite of wisdom; in book 2 he declares that one of the foundations of wisdom is "to have a definite end and form of life"; and in book 3, he details how his teachings can be applied to the different kinds of individuals comprising a state.[10] To a large extent, he internalized Montaigne's idea of wisdom as the living of one's life in harmony with oneself, an idea that epitomized Charron's notion of the natural law underlying the variety of human reasonings.[11]

The *Sagesse* is an attempt to distill a systematic moral philosophy from the relativistic experience of the world that Montaigne had expressed so eloquently. Unfortunately, though, the lessons Charron appropriated from the *Essais* were not amenable to being systematized; indeed, they became unpalatable whenever he attempted to reduce them to a logical form. A case in point is Charron's treatment of pedantry, based directly on Montaigne's essay on the subject. The latter was a critique of contemporary educational practices that, Montaigne complained, filled the student's memory rather than training his judgment. Charron transmogrified Montaigne's rambling critique by incorporating it into a systematic elaboration of the realm of reason. According to Charron, there were three great evils veiling the light of reason: religious superstition, legal and moral formalism, and, last but not least, pedantry. His definition of pedantry established a rigid distinction between *science* and *sagesse,* the former being based on memory and the latter on judgment, faculties that Charron claimed were mutually exclusive.[12] Thus, "learning" became for him the antithesis of "wisdom," a conclusion that horrified not only the scholastics, as he had intended, but also the humanists, with whom, as a moral philosopher, he was fundamentally in sympathy. Indeed, he found himself having to assuage the latter in his preface to the second edition of the *Sagesse.*[13] Montaigne's literary finesse had enabled him to get away with statements that Charron's methodological rigor made unacceptable, thus exacerbating the problem he was trying to resolve.

From *preud'hommie* to Religion

The inspiration for the composition of the *Sagesse* lies in its second book, which Charron wrote first, having originally intended to publish it as a free-standing work.[14] Here he attempted to drive the wedge of relativism between religion and *preud'hommie,* or moral integrity, in the hopes of fostering civil peace in an age of religious war. He argued that the diversity of religious practices precluded their being the basis for morality, that this diversity was born of custom, and that religious truths had to be accepted on faith alone, thus clearing the way for a moral science based on reason.

The fideism that enabled Charron to distinguish between religion and morality derived from the "Apology for Raymond Sebond," where Montaigne had argued that because of the weakness of reason, Christian truths had to be accepted on faith alone.

Charron assumed that his audience would find the novelty of his book not in its derivative content but in its systematic form, which represents moral philosophy as a tree diagram with symmetrically arranged limbs, branches, and even twigs.[15] Although he expected to be misunderstood by "malicious people of middling ability," presumably scholastic philosophers, he was unprepared for the controversy excited by his systematizing, which had the effect of highlighting the relativistic implications of fideism. Not until the second edition of the *Sagesse* did Charron begin to suspect that others might regard the distinction between religion and *preud'hommie,* which had seemed so obvious to him, as "new and strange."[16]

The initial chapters of book 2 laid the groundwork for Charron's provocative distinction. He began by establishing that skepticism was fundamental to the attainment of wisdom. Like Montaigne, he regarded skepticism as an antidote to worldly vices, not the least of which was religious violence: "In brief, [skepticism] keeps the mind in peace and tranquility, far from agitations and vices, which proceed from the conceit that we have knowledge of things; for from the latter spring pride, ambition, immoderate desires, obstinacy in opinion, presumption, love of novelties, rebellion, and disobedience. Where do troubles, sects, heresies, and seditions originate but from men fierce, obstinate, and resolute in opinion?"[17] Charron defended the skeptical position—whether Academic or Pyrrhonian—as being the opposite of heresy, for it cleansed the mind of dogmatic opinion in order better to receive the Divine Word. Indeed, he likened the sage, elevated by his skepticism above the vicissitude and variety of things, to the image of God on earth.

Skepticism not only prepared the mind to receive truth but also served as the means of searching for it. Charron's formulation of this position is clearly indebted to Montaigne's in the "Apology," but he did not so much borrow the latter's skepticism whole as modify it to suit his own purposes. Charron intentionally chose to blur the distinction between Pyrrhonian and Academic skepticism that Montaigne had popularized. There is little difference, he maintained, between the *ataraxy* of the Pyrrhonians and the indifference of the Academics; both reflect the suspension of judgment necessary for the attainment of wisdom. Charron regarded this intellectual stasis, not as an end in itself, but rather as a means of facilitating the mode of reasoning *in utramque partem:* "There are here three things that maintain, cause, and conserve one another; i.e., to judge of all things, not to be married or bound to any, to continue open and ready for all. By 'judging' we do not mean to resolve, affirm, or determine: this would be contrary to the second, which is not to bind ourselves to anything. Rather we mean to examine and ponder the reasons and counter reasons on all sides, the weight and merit of them, and thereby work out the truth."[18] The ability to "work out the truth" implies a standard of judgment, based ultimately on the positive assertion of ignorance. Charron's motto, *Je ne sçai*—in conscious contrast to his predecessor's *Que sçai-je?*—proclaims the certainty of one's own ignorance, the prelude to reasoning on both sides.[19]

By exercising the mind *in utramque partem,* one can strengthen the "equity and universal reason that shines in every one of us," thereby attaining a universal standard of judgment. Charron identified this standard with the "law of nature": "He who works according to it, works truly according to God, for it is God, or at least, his first fundamental and universal law, which brought it into the world, and which came first from God; for God and nature are to the world, as to a state is the king—its author and founder—and the fundamental law that he has made for its preservation and government. . . . This law of light is essential and natural in us, and therefore it is called nature, and the law of nature." The notion of an innate standard of judgment synonymous with "nature" was a commonplace derived from numerous Stoic and Neostoic sources, but it was also reinforced by Charron's training in civil and canon law. The former emphasized the Roman concept of *jus naturale,* law based on natural reason, while the latter identified this concept with the law of God revealed in human reason. This plurality of sources no doubt helped confirm Charron in the conviction that he had found the touchstone of reason.[20]

The theme of following nature had received its most eloquent vernacular expression in book 3 of the *Essais,* from which Charron borrowed extensively. He echoed Montaigne's idea that wisdom manifests itself in a harmonious life, and that one can achieve this harmony by living simply and naturally, "whereby one acts according to God, according to himself, according to nature, according to the universal order and *police* of the world, quietly, sweetly . . . like a ship propelled only by the natural current of the water."[21] This emphasis on living naturally also led him to borrow heavily from Montaigne's praise of the *vulgaire,* who attained sagelike tranquility without any studied effort.

Yet Charron's idea of nature was fundamentally different from Montaigne's. The latter had encouraged each individual to follow his *own* nature, whereas the former subordinated each individual's particular nature to a general law of divine origin. One needed to know oneself and one's own particular nature in order better to overcome its deficiencies and better to live in accordance with the universal ideal. Consequently, despite praising the naturalness of the *vulgaire,* Charron nonetheless disdained their incapacity for self-improvement and never accorded them the same respect as had his predecessor. For Montaigne, the natural life was a harmony of sometimes discordant sounds—"sweet and harsh, sharp and flat, soft and loud"—whereas for Charron it was an orchestration of divinely inspired notes, all in the same key.[22]

This composition did not always play well to Christian audiences accustomed to the blasts of original sin; indeed, it sounded suspiciously Pelagian to them. In response to criticisms that he had attributed too much to the power of nature unaided by God, Charron added a passage to the second edition about how the grace of God was the capstone of natural goodness. This stipulation, however, had been implicit in his idea of nature as God's first and fundamental law; he amplified it simply in order to help those in his audience who were hard of hearing. The undertone of the divinity perceptible in the *Sagesse* qualifies Charron as a "partial fideist."[23] Unlike Montaigne, he did not make a strict separation between faith and reason; ultimately, his idea of earthly wisdom was connected to that of a heavenly God. By equating the universal law of nature with the light of the divinity, he had given the separate realms of faith and reason the same sovereign.

Charron's partial fideism was a response to Montaigne's more extreme relativism. Throughout the *Sagesse,* Charron took every opportunity to mitigate this relativism. For example, we have already seen how he formulated his skeptical motto in conscious contrast to Montaigne's, and how he carefully circumscribed the latter's call to follow nature. Charron's relativizing insights always aroused normative impulses. His systematizing mind would not admit of an absolute distinction between faith and reason, because that would have excited the very sense of relativism he was trying to tame. The irony is that Charron's partial fideism would ultimately incite greater relativism than did Montaigne's complete fideism.

Having laid the foundation for wisdom in the initial chapters of book 2 of the *Sagesse,* Charron began to erect the actual edifice in the fifth chapter, on piety. Although he granted that piety was a necessary component of wisdom, he admonished his contemporaries not to confound the two. Furthermore, he went on not only to distinguish religion from *preud'hommie* but also to subsume the former under the latter: "La religion est posterieur à la preud'hommie."[24] In other words, moral integrity engenders religious sensibility, rather than the reverse. The import of this statement might not have so surprised Charron's contemporaries—raised on a steady diet of pagan moral philosophy—had not the uncompromising way in which he expressed it confronted them with a relativism they were reluctant to consider. Charron was not so reluctant, however, because he had overcome relativism with partial fideism, which enabled him to assert a distinction between faith and reason in practice while denying it in theory. He could thus use relativism to goad his audience toward a systematic moral philosophy. In the chapter on piety, he felt free to pursue the consequences of relativism to their extremes, thinking that they would ultimately illuminate new norms.

Because piety held first rank in the duties of the wise man, Charron needed to define the nature of true piety, lest religious zeal lead one into error. He accomplished this through a comparative history of religions that stunned the more devout Christians in his audience. Despite the "fearful" diversity of religions, the principal ones sprouted from the same Middle Eastern soil, shared many of the same roots, and grew through the same stages. Even their practices, when viewed from a critical perspective, appear remarkably similar: "All find and furnish miracles, prodigies, oracles, sacred mysteries, holy prophets, holidays, and certain articles of faith and belief necessary for salvation."[25] And this similarity is not coincidental, for each religion has arisen from its predecessor, whose principles were adapted to new purposes: "Now as they are born one after another, the younger always builds upon the older and previous one, which it neither improves nor condemns from top to bottom, for then it could not be heard or take footing; but it only accuses [its predecessor] either of imperfection or of having come to an end, and by this means it comes to succeed it and to perfect it, and thus to overthrow it little by little, and enrich itself with the spoils thereof."[26] Thus, the Hebrews drew sustenance from the Egyptians and other Gentiles, the Christians from the Hebrews, and the Moslems from the Hebrews and Christians together.

These historical observations hardly served to affirm the superiority of the Christian religion. The author of *Les Trois Veritez* did not feel obliged to cover this ground again, referring those desirous of such affirmation to the "second verity" of the earlier work. Partial fideism freed him to establish the office of piety in the secular realm of wisdom. But as he relentlessly pursued this goal, he unwittingly demonstrated how the distinction between faith and reason could be inimical to organized religion.

"All religions have this in common, that they are strange and horrible to common sense."[27] Consequently, Charron argued, reason must submit to faith if religion is to be held in proper reverence; and hence, all religions have claimed to be based on revelation. Yet despite these claims, religions are really received from human rather than divine hands: "Nation, region, and place bestow religion . . . we are circumcised, baptized, Jewish, Moslem, or Christian before we know we are men."[28] If we have truly received religion from the hands of God, lamented Charron, we would surely demonstrate greater devotion to him. The piety of a sage, guided by the divine light of reason, must be the product of something more than a mere accident of birth, which confirms him in a religion that is itself, at least to some extent, a historical accident.

True piety transcends the observance of specific rituals and aspires to the contemplation of the divinity. Of the many diverse religions and manners of serving God, wrote Charron, those seem to be the most noble that draw the soul inward to the contemplation of "the first cause of all things and the being of beings," without attempting to prescribe specific forms of devotion. Charron even suggested that of the idolatrous religions, those identifying their divinity with the sun were the most excusable, because the sun is the image of perfection.[29] Had he not already established his orthodoxy in *Les Trois Veritez,* remarks like these might tempt one to label Charron a Socinian.

Superstition is often confused with piety, "like the wolf that has a fair resemblance to a dog, but is of a totally contrary spirit and humor."[30] Charron caricatured the superstitious as importuning God with prayers, vows, and offerings, as inventing miracles and credulously accepting those invented by others, and as interpreting natural phenomena as divine signs. This behavior is blasphemous because it circumscribes God's will with man's own judgments and humors. One should note, however, that what Charron decried as the rituals of superstition, others might justifiably praise as the devotions of belief. He was unable to accept them as devotions because piety had become for him something wholly cerebral.

This development reflects Charron's need to circumscribe Montaigne's relativism by pushing it to its logical conclusions. In the "Apology," Montaigne had lamented: "We are Christians by the same title that we are Perigordians or Germans"; surely, he chided, this is no way to receive the one true religion. He had, in the same breath, voiced a profound sense of religious relativism and tempered it with religious orthodoxy. At no point did he ever suggest that one ought to shed the external trappings of religion in order to discover the true nature of piety; he was far too much of a relativist to forsake the refuge of ritual. Charron echoed both Montaigne's relativism and his lament, but then he abandoned the latter's sensible conclusion for a more logical one: if religion is a matter of habit, then we must pare away the accident of ritual to reveal the essence of piety. It has little in common with organized religions; they are far too diverse and contradictory. Instead of being embodied by a specific form of worship, its essence resides in the more general mode of contemplation, which is nothing other than the supreme manifestation of the universal law of nature, that spark of reason implanted by God in all mankind.

As the first reflection of the divine light, piety necessarily precedes religion. Charron's deduction here seems both obvious and innocuous, but its consequences are insidious. If piety precedes religion, so too does *preud'hommie.* It flows from the same fountainhead as piety, being animated by a spark of that divine light contemplated by the sage; and as the product of the universal law of nature implanted by God, *preud'hommie* is by definition the source of all virtue. Charron relegated religion to the status of "a special and particular virtue," distinct from all the others. Indeed, it is subsumed under one of the four cardinal virtues, justice, which teaches us to render to each thing whatever is appropriate to it. Religion is nothing other than the particular human virtue of rendering obeisance to God, and it varies according to habit and custom.[31]

Charron drove the wedge of relativism between religion and morality in order to distinguish true piety from dogmatism. France had been torn apart by more than thirty years of doctrinal strife in part because men had confused *preud'hommie* with religious devotion:

> Not having any experience, image, or conception of *preud'hommie* other than for the sake of religion, and thinking that to be righteous is nothing other than to be careful to advance and make the most of their religion, they believe that anything, whatever it may be—treason, perfidy, sedition, rebellion, and any offense to anyone whomsoever—is not only lawful and permitted when colored by zeal and concern for religion, but even praiseworthy, meritorious, and canonizable if it serves the progress and advancement of their religion at the expense of their adversaries.[32]

Even Charron himself had once been guilty of excessive religious zeal, and he wrote the *Sagesse* in order to reveal the nature of this error. He complained that the confusion of *preud'hommie* with devotion spawned a "piety" that was little more than partisan passion, and an "integrity" that was nothing but an accident of belief. Moreover, those implicated in this error were the enemies of true wisdom, because they brooked no contrary opinions; their religious zeal precluded the skeptical habit of reasoning *in utramque partem* necessary for discerning the law of nature.

Like Montaigne, Charron used relativism as a weapon to combat all forms of dogmatism, which he decried as an *esprit municipal,* a narrow-mindedness that elevated local usage to the level of absolute truth.[33] Montaigne, however, had recognized that this weapon was double-edged, and wisely chose not to wield it systematically, for fear of wounding himself in the process. Charron had no such fear because he was a partial rather than full fideist. Had he maintained Montaigne's strict separation between faith and reason, he might have been deterred from using relativism to pare away local usage in order to reveal the universal law of nature; like Montaigne he might have despaired that reason alone could find any "bean in the cake." But partial fideism guaranteed that his search would be rewarded, for the law of nature derived from God—faith and reason shared the same sovereign. This conviction not only anchored him amidst relativity but also enabled him to use it as a means of cutting through complexity to clarity.

Ironically, Charron's partial fideism laid the foundation for what was, in effect, a wholly secular moral philosophy. After he had tied wisdom to a concept of natural law emanating from the divinity, he was free to ignore God and focus on man. Indeed, God's agency is hardly apparent in the first edition of the *Sagesse*. In the second edition, Charron amplified the role of God as the capstone of natural goodness; and in the *Petit Traicté* (basically an apology for the first edition), he reiterated that human virtue, the law of nature, and human wisdom were all animated by God. These declarations—designed to affirm that his was only a *partial* fideism—underscore just how well his argument worked without them; they are simply tacked on, without any emphasis or explanation. Charron probably assumed that no explanation was necessary, for the centrality of God to his moral system was self-evident. But given his de facto silence about the divine sovereign of faith and reason, Charron in effect subordinated the former realm to the latter when he reduced true piety to an affair of the head rather than the heart.

Charron's partial fideism ultimately exacerbated the problem of relativism that it was supposed to have resolved. The virtual absence of the divinity from what would later become book 2 of the *Sagesse* necessitated that Charron place his ethical system in a larger conceptual framework that would both explain and justify it in explicitly human terms. Thus, he decided to augment his originally free-standing argument with two additional books. In what became book 1, he tied his moral philosophy to physiological theories, and in book 3, he applied it to specific political circumstances. In short, partial fideism increased Charron's need to systematize human experience.

The Project of Humbling Man

The notion of *preud'hommie* rested on the skeptical assumption that reason did not have direct access to truth. Charron's new moral philosophy was thus predicated upon "self-knowledge"—that is, knowledge of human weakness. When he wrote book 1, he made this theme explicit. In so doing he was merely pursuing systematically the implications of his initial insights, as was his wont. Like his previous effort, book 1 was also based heavily on the *Essais,* from which Charron adapted his conception of self-knowledge and its utility. He gave Montaigne's remarks on the vanity, inconstancy, and weakness of man powerful, systematic expression. This indictment of man serves to sweep the reader forward into a comparison between man and animal, borrowed largely from the "Apology for Raymond Sebond," that dethrones man utterly, casting him into the flux of the world along with all of God's other creatures. Having been reduced to his proper place in the universe, man is then subjected to a detailed analysis explaining the causes of the human condition. For Montaigne, self-knowledge led to self-acceptance, whereas for Charron it led to self-transcendence; that is, it served as the prelude for the project of moral reformation in book 2 that would provide certainty amidst flux.

The attack on human presumption in book 1 had the unintentional effect of heightening the problem of relativism. Montaigne's genial, rambling critique, although implicitly more far-reaching, appears tame in comparison to his successor's systematic onslaught, which methodically cut man adrift from all of his traditional, normative anchors. Charron was at first oblivious to the real dimensions of the relativism highlighted by his polemic because he simply used it as a goad toward a new orientation in the world; it was subordinated to the moral science in book 2 that would make the transcendence of relativism possible. Later, in the second edition of *Sagesse,* he found himself having to deal with the demons he had so blithely unleashed.

After opening book 1 with an exhortation to self-knowledge, Charron launched an attack on human presumption that begins with the second chapter of the first edition, on vanity, "the most essential and proper quality of human nature."[34] His chief concern was to show that vanity was not a personal vice but an integral part of human nature. This chapter might appear to be one of the traditional variations on the Christian theme of original sin; indeed, Charron even concluded with a quotation from Paul's "Epistle to the Romans."[35] The theme of original sin, however, served to goad man toward the true faith; whereas Charron's vigorous and systematic attack on man serves to deny him the comfort of that refuge.

Vanity is nothing other than a symptom of human weakness and frailty, which Charron analyzed in the next chapter. Perhaps the greatest proof of man's weakness lies in the fact that even his good actions are tainted by bad ones, and this admixture is especially evident in religion, "which aptly shows that all human custom and conduct is framed and made of diseased parts."[36] Charron pursued this argument by means of a comparative analysis of religions that subjected all faiths to the same kind of scrutiny, be they pagan, Hebrew, or Christian. Citing the prevalence of sacrifices in the ancient world, even among the Hebrews, Charron declared that all the most solemn acts of religion bear the shameful marks of human weakness, as evidenced by the conceit that grace could be bought with blood. Another principal feature of religion is penitence, which also bears the human stain, because it necessarily presupposes sin, just as the practice of swearing religious oaths presupposes man's infidelity. "These are good," concluded Charron, "because they are necessary, and not the reverse."[37] In effect, the analysis of these practices denied man the comfort of religion; instead of taking satisfaction in acts of devotion, he was encouraged to see them as proofs of his own weakness.

Charron continued to develop this theme through several more chapters, culminating his onslaught with a chapter on presumption. This was one of Montaigne's favorite topics, to which he had devoted an entire essay. Whereas Montaigne's composition demonstrates how self-study can provide a point of orientation in a complex world, Charron's employs many of the same arguments to denigrate man in a systematic, unrelenting way. Charron derived from his predecessor's essay the initial, organizing principle of his chapter, distinguishing between the presumption of estimating oneself too highly and that of not estimating others highly enough. Characteristically, though, he went on to divide these two types of presumption into their hierarchically ordered subsets.

He analyzed the presumption of not estimating others highly enough with regard to man's attitudes toward God, the universe, and the world of nature. The prevalence of superstition proves that man does not estimate God highly enough. The unwarranted assumption that the heavens and earth were made for man proves that he measures the vastness of the universe only by his own limited capacity. And the conceit that he is something more than an animal proves his disdain for nature. Charron concluded that man is a truly ridiculous and miserable creature, "lodged in the last and worst level of this world, farthest from the celestial vault, in the sewer and sink of the universe, with the mire and dregs, with animals of the worst condition, subject to receiving all the excrement and filth that rain and fall upon his head from above, regarding only that and having to suffer calamities that befall him on all sides."[38]

This diatribe had the unintentional effect of calling religious orthodoxy into question, and Charron found himself having to retreat a bit from the complete denigration of man: "Now all this in no way abrogates the common doctrine that the world was made for man, and man for God."[39] But, he continued, it is presumptuous to think that God created the world *only* for man. As he moved on to consider the presumption of estimating oneself too highly, Charron once again threatened to run afoul of organized religion when he charged man with believing things he had not properly understood and with forcing others into the same beliefs. "Whoever believes something thinks it an act of charity to persuade someone else of it," using *la force, le fer, et le feu* where other means of persuasion fail.[40] This thinly veiled indictment of excessive religious zeal culminates with an attack on the very practices over which Christians fought, many of which, argued Charron, are really pagan survivals authorized by usage. Religious ritual is rooted not in divine truth but in habit and custom: "There are so many kinds of religion in the world, so many superstitious customs—even within Christendom—that have survived from paganism, and from which one has hardly at all weaned the people."[41] Human presumption was so pervasive that it infected the very nature of Christian observance, denying man even this foothold in the morass of opinion.

Charron delivered the coup de grace to human presumption in the next chapter—a comparison between man and animal— inspired by Montaigne's treatment of the same subject in the "Apology." The purpose of this chapter is not only to complete the reduction of man's pretensions but also to identify the source of his vanity. The one feature distinguishing man from the other animals—his *esprit,* or rational faculty—is not worth the trouble it causes him, entailing "inconstancy, irresolution, superstition, fear of the future, ambition, avarice, envy, curiosity, slander, lying, and a world of unregulated appetites, of discontent and vexation."[42] The process of humbling man, which culminates in this chapter, consisted of depriving him of accepted norms, especially religious ones, and casting him adrift in the world.

Having disoriented man, Charron now isolated the source of his vanity in order to lay the foundation for his reorientation. This task was facilitated by a system of classification that explained the causes of human weakness, not only in man in general, but, more so, in each individual. Here is where Charron seems to have internalized Montaigne's insight that one's individual nature and circumstances provide a point of orientation in a complex world. But Montaigne had preached acceptance of one's relative condition and, implicitly, of relativism in general, whereas Charron sought to transcend both by means of systematic analysis. In other words, he had undermined accepted norms in the initial chapters, thinking that the relativism he encouraged could be used to sustain a new moral philosophy, one cultivated by the individual to suit his own special requirements.

Charron laid out the basis for his system in a general discussion of the soul, which begins with a nod to the diversity and complexity of this subject: "Here is a most difficult matter, treated and worked over by the most learned and wise, but with a great diversity of opinions, according to the diversity of nations, religions, professions and judgments, without clear accord and resolution."[43] Implicitly, Charron's analysis would serve to cut through this complexity, locating in the soul itself the source of so much erroneous thinking. In this analysis he made use not only of Bodin's version of climate theory but also of Juan Huarte's version of the theory of humors, which enabled him to make his explanation specific to individuals.

Humor theory ascribed one's temperament to an admixture of four humors in the brain: the hot, the cold, the dry, and the humid. Charron attributed the source of man's misfortune to the fact that the three faculties of the rational soul—understanding, memory, and imagination—require conflicting humors. The faculty of understanding, for example, depends on the "dryness" of the brain, which increases with age and predominates in southern regions. The admixture of humors according to climate guarantees that one cannot hope to achieve excellence in all three faculties, and that the predominance of one is at the expense of the others; it also explains why the faculties of the soul manifest themselves in so many forms. Implictly, Charron explained human diversity with a form of reductionism based on humor and climate theory, which enabled him to classify individuals and, thereby, to suggest the means of remedying their shortcomings. In other words, he focused on individuality in order ultimately to transcend it.[44]

The theme of the systematic reduction of diversity runs throughout book 1. It is as if every admission of diversity evoked in Charron the desire to systematize and, hence, to transcend. This pattern is nowhere more apparent than in the final section of book 1, on the varieties of men and the differences between them. The section begins with an introductory chapter that, in Charron's typical manner, distills order from the apparent chaos of human diversity, dividing the subject into a hierarchy of topics for analysis in subsequent chapters.[45] At the apex of the hierarchy is the natural cause of human diversity, namely, climate. Here Charron borrowed extensively from Bodin's climate theory in the *Methodus* and *République,* working out in great detail the theme he had first mentioned in the earlier chapter on the soul.[46] Although virtue could not transcend this effect of nature, he concluded that it could nonetheless "sweeten, temper, and reduce the extreme to a mean."[47]

Charron then moved on to distinguish between three general types of men, regardless of climate: the common herd, the dogmatists, and the truly superior minds that judge according to truth rather than opinion. These differences he attributed to temperament (that is, humor theory), upbringing, and experience.[48] The bulk of this concluding section of book 1 treats the "accidental" differences between human beings that derive from the circumstances of their existence. Here Charron attempted to bring order to the diversity of individual lives, for it was on the basis of the individual and his circumstances that moral reformation would proceed. Accidental differences were social ones, society being divided according to the principle that some command and some obey. This principle was, in turn, subdivided according to private and public matters, concerning the family and larger corporate groups on the one hand, and the state on the other. Charron then proceeded to analyze affairs of family and state into their smallest units, such as the relationship between husband and wife, parent and child, master and servant. The reduction of diversity thus follows a bifurcating place logic.[49] Although this was the standard sixteenth-century response to the problem of relativism, Charron believed that he was doing something new by applying it to the field of moral philosophy. Classification would enable the individual to tailor his behavior to his circumstances, using the moral ideal outlined in book 2 as a guide for his personal reformation.

Toward a New Consensus

Book 3 of the *Sagesse* served to prove that moral reformation was possible for each and every person, regardless of his circumstances. Like book 1, it was the logical outgrowth of the skeptical moral philosophy outlined in the second book of the *Sagesse*. In the latter, Charron had substituted moral for metaphysical rationalism, as epitomized by his declaration that true *sagesse* was "the excellence and perfection of man as man."[50] This subject necessitated a moral science that took the particular into account, for "man as man" was defined by the diverse and various forms of his existence.

The third book was not only the consequence but also the capstone of Charron's new moral stance, demonstrating that social consensus could be reestablished after the Wars of Religion. Charron regarded the breakdown of consensus as an intellectual problem born of the confusion of faith and reason, which led Catholics and Huguenots to talk past each other. If one could separate these two realms, a new consensus could be established that would enable both sides to communicate. Given his rejection of metaphysics in favor of moral philosophy, Charron assumed that any communication would have to take place *in utramque partem*, using accepted cultural norms to arbitrate between contrasting positions. But without consensus about the nature of these norms, the discourse *in utramque partem* threatened to degenerate into radical skepticism, the possibility of which Montaigne had already demonstrated. Charron intended book 3 as proof that consensus could be reestablished, and reasoning from both sides rehabilitated, in the face of civil war and radical skepticism.

In book 2, he had already grounded the moral realm in a thoroughgoing concept of nature, anchored at one end to the deity; now, in book 3, he secured it at the other end to the individual. God ruled the world through the vice-regency of nature, which was animated by the divine light of reason. This whole natural system ultimately devolved upon the individual, in whom the spark of the divine light was modified by the effects of bodily humors and climatic zones, themselves natural forces. It was on the basis of the individual that social and, ultimately, political consensus would be rebuilt. Charron likened the individual to a "republic" ruled by a sovereign (understanding), who delegated authority to lesser magistrates (faculties like imagination).[51] And it was only natural for Charron to progress from the task of governing this republic to that of larger entities, the family and the state, which were patterned after the soul. Given his view of the individual as microcosm, it is not surprising that Charron organized book 3, concerning civil life, according to the cardinal virtues of prudence, justice, fortitude, and temperance. The science of politics was thus subsumed under moral philosophy, which, in turn, was the function of a natural philosophy accessible to reason.

The reestablishment of consensus, and the rehabilitation of the argument *in utramque partem,* required the imposition of order upon diversity. The first chapter of book 3, on prudence, provides the model for accomplishing this goal. Prudence, Charron declared, is the "superintendent" of all the other virtues, because it entails knowledge of what to seek and what to avoid. It concerns the "triage" of things, the initial and most fundamental act of ordering the chaos of reality.

Prudence is so universal a virtue, related to every aspect of human affairs, that it appears to be as infinite as its individual manifestations. These particular cases, Charron explained, cannot be reduced to a science of prudence, because there is insufficient similiarity between them; change even the most minute and insignificant details of a case and one changes the case itself. Also, even if one can establish similarities between cases, the applicability of the counsel thus derived is contingent upon fortune; hence, good counsel can engender bad results, and vice versa. Charron thus found himself confronted with the very problem Montaigne had expressed in the first chapter of the *Essais,* namely, that by the same means we can arrive at diverse ends. "Prudence," Charron declared, "is a sea without either bottom or brink, and which cannot be limited and prescribed by precepts and advisements."[52] Amidst such diversity, how could one engage in triage?

Confronted with the problem of relativism in so stark a form, Charron gave way most fully to his classificatory impulse, with its rigid adherence to bifurcating logic. He began by invoking the principle of difference, distinguishing the instances of prudence by "kind" and "degree" as a prelude to separating the genus into its species. The degrees of prudence correspond to the two types of sages, those who follow their own light in human affairs and those who know how to recognize and follow the light of others. The kinds of prudence are distinguished according to "persons" and "affairs," the former being divided into "public" and "private" prudence, and the latter into "ordinary" and "extraordinary." These are in turn subdivided; for example, public prudence is distinguished according to matters of war and peace. The aim of bifurcating analysis was to determine the type of prudence appropriate to any given situation; after the appropriate field for deliberation had been established, one could begin to examine the situation *in utramque partem,* using the general guidelines set forth in book 2 for the proper use of reason.

The mode of thinking on both sides of a question was implicit in Charron's motto—*Je ne sçai* is an unequivocal statement of ignorance, implying the existence of a standard of judgment to be revealed by arguing *in utramque partem*. This mode of reasoning was so much a part of his intellectual world that he simply took it for granted, without feeling the need to describe its application in detail. Occasionally in book 3, though, he led the reader up to this kind of reasoning as, for example, when he described how to exercise one's judgment on historical matters. Echoing Montaigne, Charron declared that it was not enough to know that Cato killed himself at Utica in order to avoid capture by Caesar; rather, one should also be able to "make the case" for his doing so—that is, to judge whether his action merits praise or blame.[53] The traditional means of "making a case" was to argue it from both sides. Given the underlying importance of the argument *in utramque partem,* it is not at all surprising that the final chapter of the *Sagesse* concludes with a panegyric of eloquence, the rhetorical complement to this dialectical technique.

On those occasions when Charron actually elaborated arguments *in utramque partem,* he did so to shake his readers from their complacency and show them how his skeptical methodology could reveal the world in a new light. For example, he speculated that the custom among some nations of having children eat their parents might not be as horrific as it seemed when examined both from the perspective of the parents (who were thus spared the pain of old age) and of the children (who were spared the sight of their parents' decrepitude).[54] For the most part, though, he left the actual determination of precepts to his readers, each of whom would have to take into account the particular circumstances of his own existence. Charron intended to provide a general methodology—empty of specific content—that would point the way toward wisdom, for in a relativistic world, universal precepts were not just useless but meaningless. Rather than setting one's life to a certain and constant course, in the manner of a Stoic sage, one had to arbitrate continuously among options, using the light of reason to clarify the nature of one's obligations in ever-changing circumstances.

Yet Charron did not abandon himself to casuistry.[55] Although the sage determined his actions on a case-by-case basis, he always acted in accord with reason, the universal law of nature, which derived ultimately from God. True wisdom, being a reflection of the divine light, was something other than mere rational calculation; rather, it was informed by *preud'hommie,* the moral integrity born of knowing and doing the good: "*Preud'hommie* without prudence is foolish and indiscreet; prudence without *preud'hommie* is only finesse."[56] *Preud'hommie,* in turn, entailed piety, the contemplation of the divinity. Thus, every action of the sage was, if reasonable, also natural, moral, and divinely sanctioned.

In book 3, Charron ultimately sought to regulate the political world with this moral economy. Nowhere is this more apparent than in the second chapter, where he discussed the duties of the prince. Here Charron borrowed heavily from Lipsius's *Politica,* which begins with the assertion that one cannot be a good citizen unless he is an honest man; Charron's own notion of politics reveals the same moral underpinning. He applied bifurcating logic to define the various fields of princely prudence, which were themselves contingent upon the temperament of his subjects and the institutions of his state. With the prudential fields thus established, Charron granted the prince a wide latitude of action, acknowledging that "the justice, virtue, and probity of a sovereign go after another manner than that of private men."[57] Nonetheless, he cursed the doctrine that labeled any useful action by the prince as honorable. In order for a useful action to be honorable, and hence wise, it must be to defend rather than offend, to preserve the state rather than augment it, and to shield the prince from deceits rather than practice them for their own sake. Whereas Machiavelli had subordinated morality to politics, Charron did the reverse. The duties of both sovereign and subject, although contingent upon their different circumstances, were nonetheless always regulated by the divinely inspired law of nature.

It has been convincingly argued that, in his rationalistic rather than casuistic political philosophy, Charron was a precursor of Hobbes and of the independent morality of the Enlightenment.[58] The chief difference between Charron and his successors was that his rationalism derived from a deity, albeit one whose presence was hardly apparent in the *Sagesse.* Yet we must not thus dismiss the importance of the deity for Charron. It enabled him to elaborate what, in the hands of others, would become an independent political and moral philosophy. In a sea of relativity, the idea of the deity served as his ultimate lifeline. Without it, he would have found unthinkable those propositions that were destined to unsettle his contemporaries. And as his critics increasingly decried his relativism, he secured the lifeline all the more tightly.

The Demons Unleashed

Charron was genuinely surprised by the controversy his work excited after its publication in 1601. Of course, he had expected to be attacked by scholastics for his skeptical rejection of metaphysics, but he had not anticipated that others, more humanistically inclined, might question his fideism and all that ensued from it. Rather, he assumed that they would find the novelty of his work less in its derivative content than in its systematic form, which brought order to the apparent chaos of moral philosophy. But it was precisely this form that fueled the controversy by heightening the relativism Charron thought he had tamed.

His systematic analysis of the human condition in book 1 had used skeptical relativism as a goad toward the universal program of moral reform outlined in book 2. This program, too, relied on skeptical relativism to cleanse the mind of religious dogmatism in order to illuminate the law of nature, man's secular guide amidst complexity. Partial fideism underlay Charron's distinction between faith and reason; the law of nature emanated from the divine absolute, which provided the ultimate counterpoise to relativism. But partial fideism in effect freed him to subordinate faith to reason as he systematically pursued the distinction between the two, thus obscuring the role of the divinity. Charron's critics feared that his new moral philosophy was anchored to the divinity by too slender a thread.

That they perceived this problem so quickly is a tribute to Charron's methodical clarity. In response to their criticisms, he began almost immediately to revise the *Sagesse*, a process that again reveals the tension between his relativizing insights and normative impulses. He probably set to work intending only to bolster some of the more controversial points of his argument, responding to specific criticisms of his orthodoxy without, however, budging from his relativistic view of the world. In all likelihood, though, this shoring up of his argument made its relativism all the more stark, and Charron was forced to recognize that his new moral system was threatened by the very problem it had supposedly resolved. He thus felt impelled not simply to respond to specific criticisms but also to reorganize the entire work in order to mitigate the impact of relativism.

Statements of religious relativism in the *Sagesse* drew the most fire from his contemporaries. As a cleric, Charron was very sensitive to charges of undermining orthodoxy, and he probably began by revising those statements to make his adherence to church doctrine explicit. The ambivalent nature of these revisions is most apparent in the chapter on piety in book 2, which was the chapter most extensively rewritten. For example, in the first edition he had stated baldly that religion was a matter of custom: "We are circumcised, baptized, Jewish, Moslem, or Christian before we know we are men." He retained this statement in the second edition, but he prefaced it by distinguishing between true and false religions; although both are maintained by habit, true religions are received through Revelation: "The true, as they have another jurisdiction, so are they both received and held by another hand. . . . As for their reception, the original and general publication and installation of them has been 'with the aid of the Lord, who followed up his words with miracles.'"[59] In an age of doctrinal strife, the plural reference to "true religions" did little to soften the impact of the original statement that all religions are maintained by force of habit. Despite intense criticism, he could not deny the relativism that had impelled him to articulate a new moral standpoint.

The reinforcing of his relativistic insights served to reawaken his normative impulse. Charron's piecemeal response to criticism led him to realize that the bulwark against relativism could not simply be shored up with scattered statements of religious orthodoxy. Thus, in addition to revising the content of the *Sagesse,* he also revised its form, completely reorganizing book 1. These structural changes, designed to emphasize the normative role of the deity in the new moral philosophy, represent a retreat into classification. Implicitly, Charron acknowledged that his new moral science could not alone withstand the full force of relativism, and he now sought to anchor it in the traditional notion of the Great Chain of Being.

In the second edition of book 1, he linked his moral philosophy to the hierarchy of creation. The opening exhortation to self-knowledge culminates in the second edition with an actual outline in tabular form of the "five considerations of man and the human condition." This leads directly to an entirely new second chapter introducing the "first consideration of man"—concerning his creatural nature—that begins with his creation by God and his subsequent reproduction by natural means. The addition of this chapter was an attempt to maintain orthodoxy by explicitly positing the relationship between creature and Creator, and by implicitly affirming the linkage between the deity and Charron's secular moral philosophy.

This revision was, however, more than just another nod to orthodoxy; rather, it sounded a retreat from the relativism with which Charron had originally launched his moral offensive. The stunning assault on the vanity, weakness, and presumption of man that had spearheaded Charron's argument for self-knowledge in the first edition was now transposed to the center of the book, where it comprised the fourth consideration of man; in effect, it was buried. Furthermore, it was detached from the comparison between man and animals, which had originally served to deliver the coup de grace to human presumption; that comparison now became the "second consideration of man." The offensive that had originally forced the reader into a new moral stance was broken up, its elements scattered, and its impact blunted.

From a polemic against the vanity and weakness of man, book 1 was transformed into a logical analysis of the human condition. The first consideration of man, regarding his creatural nature, leads to the comparison between man and other creatures. In theory, this "second consideration" serves to separate out the specifically human characteristics that would then be subjected to further analysis (in practice, it is ill suited to this logical task, because its original, polemical content remains unchanged). The brief, third consideration of man serves to lay out the general nature of human life—its stages and length—as a prelude to the fourth consideration, regarding the moral qualities man brings to his life. The fifth consideration completes the analytical process, extending it to the particular circumstances of human existence, which cannot be further subdivided. The original project of humbling man had given way to the task of classifying him, thus transforming a polemic into a "science" of man that positioned him in the hierarchy of Creation.

Although Charron had began revising the *Sagesse* with the intention of strengthening the ties between his secular moral philosophy and the deity, he only succeeded in further weakening them. His initial, piecemeal revision of the most egregious statements of religious relativism had left their impact virtually undiminished. The only way to mitigate them was to reinforce his partial fideism, linking the secular realm more closely to the divine sovereign. But a simple reiteration of partial fideism was, in and of itself, no longer a sufficent response to Charron's critics; rather, he had to prove that the threat of relativism was not as great as they had feared. He did so through a classification of the human condition in book 1 that explicitly linked creature to Creator. Ironically, the net effect of this "science" of man was to increase the subordination of faith to reason by reducing the deity to the logical status of a genus.

It was subsequently easy for both Charron's admirers and critics to make the *Sagesse* appear more secular than he had intended by taking its arguments out of their elaborate context. Among his admirers were the so-called *libertins érudits*—men like Guy Patin, Gabriel Naudé, and Pierre Gassendi—who were suspicious of all forms of dogmatism, religious as well as philosophical. They extracted Charron's skepticism and his notion of following nature from the context of his partial fideism, thus making his new morality appear to be independent of the divinity. Largely in response to his admirers, his critics, too, dismembered his philosophy, subjecting his skepticism in particular to intense criticism. In a vituperative attack on Charron, François Garasse branded his skepticism a form of atheism, and even the more restrained Marin Mersenne implied that the *Sagesse* was a "seminary of irreligion." Not surprisingly, the foremost work of this Catholic priest would soon become known as the "breviary of the libertines," for when its arguments were taken out of context, they pointed the way toward life without God, in a world where each individual devised his own moral standards.[60]

Charron was trapped at the threshold of modernity. He could not ignore the problem of relativism, which had now become the dominant concern of moral philosophy, but he had no effective means of addressing it. Full acceptance of relativism was unthinkable, and retreat into classification had proved to be unworkable. He needed an anchor more secure than Montaigne's free-floating self, yet the one he found was loosed by the very relativism it supposedly restrained. The failure of classification would soon, however, impel Descartes to search for a new way of addressing this apparently intractable problem.

CHAPTER 5

THE ORDER OF THE SCIENCES

Into the Cul-de-Sac

Relativism was an increasingly difficult problem for an early modern mind trained to distill universal moral norms from the diversity and variety of human existence. The growing awareness of diversity increasingly undercut the ability to generalize about the world. In response to this problem, early modern thinkers tended to branch off in two directions from a shared taxonomic path. One group, represented by the neo-Bartolists, followed a metanormative route, seeking the similarities underlying apparently diverse entities; the other, which we have been tracing, sought to understand the uniqueness of these entities in their own terms. Given the tools and techniques available to the early modern mind, however, the latter path led, ultimately, to an intellectual cul-de-sac.

The program of historical and cultural taxonomy proposed by La Popelinière, Vignier, and Pasquier organized complexity around a notion of causation that was increasingly called into question by the very experience of relativism. Montaigne was the first to reject this kind of taxonomic thinking, leaving him with no alternative but to turn the mind away from the impossible task of knowing the world and toward the practicable one of knowing itself. Following Montaigne's lead, Charron had also realized that traditional normative ideals were no longer appropriate guides for life in a complex world, and that the individual had to find a point of orientation tailored to his own unique needs.

Whereas Montaigne's path had led toward the full acceptance of relativism, with a free-floating self as one's only guide in an infinitely complex world, Charron had tried to show how each individual could follow the universal law of nature down his own chosen path. But in so doing, Charron unwittingly lost the divine compass that would enable the individual to find his natural bearings in life. In the final analysis, his systematic attempt to chart a course through the diversity of circumstances and moral options led, not to *sagesse,* but back to the problem of relativism.

Descartes, too, would attempt to establish a new form of *sagesse* appropriate for life in a complex world. But unlike Charron, he chose to pursue this ideal in a new direction, toward rather than away from *science.* For Charron, the diversity of learned opinions had obscured the path toward wisdom, which he had explicitly distinguished from that of learning. While Descartes also dismissed this diversity, he did not make Charron's distinction between learning and wisdom; instead, he conceived of a new kind of *science,* one that would show the way through the morass of opinion to a revitalized *sagesse.*

He started from the point that Montaigne had first reached. The latter had recognized that, in a world where reason did not have access to normative truths, the alternative to complete skepticism was to base knowledge on what was actually accessible to the mind, namely, itself as reflected by its operations in the world. From this point he had proceeded blithely toward a full acceptance of his individuality and the relativism it entailed. Descartes chose a different direction. Starting from the act of thinking, he moved, not outward toward an acceptance of the world, but inward toward a logic abstracted from all worldly contingencies. This logic was the basis for a program of learning that would reorient the sciences toward a new form of wisdom—one infinitely more practical and beneficial than the vain moralizing of the philosophers—ultimately entailing a fuller engagement with the world.

This inward path toward a new logic did not lead in the direction Descartes had anticipated. Instead of revitalizing *sagesse,* he unwittingly contributed to the permanent disjunction of the natural sciences, unified under mathematics, from the human ones. In other words, he reified the problem that he had tried to resolve. The difficulties inherent in his undertaking virtually precluded any further systematic attempts to resolve the problem, until the advent of an idea of historical development in the eighteenth century laid the foundation for the human sciences.

The Drift into Skepticism

Descartes had to some extent inherited the problem of relativism from Montaigne and Charron. Although he was was notoriously reticent about his sources, the *Discours de la méthode* in particular bears the traces of many ideas popularized by his two skeptical predecessors.[1] For example, his reaction to his humanist eduation at the Collège de La Flèche betrays the same impatience with commonplace thought characteristic of the *Essais,* which probably served to mirror his own frustration. His subsequent abandonment of learning in favor of travel reflects not only Montaigne's advice in "Of the Education of Children" but also his disdain for erudition in "Of Pedants," a disdain echoed by Charron. Indeed, in part 1 of the *Discours,* Descartes describes nothing less than a quest for the kind of *sagesse* that Montaigne and Charron had popularized. And some scholars have even implied that the method enabling him to make sense out of the world may reflect the influence of Charron's regimen, in book 2 of the *Sagesse,* for cleansing the mind.[2]

But the autobiographic portions of the *Discours,* for all their tantalizing allusions, were the work of a forty-year-old man. It was only natural for him, casting a backward glance at the formation of his mind, to describe that process with reference to the ideas of his famous predecessors, who were still very much in vogue. One may justifiably question whether Descartes, as an adolescent schoolboy, ever had the opportunity (let alone the desire) to read and internalize the writings of Montaigne and Charron. The seeds of his mind were nourished in a different kind of soil.

Descartes himself traced the germination of these seeds back to a humanist education that left him mired in diversity, yearning for certainty. Some scholars dismiss this account as attributing mature ideas to a youth who could not possibly have entertained them. Some even go so far as to dismiss the autobiographic portions of the *Discours,* in whole or in part, as being duplicitous—contrasting, for example, Descartes's criticism of Jesuit education in the *Discours* with his praise of it in his correspondence. But Etienne Gilson's meticulous dissection of the *Discours* reveals that Descartes (who was, after all, a philosopher's philosopher) chose his words very carefully indeed when describing the intellectual attitudes of his youth and generally did not confuse them with his mature ideas.[3] And a careful consideration of his educational experience reveals how he could have valued its combination of intellectual discipline and flexibility while dismissing its pretense at providing moral certainty. Besides, we have already seen how Montaigne's education laid the foundation for his skeptical crisis. It should hardly be surprising that Descartes, who set for himself the task of resolving that crisis, was impelled to do so by a remarkably similar educational experience.

Descartes was born a sickly child to a minor noble family of Touraine in 1596.[4] Perhaps on account of his ill-health, he remained with his family for an unusually long time, probably until the age of ten, during which he may have studied Latin with a tutor, as was common practice. He was finally enrolled in the Jesuit Collège de La Flèche by 1606.[5] The Jesuits had returned to France only three years earlier, after their banishment during the last phase of the civil wars. Almost immediately upon their return, Henri IV authorized the establishment of the Collège de La Flèche, designating it for the instruction of his nobility.

The Jesuits brought back with them a coherent educational curriculum that extended from primary schooling to the study of philosophy and theology, the tried-and-true product of fifty years of pedagogical experience. Loyola had laid the foundation for this curriculum in the fourth part of the *Constitutiones Societatis Jesu,* composed around 1550. He had envisioned that his general statements about the nature and purpose of Jesuit education would be supplemented by more specific rules concerning the details of educational practice. These rules were first compiled by a committee of Jesuit pedagogues in the *Ratio studiorum* of 1586, which was revised in 1591 and 1599. The *Ratio* of 1599, in conjuction with part 4 of the *Constitutiones,* gave definitive shape to Jesuit education for the next two hundred years.[6]

The organization of the Jesuit colleges was ultimately based on the medieval model of the University of Paris, onto which Loyola grafted the *studia humanitatis.* He foresaw that the future of the society depended on its ability to recruit youths, whom it would have to educate not only that they might better know and serve God, but also that they might set a good moral example for others unable to follow the regimen of the Jesuits. Heading the proposed curriculum for this dual-purpose education was the study of "the humane letters of the different tongues," namely, Latin and Greek grammar and rhetoric, to which Loyola also added the more traditional studies of logic, natural philosophy, ethics, metaphysics, and theology.[7] He thus accepted the notion, commonplace among humanist pedagogues, that the study of letters was the basis for a moral education, which he adapted to the spiritual goals of the society.

We have already seen how the humanist program of education united a normative view of the world with a skeptical mode of thinking by organizing knowledge in notebooks and utilizing it in disputations. These educational techniques were well established by the mid sixteenth century, and were incorporated into both the *Constitutiones* and the *Ratio* of 1599. Like the humanists, the Jesuits inculcated these techniques while leaving unexamined the moral assumptions on which they were based. Earlier in the century, however, humanist educational practice had been facilitated by the widespread acceptance of ancient norms that would increasingly be called into question by the end of the century, which had witnessed the Reformation, the discovery of the New World, advances in classical scholarship, and the dramatic spread of printing. The corrosion of the normative view of the world on which humanistic education was based would naturally tend to induce the same kind of skepticism that had troubled Montaigne.

If the form of Jesuit training in language and letters was no different from that of humanist schools, the content was at least slightly different. In addition to the standard works of classical poetry, oratory, moral philosophy, and history, students also studied the catechism extensively in both Latin and Greek. The Jesuits hoped by this means to remedy what they perceived as a deficiency in humanist education, namely, that it furnished the mind without nurturing the soul. This deficiency would be further remedied by daily devotional exercises, the elaborate observance of religious festivals, and periodic religious retreats. Students were also divided into "congregations," religious fraternities devoted to piety and good works. For a student body destined solely for the order, the religious content of Jesuit education would have sufficed to adapt its humanist form to Christian needs.[8]

Loyola and the early Jesuit pedagogues had not, however, foreseen the extent to which their educational mission would reach beyond the order. Although they made hardly any provision for lay students, the latter quickly came to predominate. Lay students were not expected to complete the whole curriculum, which culminated with a four-year course in theology; if they enrolled beyond the course in humane letters, they generally left after the study of philosophy. We should note that the latter course of study was also the optional capstone in many humanist schools. Lay students in Jesuit schools thus received little more than a basic humanist education in a Catholic environment. This education inculcated the skepticism characteristic of the Ciceronian orator at a time when the commonplaces designed to hold that skepticism in check were being undermined by the growing awareness of the diversity and complexity of the world.

Descartes would ultimately derive his solution to the problem of relativism from the principles of mathematics, to which he was first introduced at the Collège de La Flèche. After students had graduated through the six classes that began with grammar and culminated with rhetoric, they had the option of pursuing a three-year course in philosophy. They studied logic in the first year, physics and mathematics in the second, and metaphysics and ethics in the third. The entire course of study was based strictly on Aristotelian doctrine, the inculcation of which necessitated only a slight departure from the educational practice in the lower classes.[9]

The chief instrument of instruction in philosophy was the *lectio,* in which the professor dictated his explication of the Aristotelian text under consideration. Although students were required to keep meticulous notes, these did not take the form of commonplace collections; they provided the material for problem-solving and logical analysis rather than for literary composition. But the competitive spirit fostered by humanistic education carried over into the study of philosophy. The professor's theses were driven home through the daily repetition of previous lectures, in which students in the third year drilled those in the second, and students in the second those in the first. Students were also tested in weekly and monthly disputations. In the weekly disputations, one student would be assigned the task of defending a thesis and another that of attacking it; every week they would switch roles. Monthly disputations followed the same pattern, but the defendant had two adversaries, one from his class and one from a more advanced class.[10] Like their younger counterparts studying grammar and rhetoric, students in philosophy were trained to be facile in the manipulation of a body of truth, the validity of which remained unquestioned.[11] The form of Descartes's course in philosophy reinforced the pattern of thinking inculcated by his rhetorical training.

The mathematical content of Descartes's course in philosophy did little to offset its disputatious form. Mathematics played only a small role in the curriculum, supplementing the study of physics in the second year, just as ethics supplemented the study of metaphysics in the third. Second-year students received only forty-five minutes' instruction in mathematics daily. The professor would commonly explain the elements of Euclid, along with "other matters which students are glad to listen to," such as geography and astronomy.[12] Students were tested on their lessons only infrequently, in monthly or even bimonthly problem-solving competitions. Training in mathematics seems to have been far less rigorous than that in logic and metaphysics, perhaps because mathematics did not readily lend itself to the cause of religious orthodoxy.

Yet despite its politico-religious agenda, and its strict discipline, Jesuit education could be tailored to the individual needs of the student and left considerable room for dispassionate intellectual inquiry.[13] Descartes himself seems to have benefited from this flexibility, and, probably on this account, he praised the Collège de La Flèche in his correspondence and recommended that a friend send his son there.[14] For example, the *Ratio* stipulates that students demonstrating special aptitude for mathematics continue to study it beyond the second year in private lessons, as Descartes no doubt did. Furthermore, the Jesuits were willing to bend their strict discipline, which required that students awake at 5 A.M., to accommodate an obviously gifted student who did his best thinking while lounging in bed in the morning.[15] Finally, the rigorous training in traditional philosophy, reinforced by constant exercises in disputation, may well have forced the young Descartes to know his assertions clearly and to articulate them logically, perhaps contributing to the step-by-step method of analysis in the *Discours*. Descartes could thus praise the Collège de La Flèche while nonetheless complaining that it failed to provide the kind of practical moral guidance necessary for life in a complex world.

Part 1 of the *Discours* recounts Descartes's youthful dissatisfaction with a humanistic education that had failed to fulfill its promise: "From my childhood I have been nourished upon letters, and because I was persuaded [*et pource qu'on me persuadait*] that by their means one could acquire a clear and certain knowledge of all that is useful in life, I was extremely eager to learn them."[16] The promise was not of scientific but of moral "clarity" and "certainty," the moral utility of humanist education being a long-established commonplace. Descartes's experience of relativism, however, undermined this commonplace.

In a brief, but thorough, critique of the Jesuit curriculum, Descartes showed how his chiefly humanistic education had failed to provide him with moral guidance in life. The study of ancient literature—especially history—served not to inculcate universal norms of behavior but rather to demonstrate the relativity of customs and observances. Indulgence in this kind of commerce with the ancients, despite its benefits, could make one a stranger to one's own world. And inaccuracies in even the best historical accounts called into question the value of history as the *magistra vitae:* "Those who regulate their conduct by examples drawn from these works are liable to fall into the excesses of the knights-errant in our tales of chivalry, and conceive plans beyond their powers."[17] Historical Pyrrhonism and relativism thus combined to undermine the whole commonplace view of the world.

None of the other subjects in the curriculum offered Descartes an alternative means of orienting himself. Rhetoric only seemed to embellish the innate gift of eloquence. Theology was based on revealed truths beyond human comprehension. Philosophy was such a welter of diverse and contradictory opinions, often concerning the same subjects, that one could not even establish their verisimilitude. And the sciences derived from philosophy, notably jurisprudence and medicine, were similarly tainted by doubt. Only mathematics seemed to offer clarity, and Descartes thus delighted in it; but he did not foresee that it might have any application beyond the mechanical arts.

Skepticism about the efficacy of this education to provide him with moral norms led him to abandon the study of letters "as soon as I was old enough to emerge from the control of my teachers."[18] Presumably, he would have reached this point around 1616, after receipt of his degree in law from the University of Poitiers, where the philological approach to the *Corpus juris civilis* would have culminated his study of "letters." The problem Descartes experienced was similar to that expressed by Montaigne in the first of his essays, namely, that of finding practical guidance in a complex world where traditional norms no longer seemed to hold true.

The ease with which this youth of twenty dismissed traditional wisdom might appear surprising when one recalls the difficulty that Montaigne had as a man of forty in reaching the same conclusion. Indeed, there is no indication that the youth endured anything resembling the man's skeptical crisis. But this difference between the two is less incongruous when we consider that they were separated by more than a generation, during which the world had become yet more complex, while the system of education had remained virtually unchanged. By 1616 the disparity between moral ideal and worldly reality was more glaringly apparent to a precocious student than it had been to a man in his maturity some forty years earlier, enabling the student to dismiss traditional wisdom with hardly a qualm.

Modern scholars attribute Descartes's skepticism to a *crise pyrrhonienne* induced by his reading of skeptical authors. This crisis supposedly culminated in 1628 with his retirement to Holland to reflect undisturbed upon the problem of establishing an unshakable criterion of truth.[19] Surprisingly, however, there is no conclusive evidence that Descartes ever experienced a *crise pyrrhonienne*. Indeed, once we understand his skepticism in terms of the breakdown of the normative mode of thinking inculcated by his education, there is no longer any need to posit such a crisis. In essence, he was a skeptic from his youth, long before any exposure to Pyrrhonism could have raised the issue of finding a criterion of truth. Indeed, this issue—although of undeniable importance for Descartes—was the philosophical expression of a problem of relativism arising from his education. In contrast to traditional accounts of Descartes's thought, the following analysis will focus not on the specific issue of the criterion of truth but on the more general problem of relativism that provided the context for this issue, a context in which we shall view the development of his thought.

From the Science of Order to the Order of the Sciences

Having failed to find moral certainty through erudition, Descartes sought it in the book of the world, traveling as a gentleman in military service. His decision to travel was not in the least bit unusual, Montaigne and Charron having already popularized travel as an antidote to provincialism; and his decision to do so as a soldier was entirely in keeping with his status as a nobleman. Indeed, the Jesuits encouraged young noblemen to complete their education by exercising their true profession in the service of king and country, preferably against the infidel.[20] In a Europe on the verge of the last and most destructive phase of its religious wars, there was no shortage of armies in which to serve. Descartes first joined the Protestant forces of

Prince Maurice of Nassau in Holland, who was preparing for war against Spain; then he joined the Catholic forces of Maximilian, duke of Bavaria, who was preparing to fight the Prostestants in Germany. He could make this turnabout with a clear conscience because he was serving first against the political and then against the religious enemies of his king. In reality, though, this situation merely provided him with a convenient excuse for travel, of which he took full advantage in his heartfelt quest for moral guidance: "And it was always my most earnest desire to learn to distinguish the true from the false in order to see clearly into my own actions and proceed with confidence in this life."[21] Although his assumption that experience could compensate for the deficiencies of reason was commonplace, his belief in the sole efficacy of his own judgment was unusual.

Unfortunately, the book of the world offered him no greater certainty than the world of books, the diversity of customs being just as bewildering as that of philosophical opinions. At this point of confusion in his life, Descartes found a mentor in the Dutch physician and savant Isaac Beeckman. The young Descartes met Beeckman late in 1618, while Maurice's army was quartered at Breda. Beeckman was eight years older than Descartes and, as rector of the College of Dordrecht, had already established a reputation for himself as a man of learning, with a special interest in natural science and mathematics. It was Beeckman who reawakened Descartes's own interest in mathematics, thus providing a focus for the younger man's diffuse yearning for certainty.[22]

Under Beeckman's influence, Descartes enjoyed a year of intense creativity, which culminated with his famous meditations in the *poêle,* or stove-heated room, in Germany on 10 November 1619. During this period he worked on the fall of bodies, on the pressure of liquids, on music as a science of proportions, on abstruse mathematical problems, and even on the passions of the soul.[23] In a letter to Beeckman of 26 March 1619, Descartes announced that he would soon offer the world "an entirely new science" for the solution of arithmetical and geometrical problems.[24] No doubt, the seeds of analytical geometry—correlating arithmetic and geometry, two sciences in the *quadrivium* previously thought to be distinct—germinated during this period.

Descartes, though, was not narrowly concerned with solving mathematical problems but more broadly with distinguishing true from false "in order to see clearly into my own actions and proceed with confidence in this life." In other words, he was seeking the moral orientation that his education and travels had failed to provide. His insights into mathematics only served to stimulate this broader concern, which began to manifest itself in his curiosity about various schemes for ordering knowledge. An understanding of the order of knowledge could provide a reliable basis for action in the world.

A letter to Beeckman in April 1619 reflects the general interest in a science of order that underlay Descartes's specific research. Here he describes meeting a follower of Raymond Lull—the thirteenth-century author of an art for the solution of all problems—who claimed to be able to discuss any conceivable subject with ease. Descartes was intrigued enough to ask Beeckman whether Lull's art was worth investigating.[25] The yearning for a universal science of order also may have led him to flirt briefly with the Rosicrucians, a secret society claiming to have the mystical key to knowledge.[26] And, most instructively for us, the same desire probably inspired him to read Lambert Schenkel's *De arte memoria.*

Schenkel's treatise ostensibly elaborated classical schemes for the spatial organization of knowledge in *loci,* the visual representation of which would aid in the recall of their contents. For example, "places" might be correlated with the separate rooms of a building, in each of which a human figure, providing an allegorical representation of a specific body of knowledge, would be imagined, with various aspects of the figure depicting the subdivisions of knowledge. The room, the figure, and its aspects were all designed to trigger the memory. Descartes probably did not know, however, that Schenkel's traditional mnemonic served to disguise an occult scheme for divining the mystical unity of knowledge, which was attributed to celestial "causes." In occult mnemonic schemes, the influence of these causes pervaded and unified the bodies of knowledge subsumed under them, providing the mystical key to knowledge and bringing the mind into harmony with the cosmos.[27]

Descartes's drive for order is apparent in his reaction to Schenkel's mnemonics, recorded in a notebook under the rubric "Parnassus," whose entries probably date from between January and April 1619.[28] Here he seems to have seized intuitively upon Schenkel's concern with the "causes" of knowledge:

> On reading through the profitable trifles of Lambert Schenkel . . . I thought of an easy way of making myself master of all I discovered through the imagination. This would be done through the reduction of things to their causes; since they all reduce themselves to one, it is obviously not necessary to remember all the sciences. When one understands the causes, all vanished images can easily be found again in the brain through the impression of the cause. This is the true art of memory, radically different from [Schenkel's] nebulous art. Not that his is without effect, but it uses up too much paper and does not rest upon the right order. That order consists in forming images dependent on one another. His omits this, which is the key to the whole mystery.[29]

The images Descartes referred to were the visual representations of the sciences (traditionally conceived of as allegorical figures), which could be called to mind by recollection of their causes. Presumably these were not mystical "causes" but rather first principles, all of which could be reduced to one. For Descartes, the purpose of this mnemonic exercise would be to grasp the interrelationship between the sciences, and hence the order of reality.

His reflections on mnemonics offer perhaps the earliest indication of the emergence of a new pattern of thinking. The notion that interlinking images formed the key to the art of memory, and that they all derived from a single cause, is suggestive of his subsequent insight into the order of the sciences, all of which could be apprehended by the mind in the same manner with which it grasped mathematics. But the order of the sciences was apparently expressed within a traditional conception of the science of order. Although he barely sketched out his observations, they still seem to rest upon the generic concept of classification by shared characteristics; an implicit notion of substance underlay the ability to reduce things to their causes, all of which would ultimately devolve upon a single one. Indeed, Descartes's proposal for the reform of mnemonics is strikingly reminiscent of La Popelinière's proposal for the reform of history, which was predicated on a knowledge of causes that devolved ultimately upon a single cause or first principle embodied in the origins of human society. Both authors modified the traditional classificatory view of the world in response to the problem of relativism.

Descartes's quest for the order of knowledge culminated with his experiences in the stove-heated room in Germany on 10–11 November 1619. He had left Holland for Denmark in April 1619, one month after having announced his intention of founding "an entirely new science." He had planned to continue on to Poland, Austria, and Hungary; but in all likelihood, he cut his travels short by the summer, when he went to Germany to attend the imperial coronation of Ferdinand II. Probably soon thereafter, he joined Maximilian's forces to fight for the Catholic cause. With the end of the campaign season, he took up winter quarters in his *poêle,* perhaps near Neuberg or Ulm. The respite from travel and military obligations provided him with the opportunity for more intense reflection upon the "entirely new science," which had no doubt been much on his mind during his travels. A period of persistent, and even obsessive, contemplation climaxed with the intellectual vision of a "wonderful science" on 10 November, followed by a night of awful, revelatory dreams that gave divine sanction to the lifelong pursuit of this vision.[30]

What Descartes meant by a "wonderful science" remains unclear, although we may safely speculate that it was related conceptually to analytical geometry. Quite possibly he was inspired by the vision of what he would later term a "universal mathematics," a science of proportion that would encompass the whole *quadrivium*—not just arithmetic and geometry but also music and astronomy—as well as related arts like optics and mechanics.[31] This possibility is supported by his elliptical notes under the rubric *Praeambula,* or "Preliminaries," to which he had appended the motto "The fear of the Lord is the beginning of wisdom." These notes date from soon after his meditations in the *poêle,* and the motto probably refers to his night of revelatory dreams.[32]

One of these "preliminaries" describes the hidden unity of the sciences: "The sciences are at present masked, but if the masks were taken off, they would be revealed in all their beauty. If we could see how the sciences are linked together, we would find them no harder to retain in our minds than the series of numbers."[33] The reference to mnemonics is very striking; it recalls his previous comments about the art of memory and suggests that a powerful urge to order all knowledge underlay his vision of a "wonderful science." The order he conceived of, though, was no longer characterized by interdependent "images" but rather by a "series of numbers."

In the *Discours,* he would subsequently amplify this notion of order in the four deceptively simple rules of his new logic: to accept as true only what he apprehended so "clearly" and "distinctly" that there was no room for doubt; to divide each problem into as many parts as possible; to think in an orderly manner, from simple to complex; and to make the "enumerations" so complete as to omit nothing. The resulting "long chains of reasonings" expressed relations between entities that were characterized by proportions—"greater," "lesser," and "equal"—rather than grouping entities by shared properties. Descartes assumed "that all the things which can fall under human knowledge are interconnected in the same way"; in other words, he assumed that his new logic provided insight into the structure of reality.[34] In his view of the world, the sciences were linked like a "series of numbers" reflecting the sequential nature of human knowledge, which he elaborated in a plan of study that began with the new logic and culminated with morals.

This new intellectual orientation served the same purpose as the old one, namely, the attainment of wisdom through an understanding of the order of reality. The "Preliminaries" begin with this moral goal, expressed in the motto that fear of the Lord is the prelude to *sapientia;* and they conclude with it, when Descartes noted that even those without exceptional abilities can "arrive at a correct judgment of the value of things."[35] Furthermore, it is reflected in the *Discours,* where Descartes claimed to have continued traveling for nine years after the winter of 1619–20 in order to "amass a variety of experiences to serve as the subject matter of my reasonings."[36] Descartes's concern with an art of living resembles that of Charron and Montaigne. Indeed, much like them, he distinguished between mere erudition on the one hand and genuine *sagesse* on the other. But this distinction had led Charron, at least, explicitly to reject *science,* whereas Descartes sought to reform it and thereby reunite it with *sagesse.*

The new logic serving as the basis for this reformation began with the systematic doubt of all that was not apprehended clearly and distinctly. This standard was too stringent for moral truths, which were as diverse and contradictory as the opinions of the philosophers. In order to live and act in the world while seeking *sagesse,* Descartes adopted a "provisional morality" that entailed obeying the laws, customs, and religion of his country.[37] The clear implication in his use of the adjective, though, was that this morality would eventually be superseded by one accessible to all those who had internalized the new method. In other words, *science* would culminate with *sagesse,* the attainment of a universal moral code supplanting the diversity of habit and custom.

The Experience of Certainty

His account in the *Discours* notwithstanding, Descartes did not formulate the four simple rules of his new logic until long after leaving the *poêle.* Continued military service may have taken him to Silesia and Poland in 1621, after which he returned briefly to France; in March 1623 he left for Italy, where he traveled for over two years. By 1626 Descartes had settled in Paris for a largely uninterrupted stay, until his departure for Holland in the autumn of 1628. Although he pursued his vision during these travels (as the evidence of his notebooks indicates), he did not attempt a systematic formulation of his logic until settling in Paris, during which time he probably composed the *Regulae ad directionem ingenii.* He conceived of thirty-six "rules for the direction of the mind," divided into three equal groups, but he completed barely half the project before abandoning it. Perhaps he decided that three dozen rules were too many. In fairness to his account in the *Discours,* though, all the rules he completed basically reduce to the four simple ones, thus indicating that he had the fundamentals of his logic in mind long before finding a satisfactory means of expressing them.

Despite being unfinished, the *Regulae* offer a more robust analysis of Descartes's method than does the *Discours,* which he intended merely as a cursory introduction to his new way of thinking.[38] In particular, they provide greater insight into the nature of the "clear and distinct ideas" that lie at the foundation of his logic. These reduce in the *Regulae* to what he variously called "simple natures" or "simple essences." We shall later try to determine what he meant by these terms, which he never clearly defined; for the present, though, suffice it to say that these "simples" are the subject of intellectual "intuitions." Descartes defines intuition, in contrast to the deceptions of sense and imagination, as "the conception of a clear and attentive mind, which is so easy and distinct that there can be no room for doubt about what we are understanding."[39] In Rule Three, he provides several examples of "clear and distinct" intuitions: "Thus everyone can mentally intuit that he exists, that he is thinking, that a triangle is bounded by just three lines, and a sphere by a single surface, and the like."[40] Intuition provides immediate access to truths, bypassing the senses and the imagination.

The "main secret" of Descartes's method in the *Regulae* is that all things can be arranged serially in what he would later describe in the *Discours* as "long chains of reasonings" extending from the simple to the complex. The links in a chain are deduced from the initial truth grasped by the intuition. This "simple" provides an absolute point of reference, to which subsequent deductions are relative. Descartes describes the relationship between the links of the chain in terms of the interval—be it greater, lesser, or equal—that separates them from each other. For example, twice 3 is 6, twice 6 is 12, twice 12 is 24, and so on; from this one can deduce that the ratio between 3 and 6 is equal to the ratio between 6 and 12, between 12 and 24, and so forth; thus, these numbers are "continued proportionals" in the ratio of two to one. This ratio is a "simple"—the direct intuition of a proportion—from which increasingly complex applications can be deduced, enabling the mind to order all objects in the series, n, $2n$, $4n$, $8n$. . . . From this ratio one can deduce others that, taken together, would illuminate "the essential core of the entire science of pure mathematics," namely, the principle of proportion upon which mathematics is based. The key to this kind of serial reasoning is the proper identification of the "simple": "The secret of this technique consists entirely in our attentively noting in all things that which is absolute in the highest degree."[41]

Modern readers may be unimpressed by the "main secret" of Descartes's method. One commentator, for example, remarks that Descartes should have reserved that title for his practice of reducing all scientific problems to mathematical form.[42] Although this remark may be true from our perspective on the development of modern science, Descartes's perspective was on his break with the traditional logic of substance: "All things can be arranged serially in various groups, not insofar as they can be referred to some ontological genus (such as the categories into which philosophers divide things), but insofar as some things can be known on the basis of others."[43]

Serial reasoning is the basis for all knowledge derived from the intuition of simple essences: "But, as we have frequently insisted, the syllogistic forms are of no help in grasping the truth of things. So it will be to the reader's advantage to reject them altogether and to think of all knowledge whatever—save knowledge obtained through simple and pure intuition of a single, solitary thing—as resulting from a comparison between two or more things. In fact the business of human reason consists almost entirely in preparing for this operation."[44] Comparison entails noting the existence of some commonality uniting the mental objects under consideration: "But I cannot get to know what the proportion of magnitude between 2 and 3 is without considering some third term, viz., the unit [*unitate*] which is the common measure of both."[45] This "unity" underlies not only the two objects under consideration but also all others in the ratio of two to three, which can be ordered as a series. Unity is thus a defining characteristic of simple essences, which are proportions describing the relations between mental objects in a series.

Descartes elaborates on this notion of unity by distinguishing between "contingent" and "necessary" unions. Contingent unions are incidental to the objects under consideration, whereas necessary ones are inseparable from the objects, such that neither object can be conceived of "distinctly" without the assumption of unity. The proposition, "I am, therefore God exists," exemplifies a necessary union, in that the finitude of the ego assumes the "infinity" of God, here conceived in terms of an indefinite series deduced from a simple essence.[46] Descartes had indeed left the traditional way of thinking far behind when he defined God, not as the source of all qualities, but as a proposition in a process of serial reasoning!

Instead of anchoring his intellectual process to an abstract, ontological given, Descartes based his logic on simple essences apprehended by intuition. In other words, any logical series ultimately devolves not upon a "timeless" truth, as it were, but upon an actual "moment" of truth that cleanses the "attentive" mind with clarity. The self-conscious *experience* of certainty is thus the touchstone of his new logic. Descartes repeatedly stressed the experiential nature of certainty in his subsequent defense of the famous *cogito* against the charge that it was merely a syllogism: "If [someone] were deducing it by means of a syllogism, he would have to have had previous knowledge of the major premise 'Everything which thinks is, or exists'; yet in fact he learns it from experiencing in his own case [*ex eo quod apud se experiatur*] that it is impossible that he should think without existing."[47] The *Conversation with Burman* asserts this point even more forcefully: "I am attending only to what I experience inside myself [*attendo quod in me experior*]—for example, 'I think therefore I am': I do not pay attention in the same way to the general notion 'whatever thinks is.' As I explained before, we do not separate out these general propositions from the particular instances; rather, it is *in* the particular instances that we think of them."[48] In other words, universal premise and particular instance fuse in the *cogito* to form a single living moment of truth.[49]

The serial movement of the mind proceeds by means of deduction from a certainty, the results of which are necessarily true, for "the deduction or pure inference of one thing from another can never be performed wrongly by an intellect that is in the least degree rational."[50] Deduction, however, removes the mind ever farther from the freshness of the experience of truth. The more the mind relies on the memory of that experience, the greater the possibility of error, "since memory is weak and unstable."[51] On this account, Descartes sought to minimize the role of memory by constantly reviewing the logical steps in any long chain of reasoning: "I run over them again and again in my mind until I can pass from the first to the last so quickly that memory is left with practically no role to play, and I seem to be intuiting the whole thing at once."[52] Thus, in his mind, the whole series could be likened to a single moment of truth.

Descartes intended his logic to supplant the syllogistic reasoning of the "dialecticians," in which he had been trained at the Collège de La Flèche. At one point in the *Regulae,* he attributes two flaws to syllogistic logic (aside from its dependence on sensory information). First, it encourages intellectual laziness: "[The dialecticians] prescribe certain forms of reasoning in which the conclusions follow with such irresistible necessity that if our reason relies on them, even though it takes, as it were, a rest from considering a particular inference clearly and attentively, it can nevertheless draw a conclusion that is certain simply in virtue of the form." The inattentive mind, relying solely on syllogistic form, can too easily arrive at erroneous, if not inane, conclusions. Second, syllogisms are trivial, in that they merely enable the mind to deduce the truths it already beholds: "Dialecticians are unable to formulate a syllogism with a true conclusion unless they are already in possession of the substance of the conclusion, i.e., unless they have previous knowledge of the very truth deduced in the syllogism." Descartes conceived of his new logic as building upon the immediate experience of truth, which syllogisms could at best only describe but not extend.[53]

But what are the "simples" upon which this new logic is based? A consideration of this question will reveal the profound nature of Descartes's insight into the order of reality, an insight that generated such mixed results when applied to the problem of relativism. From the preceding analysis, it would appear that the simples are not mental objects but rather relations between objects; yet in the *Regulae,* Descartes seems to equivocate on this point. In Rule Six, he describes simple natures as "whatever is viewed as being independent, a cause, simple, universal, single, equal, similar, straight, and other qualities of that sort." In Rule Twelve, he offers a more elaborate definition, in which he divides them into three classes: the "purely intellectual," such as "knowing," "doubting," and "willing"; the "purely material," such as "shape," "extension," and "motion"; and the "common" ones, operative in both the intellectual and material realms, such as "existence," "unity," and "duration." In addition to these two definitions, we should recall the "simples" exemplifying intuition in Rule Three: that one exists, that one is thinking, and that a triangle has only three sides. "Simples" thus seem to embrace an unlikely collection of metaphysical notions, geometrical and mathematical properties, and intellectual and psychic states.[54]

For the sake of argument, though, we can divide these definitions into two categories, concepts and propositional relations. The simples designated in Rule Six by the terms "independent," "cause," "simple," "universal," "single," "equal," "similar," and "straight" appear to be concepts grasped by the mind without the mediation of sense or imagination. They are simple because they cannot be further analyzed, and hence are presented to the mind whole, as intuitions. Furthermore, as simples they are absolute—all straight lines, for example, are equally straight—and they imply the existence of correlative terms, such as "curved," which derive their meaning by reference to the absolute. These simples have been described by one commentator as "ontal elements" constitutive of reality; and they have been likened by another commentator to the "alphabet of reality," finite in number but capable of the innumerable combinations that account for the complexity of the universe.[55] It will suffice for our purposes to regard them as "units" of thought.

The simples designated in Rule Three by expressions like "I exist," "I am thinking," and "a triangle is bounded by just three lines" are propositional relations. They represent the immediate and necessary linkage of two elements meaningful only in relationship to each other. These elements comprise a "simple" fact, because it cannot be further analyzed; hence, it constitutes an irreducable minimum of knowledge.[56] Viewed as propositions, simples signify not "units" but the previously described "unity" of thought, characterizing the relations between two or more mental objects in a series. Propositional relations thus serve to link concepts.

Descartes's reluctance to make a rigid distinction between these two categories has generated some scholarly confusion. For example, the three classes of simples listed in Rule Twelve can be interpreted either as concepts or as propositions. One commentator notes that the third class (existence, unity, and duration) has the same "feel" as the simples in Rule Six (such as universal, single, equal, and straight); both seem to be concepts, in that they function as absolute terms to which others are relative. Yet, another commentator notes that throughout Rule Twelve, Descartes attributed the simples to things, be they corporeal or spiritual, and thus ultimately intended these terms to designate propositional relations, like "I exist."[57] Indeed, on this basis one might be tempted to regard even the concepts of Rule Six as propositions, for simples like "straight" are also predicated of things. But this move, although fully justifiable, would obscure the profound insight into the order of reality represented by Descartes's equivocations, an insight that offered a solution to the problem of relativism.

It seems that he initially wanted to treat the simples as if they were concepts reflecting the structure of extra-mental reality. This desire was only natural given his exposure at the Collège de La Flèche to Aristotelian realism, which posited that the mind had direct access to reality via the senses, from which information it derived and classified concepts. In the "Apology for Raymond Sebond," however, Montaigne had used the Pyrrhonist critique of the senses as the ultimate means of denying man access to normative truths. Descartes evidently constructed his new logic with this critique in mind, for simples like "straight" and "equal" were grasped by neither the senses nor the imagination, but rather by a mind capable of intuiting them instantaneously and in their entirety. They were "units" of thought without being concepts in the traditional realist sense.

But Descartes also recognized that every "unit" of thought was also a "unity," and he ultimately based his solution to the problem of relativism on this insight. It is implicit in the process of serial reasoning where, for example, the number 2 is both a "unit" in a series and a "unity" expressed by the ratio 2/1. In other words, Descartes realized that numbers were both concepts and propositional relations. This insight potentially enabled him to supersede the "real" with the "relational"—that is, to reduce the content of thought to logical relations that could not themselves be further reduced and were thus "simple." Implicitly, these simples could provide the mind with its touchstone of clarity, from which it could proceed to know the world with certainty.[58]

In the *Regulae,* Descartes equivocated about the nature of simple essences in part because he may not have been entirely comfortable with this insight. After all, it entailed a rupture with the realism to which he was accustomed. But in part his equivocation also served to capture—in an unfinished work—the original nature of his insight: that concepts reduced to propositional relations, that every mental object could also be regarded as a logical nexus, and thus that one could find clarity amidst complexity. After setting the *Regulae* aside and retiring to Holland in 1628, Descartes shifted emphasis toward the relational aspect of his thought as he began more fully to explore its potential for resolving the problem of relativism.

This shift is evident by the time he published the *Discours* in 1637. Here "clear and distinct ideas" have replaced the "simples." The new term reflects the chief characteristics of the "simples" without having any realist associations, which are unnecessary for an argument that has become more relational. The foremost example of a clear and distinct idea is the proposition "I think, therefore I am," which posits the necessary relationship between thinking and existing. This juncture—Descartes's logical bedrock—was doubly suited as the basis for knowledge in a complex world. First, it transformed what we would today term the "subjective" act of thinking into a mental object that could serve as the basis for certainty. Second, it expressed not a substantive truth but a propositional one that was relative to its two elements, "thinking" and "existing." Although this truth was at first alive only in Descartes's own mind, it could also come alive for anyone who considered the proposition attentively. In other words, this proposition, though both "subjective" and relative, was nonetheless universal. It thus offered an ingenious solution to the problem of orienting oneself in a complex world.

In his solution to the problem of relativism, Descartes began where Montaigne had left off. Both men had been searching for *sagesse.* Both eventually came to realize that, in a complex world devoid of apparent norms, the only real knowledge accessible to the mind was that of its own operations. Both, then, focused their attention on the mind's self-conscious experience of the cognitive moment. But Montaigne's fascination with the uniqueness of each moment compelled him simply to record its distinctiveness, whereas Descartes went on to analyze it, stripping it bare of all contextual detail in order to reveal its quintessential nature as a propositional relation. He thus distilled a logical unit, empty of content, from the very moment of cognition that lay at the heart of Montaigne's relativism. In place of the mind's rich experience of itself in the world, he had substituted the mind's bare experience of itself in isolation.

The Limits of Experience

The cognitive moment at the heart of Descartes's method provided the mind with a purely logical point of orientation from which it could extend outward toward the world by means of serial reasoning. This approach enabled him to reduce all problems to questions not simply of measurement but of logical order. In this sense, he did not simply maintain that the mind could use mathematics to know the world, but that it could apprehend the world with the same kind of certainty with which it grasped mathematics.[59] Descartes's explicit concern with an overarching certainty—traditionally interpreted solely in terms of his philosophical quest for an unshakable criterion of truth—reflects a more general attempt to use *science* to redefine *sagesse,* which had become divorced from learning with the breakdown of commonplace thought. He anticipated that the new logic of relations would enable him to reform first the natural and then the moral sciences, purifying them of the errors born of custom and opinion, and molding them into the unified structure of human knowledge that was the true image of wisdom.

In the *Discours,* he described a program of study that he would later elaborate into a "tree of knowledge," the roots of which were metaphysics, the trunk physics, and the branches medicine, mechanics, and morals. The roots and the trunk were but means to sustain and support the branches, bearing the fruit of philosophy, of which morals was the choicest: "By 'morals' I understand the highest and most perfect moral system, which presupposes a complete knowledge of the other sciences and is the ultimate level of wisdom." This new form of *sagesse,* based ultimately on clear and distinct ideas, would "dispose people's minds to gentleness and harmony" and thereby eliminate "the heresies and disagreements that now plague the world." Descartes's goal was thus worthy of a Charron.[60]

This goal, however, could not be reached by means of his new mode of reasoning. How did the mind extend outward from a point in propositional logic, via a series of quantitative relations, to encompass the qualitative world of sensation, passion, and will? In an attempt to resolve this question, Descartes ultimately based his quantitative reasoning upon qualitative assumptions, expressed in terms of the traditional vocabulary of "substance." The resulting anomaly in his philosophy would ultimately bring about the "downfall" of Cartesianism in the next century, engendering the permanent disjunction of the human from the natural sciences, and reifying the problem of relativism he thought he had resolved.[61]

The anomaly at the heart of Cartesianism is already apparent in the *Discours,* where Descartes formulated his logical bedrock in terms of the proposition *Je pense, donc je suis.* He regarded the expression *Je pense* as signifying an experience; to this extent, it can be translated in the so-called continuous present as "I am thinking" (with the caveat that this expression does *not* denote an ongoing activity).[62] Strictly construed, the "I" in this phrase is gratuitous, a mere concession to linguistic usage; what we really have is the presence of "thinking," a moment or instant of thought. Descartes's formulation simply serves to express the necessary relationship between "thinking" and "existing," the latter state being expressed by the phrase *Je suis,* positing a nongratituous "I". Descartes specified repeatedly that the existence of the ego was coterminous with the activity of thought: "I am, I exist—that is certain: but for how long? For as long as I am thinking."[63] He thus confronted two related problems: that of deducing from a discrete experience of thought/being the continuity of consciousness necessary for systematic knowledge of mental reality, and that of establishing the connection between mental and extra-mental reality, such that the truths grasped by the mind could be applied to the world.

Although Descartes ultimately based his solutions on the traditional Aristotelian way of thinking, he could have relied on the new epistemology of serial reasoning. In the *Regulae,* he had articulated his notion of "unity," the commonality enabling one to compare two or more mental objects, from which one could derive a series. This notion of "unity" underlay the conjunction of "thinking" and the "ego": the two taken together comprised a "necessary union"—a "unit" of thought—neither element of which could be apprehended "distinctly" without the other; and this "unit," in turn, presupposed the "unity" of all thoughts in the same series. In a letter to Denis Mesland of 9 February 1645, he described the "rational soul"—that which engages in the act of thinking—as if it were a "unit" and "unity" of thought. He argued that if one regarded the "body of man" simply as a quantity of matter, a change in that quantity entailed a change in the body—it was no longer, to use his expression, "numerically the same." Yet in actuality, he continued, when we speak of "the body of man," we refer not simply to a quantity of matter, but matter conjoined with a soul; the quantity of that matter may change, but it is still "numerically the same" body, provided that it remains conjoined with the same soul. Implicitly, then, the soul perceives the "unity" by which the body attached to it always remains "numerically the same," and this unity presupposed a series—the continuity of consciousness that could serve as the basis for knowledge of mental reality.[64]

From the unity of thought, he could have established the isometry between the mental and extra-mental worlds, thereby making practical knowledge possible. In the *Regulae,* Descartes had used the proposition "I exist, therefore God exists" as an example of the necessary union of mental objects, a union deduced through serial reasoning extending from the ego, ad infinitum, to God. Later, in the *Meditationes,* he would equate the assumptive God of serial reasoning with the God of infinite perfection, who guaranteed the truth of clear and distinct ideas and, ultimately, the correspondence between mental and extra-mental reality. Here he would describe the ego as a unit in a series extending from the infinite perfection of God to a "certain negative idea of nothingness" that was "farthest removed from all perfection."[65] In other words, the new epistemology of serial reasoning offered a ready solution to the philosophical problems apparent in the *cogito,* yet he chose not to rely on this innovation in the *Discours.*

Instead, Descartes explained the formula *Je pense, donc je suis* by using traditional Aristotelian terminology: "If I had merely ceased thinking, even if everything else I had ever imagined had been true, I should have had no reason to believe that I existed. From this I knew I was a *substance* whose whole *essence* or nature is simply to think, and which does not require any place, or depend on any material thing, in order to exist."[66] In other words, the ego coterminous with thinking must be the cause of that phenomenon, and as such it is a "substance" whose essential characteristic, "thinking," informs its effects. Descartes thus fell back upon the traditional notion of causation, rooted in a metaphysic of "being," which has been described most succinctly by Etienne Gilson: "That we may have causality in the strict sense of the term means that we must have two beings and that something of the being of the cause passes into the being of that which undergoes the effect."[67] By grounding "thinking" in "being," Descartes had elevated clear and distinct ideas from epistemological to ontological status. Instead of being pure relations existing in conceptual isolation, they were attributes of the thinking substance.[68]

This segue into ontology leads to his subsequent argument about the existence of God, by means of which Descartes established the continuity of consciousness and the connection between mental and extra-mental reality. If clear and distinct ideas derive from a thinking substance, the latter must be either perfect (thereby constituting its own cause) or imperfect (and thereby caused by something that has at least as much reality as the thinking substance). His ontological argument therefore devolves upon a notion of the perfect being. Since the ego is necessarily aware of its own imperfection—because, for example, it can doubt—it derives ultimately from the perfect being, which sustains its existence: "If there were any bodies in the world, or any intelligences or other natures that were not wholly perfect, their being must depend on God's power in such a manner that they could not subsist [*elles ne pouvaient subsister*] for a single moment without him."[69] The crucial word here is "subsist," which implies that God—as sustainer of the entities deriving from him—guarantees the continuity of consciousness.

Descartes elaborated on God's role as sustainer of the universe by addressing those who might remain unconvinced by his argument for "the existence of God and of their soul." Such skeptics, he reasoned, cannot then be certain of anything else. Without the assurance of God's perfection, they cannot distinguish true from false, or reality from dream, with absolute certainty: "If we did not know that everything real and true within us comes from a perfect and infinite being then, however clear and distinct our ideas were, we would have no reason to be sure that they had the perfection of being true." In other words, clear and distinct ideas are true by virtue of the existence of God, who guarantees their correspondence to extra-mental reality.[70]

When he made an ontological notion of God the guarantor of the epistemological realm of clear and distinct ideas, Descartes opened himself to the charge of circular reasoning. From a clear and distinct idea—*Je pense, donc je suis*—he had deduced the existence of God, which, in turn, assured him of the truth of his clear and distinct ideas—this is the famous "Cartesian Circle." In his subsequent response to this charge, made against a similar argument in the *Mediationes,* he more clearly explained how God, as sustainer of existence, accounted for the continuity of consciousness. Descartes argued that one did not need God to guarantee the truth of a proposition that the mind was actually engaged in perceiving clearly and distinctly. The truth of the *cogito* was thus self-evident to the *attentive* mind; but were that mind to wander, all certainty (including that of its own existence) would vanish. Only by means of God's agency as upholder of existence could the mind transcend the immediate experience of truth and aspire to systematic knowledge. By the nature of God's perfection, the clear and distinct ideas that the mind had once experienced, but to which it no longer immediately attended, were nonetheless true, including that of the mind's very existence. Descartes thus ultimately derived the continuity of consciousness, and the isometry between mental and extra-mental reality, not from a process of serial reasoning anchored in the central experience of certainty, but from, as it were, a deus ex machina.[71]

Descartes had reverted to the traditional way of thinking in order to preserve the orthodox notion of God's infinity as the positive source of all qualities.[72] This notion differed from the "privative" definition of God's infinity, represented by a series without end. The distinction here is between the "infinite" and the "indefinite": it is hard to conceive of the indefinite as the fountainhead of mental and extra-mental reality. The orthodox notion of God better enabled Descartes to substantiate and bridge these two worlds. Despite making this distinction, however, Descartes implicitly assumed that the "God" of the series and the God of Creation were one and the same. This assumption reflects his original insight in the *Regulae*—that concepts equal propositional relations, that every "unit" of thought is also a "unity," or, in mathematical terms, that every number can be expressed as a ratio. From the very beginning, he had applied this insight to the concept of God, whose infinity could be expressed mathematically as an indefinite series. In the *Discours,* he simply reversed the terms of the equation, explaining the assumptive God of the series in terms of the infinite God of Creation.

It seems as if Descartes conceived of his epistemology of serial reasoning, not as a substitute for the traditional ontological way of thinking, but rather as a supplement to it that simplified it and cleansed it of errors. In place of the many different types of traditional substances, Descartes offered two—mind and matter. And the mind that operated according to serial reasoning was ideally equipped to understand the extra-mental world of matter, whose chief characteristic, extension, could be conceived of as points along a line, the geometrical analogue to serial reasoning. For Descartes, epistemology complemented, clarified, and simplified a traditional ontology that had become overgrown with too many so-called "substances," which were merely the products of a confused way of thinking about the world.[73]

The assumption that epistemology was the basis for ontology influenced Descartes's unusual choice of an autobiographic form for the *Discours.* Of course, there were political and personal, as well as philosophical, reasons for this choice. The condemnation of Galileo by the Inquisition had made Descartes fearful of ecclesiastical censure for espousing new ideas. He chose an autobiographical form for the first presentation of his views because he could then claim, not to teach, but merely to tell of his own personal accommodation to the world: "My present aim, then, is not to teach the method that everyone must follow in order to direct his reason correctly, but only to reveal how I have tried to direct my own."[74]

This political motivation for autobiography meshed nicely with the personal desire to tell the story of the unique mind that had created a wholly new logic. The genre of intellectual autobiography, pioneered by St. Augustine, provided a model for the fulfillment of this personal desire. Descartes told his story purely as the unfolding of the idea for his new logic; consequently, he did not take the "accidental" factors of time and place into account. Where was the famous *poêle?* This and many other such historical details were unimportant for Descartes because they played no role in the formation of his method. He gave an account only of the inner path that led him from the quarrels of the philosophers to the bedrock of certainty, at which point his mind had gained a clear vision of universal truth.[75]

Descartes, however, was too well schooled in the art of rhetoric not to realize that this literary strategy also reinforced his philosophical objectives. The autobiography situated the experience of the *cogito* within a living context; it provided the existential backdrop for a philosophy that purported to pass from an isolated moment of certainty—conceived of as a mere propositional relation—to knowledge of the world. Indeed, it offered the perfect literary complement to what we would today call philosophical "subjectivism." What better way to describe a philosophy born of the experience of certainty than by framing it with an account of the mind that underwent that experience? Descartes thus appeared to articulate his method in a manner internally consistent with the touchstone of experience, where the quantitative and qualitative realms met.

Appearances, though, are deceptive, for the ego of the *cogito* is not the narrator of the story.[76] The ego is a desiccated "I," a mere unit of being coterminous with a logical juncture; it has nothing whatsoever in common with the man of flesh and blood who thought it. In order to understand how Descartes could have conflated the two, one should again recall the nature of his original insight in the *Regulae*—that concepts reduce to propositional relations, numbers to ratios, and "units" of thought to "unities." This insight was the key to the serial reasoning that would enable him to reform *sagesse* and resolve the problem of relativism. When he conflated the ego of the *cogito* with the selfhood of the thinker, Descartes had simply extended this insight to the experience of living, implying that intellectual abstraction was the nub of concrete existence. This implication was further reinforced by Descartes's very conception of *intellectual* autobiography, which enabled him to portray the mental experience of certainty as if it were also an extra-mental experience. Philosophical insight and literary form thus conspired to obscure from Descartes the fatal anomaly at the heart of his philosophy.

In the subsequent elaboration of his tree of knowledge, Descartes had difficulty convincing his contemporaries that the quantitative and qualitative realms could be bridged. This difficulty was already apparent in the three "essays"—on optics, geometry, and meteorology—introduced by his *Discours.* He could demonstrate the method convincingly in geometry, but less so in optics and meteorology, which were dependent on extra-mental referents. Largely on this account, he attempted to demonstrate the isometry of the mental and extra-mental worlds in the *Meditationes,* where the *cogito* in particular excited a storm of controversy. Undeterred, Descartes continued to pursue his program of study in the Latin and French editions of his *Principles of Philosophy,* where he laid out his approach to physics. This was the trunk of a "tree" whose branches—medicine, mechanics, and morals—he was in the process of elaborating when he died.

Descartes addressed the crucial issue of morals in his last work, *Les Passions de l'âme,* published in 1649. Here he undertook a physiological analysis of the passions and the means of controlling them, an inquiry based implicitly on the Stoic tenet that reason is the vehicle of constancy. In essence, Descartes argued that the passions are not under our voluntary control, but that we can nonetheless control them indirectly through habitual responses to their stimuli, such as the habit of deep breathing to control fear. Despite the obvious utility of this approach, Descartes's treatment of morals foundered on his inability to provide a convincing explanation of how the thinking substance of the soul interacted with the material substance of the body. His attempt to locate the site of this interaction in a particular part of the brain—the pineal gland—only incited the skepticism of his contemporaries. Even Malebranche, his greatest disciple, had difficulty accepting this explanation, and instead espoused the theory of "occasionalism," whereby the relationship between mind and body was sustained in each and every instance by the action of God's will.

Descartes's choicest fruit, providing the soul's greatest nourishment, would wither unpicked on his tree, ultimately because of the problem that lay in the very ground of his philosophy. Skepticism about his theory of the pineal gland in the *Passions,* like much of the storm over the *cogito* in the *Meditationes,* reflects the difficulty of bridging the quantitative and qualitative realms. This problem, in its many forms, undermined the whole project of *sagesse.* Ironically, the collapse of this project reified the problem of relativism by giving "science" a radically different form than "wisdom." In the medieval tradition to which Descartes was heir, *scientia* was the means to *sapientia;* the concepts extracted from sensory information were logically classified in a hierarchy, a *summa* extending from God to man and encompassing all aspects of human activity. Yet Descartes's quest for certainty led him unwittingly to base *scientia* on assumptions incompatible with *sapientia.* Whereas propositional logic could not clarify moral philosophy, it did enhance the understanding of natural philosophy. Thus, Descartes ultimately contributed to the separation of the natural sciences, unified under mathematics, from the apparent chaos of the human ones.

In his attempt to resolve the problem of relativism, Descartes had followed the only available path. Charron's difficulties had demonstrated the impossibility of reestablishing moral norms once one had fully acknowledged the diversity and complexity of the world. The only alternative was to follow Montaigne's lead, into the experience of the cognitive moment. Ultimately, however, Descartes ended up in a realm alienated from experience, in which the ephemeral appearance of the ego bore no relationship to the concrete life of the individual. Following the only plausible path, he had pursued the problem of relativism into an intellectual cul-de-sac, from which there would be no exit until the idea of historial development provided a new kind of logic for a new kind of wisdom.

EPILOGUE
RELATIVISM RESOLVED

Imagine yourself born ten years earlier or later than you were, and ask yourself whether you would consequently be a different person than you are now.[1] Most of us would answer, "Of course!"—all the while wondering how anyone could ask such an obvious question. This automatic response indicates the extent to which we do take for granted the notion that our individuality has developed in relationship to our circumstances—we assume that given different circumstances in time and space, we would have developed in different ways. We bring this same attitude to our understanding of the world, which we assume to be filled with entities—people, states, religions, cultures—that are unique because of the circumstances of their development. Indeed, we are hardly conscious of the delight we take in this rich variety of human forms, without which life would be much less interesting. In other words, we are fundamentally at home in a relativistic world; although it may sometimes present disconcerting challenges to our customs and beliefs, we have nonetheless accommodated ourselves to it by internalizing an idea of historical development.

The figures we have examined so far did not have this conceptual reflex. This is not to say that they had no idea at all of development. The essay "Of the Education of Children" clearly demonstrates Montaigne's awareness of how a personality can be shaped and molded from childhood on; and in the treatise *Le Monde,* Descartes boldly articulated an evolutionary view of creation. But these and other developmental notions did not constitute a sustained form of understanding applied to self and world. Instead, attention was focused so closely on the individuality of entities, on their *haecceitas,* that one could not perceive their development in any systematic way. The analogy here is precisely that of missing the forest for the trees. Fascination with the infinite complexity of reality led to various schemes for arranging the pieces—cultural taxonomy, moral morphology, serial reasoning—that emphasized their distinctiveness at the expense of a notion of development.

Moreover, the prevailing intellectual current reinforced the tendency to compartmentalize knowledge even as it undercut the classificatory view of the world. In a complex reality where reason did not have access to normative truths, thought necessarily turned inward, away from skepticism and toward the mind's self-conscious experience of the cognitive moment. The emphasis on intellectual experience had the effect of separating each instant of thought from the next one, regardless of how one defined the cognitive moment. Whereas Montaigne apprehended the moment in all its rich, contextual detail, Descartes stripped it down to its essence, pushing experience beyond the existential realm into a logical one even more amenable to order. We have already seen how, in regard to the problem of relativism that first prompted it, this inward turn led ultimately to a conceptual dead end.

In direct response to this situation, Giambattista Vico formulated a dramatic reassessment of experience, yielding an idea of historical development that served as the basis for a science of humanity. Vico, an eighteenth-century Neapolitan professor of rhetoric, was arguably the last great Renaissance humanist, a philologist steeped in the study not only of language but also of law. These studies bore their greatest fruit in his *Scienza nuova,* first published in 1725 and extensively revised for the posthumous edition of 1744. This eclectic work reflects the influence of many different intellectual concerns—such as contemporary debates about Creation, the age of the earth, and chronology, to name only three of the more obscure—most of which would take us far beyond our field of inquiry.[2] Nonetheless, I would like to suggest, by way of a conclusion, how Vico's idea of development emerged at least partially in response to the problem of relativism bequeathed to him by French thinkers.

Although Vico openly acknowledged the influence of such seventeenth-century legal theorists as Grotius, Selden, and Pufendorf, he did not acknowledge his apparent debt to the sixteenth-century French historical school of law. His familiarity with the *mos gallicus* is evident from repeated references to the works of Cujas, Bodin, and Hotman; and the contemporary Neapolitan interest in feudal law no doubt encouraged his reading of other French historical jurists as well, for this school had popularized the distinction between classical and medieval jurisprudence.[3] Indeed, according to Isaiah Berlin, "there is a similarity of approach, both basic and in detail, between the historical jurists, especially Hotman and Baudouin, and Vico. Distrust of narrative history, antipathy to timeless principles, whether those of Natural Law, or later, Cartesianism, [and] faith in 'philology' as a kind of rudimentary anthropology and social psychology [are] common to both." Berlin has speculated that Vico's conception of the stages of cultural development—each characterized by its own form of language and law—builds on the work of the historical jurists, whose philological study of law revealed the distinctiveness of past cultures.[4] Perhaps Vico did not acknowledge this likely debt because the philological orientation of the *mos gallicus,* and the sense of relativism it inspired, had become widespread by the eighteenth century.

We have already established that the sense of relativism arising from the *mos gallicus* did not, in and of itself, engender an idea of historical development. In Vico's case, that idea emerged at least in part from his exposure to Cartesian method, which combined with the sense of relativism to inspire a science of humanity. In his autobiography, Vico confessed to an early admiration for Descartes that, despite a subsequent turnabout, had a profound influence on his thought.[5] Indeed, the very form of intellectual autobiography with which he described the unfolding of his "new science" may have been inspired by the autobiographical form of the *Discours.* And an *esprit géométrique* pervades the whole *Scienza nuova,* which takes the form of a deductive science founded on an extensive set of axioms.

Yet Vico formulated his new science in direct response to the Cartesian one. On the basis of his initial axioms, he established the first principle of the science of humanity, "that the world of civil society has certainly been made by men, and that its principles are therefore to be found within the modifications of our own human mind [*le modificazioni della nostra medesima mente umana*]."[6] He went on to argue that one can know only what one has made and, thus, that the true realm of science is not the natural world of God's creation but the world of nations created by man. This represents a frontal assault on Cartesianism, as Vico had already made clear in an earlier work: "The rule and criterion of truth is to have made it. Hence the clear and distinct idea of the mind not only cannot be the criterion of other truths, but it cannot be the criterion of that of the mind itself; for while the mind apprehends itself, it does not make itself, and because it does not make itself it is ignorant of the form or mode by which it apprehends itself."[7] The *cogito* is a spurious moment of certainty because it simply expresses consciousness (*conscientia*) without entailing knowledge (*scientia*). Of course, the mind does "make" mathematics, but for Vico this logical realm is divorced from the human one in which the mind makes itself. The difference can be likened to "that between the act of blowing bubbles of soap and the vital act of drawing breath; by the one there is called into being an ephemeral appearance, by the other the concrete life of the organism."[8] In other words, what Descartes had regarded as the bedrock experience of certainty was not, for Vico, a genuine experience at all.

The idea that one can know fully only what one has made is a medieval commonplace; yet Vico used this maxim to express an entirely new form of knowing.[9] It is not concerned with the knowledge of facts or techniques—the "knowing that" or the "knowing how"—rather it entails a more intimate form of knowledge, a "knowing from the inside": "This is the sort of knowing which participants in an activity claim to possess as against mere observers: the knowledge of the actors, as against that of the audience, of the 'inside' story as opposed to that obtained from some 'outside' vantage point."[10] This is the kind of knowledge that comes from living—from being able to interpolate from one's own experience to that of another, and from being able to imagine what some utterly foreign experience may have "felt like." It is, in other words, a new form of cognitive experience, the direct result of the rejection of the *cogito* as a spurious moment of certainty divorced from the world. Vico's formulation defines the realm of cognition as the empathic moment when one experiences the world of human creation by means of imagination, constituting a modification of "one's own" human mind.

How does Vico's form of cognition differ from Montaigne's, which is also characterized by a high degree of empathy? Montaigne's struggle to come to grips with the horror and heroism of Cato's suicide provides a striking example of his "historical" imagination. Essaying himself on Cato's grim resolve, Montaigne determined that neither simple adherence to Stoic precepts nor a vain desire for glory, as some had supposed, could possibly suffice to explain how this man could have disemboweled himself with his bare hands. The hypothetical shifting of perspectives, in the imaginary assumption of Cato's outlook, enabled Montaigne to experience vicariously the ideas, emotion, and will of a man who welcomed suicide as the sublime test of virtue: "I believe without any doubt that he felt pleasure and bliss in so noble an action, and that he enjoyed himself more in it than in any other action of his life."[11] How is Vico's form of "knowing from the inside" different from Montaigne's in particular, and from the general Renaissance fascination with ancient personalities and their lifestyles?

In Vico's hands, the medieval commonplace—that we can truly know only what we ourselves have made—takes on a profoundly developmental aspect, distinguishing it from all previous forms of imaginative knowing. This aspect is inherent in his notion that the true realm of cognitive experience lies within "the modifications of our own human mind." Here, as so often in the *Scienza nuova,* the power of his insight strained his literary ability, making the expression bear a heavy burden. He meant not only that the act of historical imagination is self-reflective—a notion little different from Montaigne's idea of the essay—but that our mind, our very consciousness, is historically grown, and that every act of historical imagination ultimately confronts us with this, our vital nature. Montaigne had recognized that Cato's inner life was so unique that it could not be judged according to the ideal of the sage; but the difference between Cato's inner life and Montaigne's, or (for that matter) a Brazilian cannibal's, was merely one of degree. These were all variations on "man in general," a topic that subordinated spatial and temporal differences to an ideal of human nature, albeit one very broadly defined.[12] Vico, however, recognized the possibility of differences not of degree but of kind—that the inhabitants of the New World and Homeric Greece share a form of being human so radically different from his eighteenth-century Neapolitan one that they do not even appear to be "men." Once he acknowledged these kinds of differences, Vico had to define himself in relationship to them, to see them in terms of "the modifications of our own human mind."

He amplified the meaning of this expression through repeated analogies to childhood: "The most sublime labor of poetry is to give sense and passion to insensate things; and it is characteristic of children to take inanimate things in their hands and talk to them in play as if they were living persons. This philologico-philosophical axiom proves to us that in the world's childhood men were by nature sublime poets."[13] Just as the individual develops from childhood to youth to maturity, so too civil society has its successive ages of "gods," "heroes," and "men," each characterized by a special form of consciousness that pervades every aspect of life. In book 2, on "Poetic Wisdom," Vico elaborated the "master key" of his new science, that primitive men were "poets" who spoke in poetic characters, thought in poetic logic, and lived by poetic laws—"poetry" denoting imagination as opposed to reason.[14] He did not in the least romanticize this primitive poetic nature, but rather opened himself to both its vigor and its savagery, qualities so far removed from modern experience that he could only recapture them through twenty years of arduous labor.[15] The overburdened formulation with which Vico expressed the first principle of his new science thus combines several levels of meaning: it indicates that the human mind evolves in relationship to changes in civil society, that these modifications are akin to the changes in perception experienced by individuals as they mature, and that such changes can only be recaptured by a modification of the mature mind enabling it to enter the past imaginatively and experience lost forms of consciousness.

The modifications of the mind are revealed by a "philologico-philosophical" method. Vico correlated philology with knowledge of the "certain," and philosophy with that of the "true." The "certain" is the realm of facts, the simple awareness (*coscienza*) of things in their concrete specificity, that they are this or that particular way. The "true" is the realm of reason, the knowledge (*scienza*) of *why* things are this or that particular way.[16] In effect, Vico was distinguishing the mere perception of *haecceitas* from a deeper understanding of the world; he wanted to preserve the "thisness" of perception while at the same time transcending it.

He intended to accomplish this aim by combining the philological awareness of the historicity of documents—that they were written at a given time, under the press of given events, when certain practices held sway—with a philosophical understanding of universal truths revealed by reason. The truths Vico enumerated function on different levels of abstraction. For example, reason reveals that all peoples have some form of religion, marriage, and burial; that all peoples have their respective ages of gods, heroes, and men; that this universal course of history is subject to constant repetition; and, ultimately, that behind the *corsi* and *ricorsi* of history is the guiding hand of Providence, which makes human self-interest the unwitting agent in the evolution of humanity.

This philosophical perspective encompasses an idea of historical development that enabled Vico both to preserve and to transcend the "thisness" of philology. For example, by viewing the details of Roman history from the broader perspective of historical *corsi,* Vico disclosed how the conflict between patricians and plebians led to the evolution of Roman civic institutions and, ultimately, of Roman consciousness. As the age of the "gods" (characterized by primitive, isolated families) yielded to the age of "heroes," Rome emerged as a heroic commonwealth governed by an aristocracy that maintained its religious and political prerogatives through secret language and ritual. The philological analysis of ancient tales about gods and men reveals these "heroes" as "poets"; their larger-than-life, mythic mentality spurred them to excesses of virtue, discipline, and spirituality untouched by any "rational" considerations. And the analysis of Roman legal and historical writings reveals how plebian opposition gradually transformed this harsh rule by the introduction of institutions, like the census and the tribuneship, to which the patricians acquiesced solely in order to preserve their authority. These institutional changes induced changes in consciousness—manifesting themselves in linguistic usage—as the plebians ceased to regard the patricians as "heroes" and came to see them as people like themselves. Thus, the poetic age of heroes yielded to the rationalistic one of "men."

Vico regarded the particular development of Rome as but a variant of the "ideal eternal history traversed in time by the history of every nation in its rise, development, maturity, decline, and fall."[17] At first glance, the notion of an "ideal eternal history" might appear to be more compatible with an idea of unfolding than one of development. An idea of unfolding would prescribe to each nation an inherent potential, to be realized progressively over time. But Vico's "ideal eternal history" makes no such prescription. Rather, each nation follows a course of development dictated by the "modifications" of a collective consciousness that literally makes itself as it reacts to its circumstances. To the extent that mind makes itself in relationship to its world, it is not fulfilling a potential inherent in the genus "mind"; rather, it fulfills only the potential of the immediately antecedent juncture of mind/circumstance, which is itself conditioned by its predecessor, and so on. The ideal eternal history thus contains a idea of development in which humanity is indistinguishable from its history.[18]

Despite the appearance of a predetermined pattern of history, Vico insisted that both *corso* and *ricorso* flow from the mind of man, the product of his own free will:

> It is true that men have themselves made this world of nations . . . but this world without doubt has issued from a mind often diverse, at times quite contrary, and always superior to the particular ends that men had proposed to themselves; which narrow ends, made means to serve wider ends, it has always employed to preserve the human race upon this earth. . . . That which did all this was mind, for men did it with intelligence; it was not fate, for they did it by choice; not chance, for the results of their always so acting are perpetually the same.[19]

That free will generates forever and always the same pattern of history—woven of an infinitude of self-interested actions—evidenced for Vico the guiding hand of Providence, albeit one far removed from the immediate course of events.

Providence served as the ultimate guarantor of the meaning of events, without which the idea of development would have been unthinkable. Although historical scholarship had superseded providential interpretations of history derived from the Bible, no one questioned God's sovereignty over events. Even La Popelinière, Vignier, and Pasquier—who were explicitly not writing providential history—still acknowledged divine agency in human affairs. Their classification of events and institutions was fully compatible with the assumption that God created the original "stuff" from which kingdoms unfolded and that he directly controlled this process through human actors. Vico, however, removed God much farther from events. Although he acknowledged God's direct agency in the history of the Hebrews (as revealed in Scripture), he had difficulty finding it in the history of so many diverse gentile peoples. The ideal eternal history served to reveal the hand of God working, not directly upon events (as in the case of God's chosen people), but indirectly through an infinitude of unwitting human agents. The idea of development had to be circumscribed by the ideal eternal history, which itself had to be anchored to an idea of Providence, in order for the local movement of events to have any global meaning for an avowed Christian.

The idea of development contained within this providential interpretation enabled Vico to perceive history, not as a catalogue of diversity, with each entity characterized by the same degree of *haecceitas,* but rather as a vast process of the self-formation of humanity. The uniqueness of historical entities was subsumed under and ordered by this process; no entity could be understood apart from the process that defined it. Indeed, only from the latter perspective could one fully grasp the nature of an entity, its role in the evolution of a people and its consciousness. The idea of development thus served to dissolve the quality of *haecceitas* that had trapped thinkers as diverse as La Popelinière and Montaigne in the same conceptual mold, the same classificatory *episteme.* And with the dissolution of the old quality of perception, relativism ceased to be problematic. One could now look to the past for fundamental differences rather than similarities, confident that the key to self-knowledge—knowledge of the modifications of "our own" mind—lay in the understanding of how that mind evolved from radically different forms of consciousness. Far from remaining problematic, relativism now became the very ground of true knowledge, transforming diversity into the object of universal delight rather than despair or disdain.

Of course, Vico did not behold the same marvel of complexity that we do. His developmental thought is everywhere crosscut by mitigating factors, not the least of which was his inability the grant individuality its due, be it the individuality of a historical figure, an age, or a people. Vico's Rome was not shaped by historical actors and salient events but only by the inexorable movement of mind, the changes in collective consciousness arising by necessity from the previous form of consciousness. Likewise, he subordinated the uniqueness of Rome's heroic age to the nature of heroic ages in general, and the history of the Roman people to the ideal eternal history, of which Rome was but a particular instance. This intellectual characteristic led Friedrich Meinecke to conclude that Vico's conception of development was "strictly limited to the idea of mere evolution"—it emphasized internal necessity over and against human spontaneity.[20] Be this as it may (and as we saw above, it had to be this way to permit any conception of development at all), Vico's "new science" nonetheless created the possibility of an entirely new form of understanding rooted in the cognitive moment. In place of the *cogito*—a moment of self-awareness extended horizontally via the process of serial reasoning—Vico had substituted the self-consciousness of a mind that delved vertically into the experience of its own modifications. This new form of understanding the human world stands as the prototype for our own, with its richer conception of the development of individuality and its fuller acceptance of relativism.

Vico was a philosopher at heart, and thus he privileged his new form of understanding. He did not regard it merely as the product of his own rationalistic age of "men"—and hence as being relative to his own circumstances—but rather as a universal truth expressing the essence of the human condition. It remained for later thinkers, like Marx and Nietzsche, to relativize the idea of development by (in effect) turning it inward upon itself. This move, combined with the Freudian notion of the unconscious mind, contributed to a new form of historical relativism. Although Marx, Nietzsche, and Freud were not themselves relativists, their ideas about the formation of consciousness contributed to modern arguments about the mind's inability to know the past—its inability to transcend its own mode of discourse and enter "objectively" into that of others. This amplification of historical relativism has called Vico's idea of imaginative knowing into question, along with the whole concept of the human sciences.

If I had a solution to this problem, I would have written a different book; but I do think we can view it from a historical perspective that may provide us with a point of orientation. To facilitate this undertaking, I recommend that we rehabilitate Vico's notion of historical *ricorsi*. Modern readers seem unsympathetic to this notion, now that cyclical theories of history have fallen out of fashion. Vico formulated it in response to what he saw as clear parallels between the Middle Ages and Homeric Greece. Although he may have stretched the point by equating Dante with Homer, one must admit that—beneath the thin veneer of Christianity—the heroic self-assertiveness of a Roland is very much like that of an Achilles. Of course, that parallels exist between heroic ages does not mean that history moves in cycles; but by the same token, we cannot exclude the possibility that there might be other parallels between other ages. Although Vico's notion of *ricorsi* may seem quaint to us, it serves to express a nondevelopmental connection between past and present, reflecting the structural similarities between certain ages and their mentalities.

With this notion in mind, we might regard our own relativistic age as a *ricorso* paralleling the sixteenth century. We are in the midst of a broad process of decontextualization arising at least in part from changes in the technology of communication. The impact of telecommunications, culminating in the computer revolution, is difficult to analyze but everywhere apparent—we are deluged with information. Hardly an event can happen anywhere around the globe without our knowing about it almost instantaneously; and instantaneous communication only adds by the second to the backlog of data to be absorbed, a backlog stored on paper, audio and video tapes, film, microfiche, computer disks, and silicon chips. This flood of information, stored and conveyed in so many novel forms, has begun to wrench us from our traditional print culture. What the end result will be is not clear, but the academic world bears profound witness to the presence of new levels of abstraction—manifested in structuralist, poststructuralist, and deconstructive theories—reflecting the phenomenon of decontextualization. And much like our learned counterparts in the sixteenth century, we now face the problem of orienting ourselves amidst newfound complexities.

The difficulty of this task is redoubled by recent challenges to the idea of historical development that have called into question one of our basic strategies for organizing information. Some critics confuse this idea with the superficial one of progress and hence reject history as a simplistic form of understanding. Unfortunately, enough "Whig history" has been written that this charge cannot easily be dismissed, although the issue can be clarified by studies like the present one. Other critics charge history with inducing an enervating moral relativism that interferes with the ability to make value judgments. This, too, is a serious criticism, not easily dismissed, for the idea of development has indeed fostered the notion that each people and each age must be understood in its own terms rather than judged from on high. Yet it might be useful here to distinguish between moral relativism and pluralism, for one can acknowledge the existence of other values without necessarily calling one's own into question.[21]

But the most serious challenge comes from the structuralists, poststructuralists, and deconstructionists who question whether "objective" knowledge of the past is possible. Taken as a group, these critics have attacked the form of imaginative knowing that has been the basis for the human sciences; they are skeptical of the ability to enter into and experience past forms of consciousness. In other words, they have cast doubt on the developmental process that Vico described as the modifications of "our own" human mind. This challenge in particular threatens to undermine the very basis for historical understanding at a time when we are most in need of strategies for organizing information.

The experience of our parallel age indicates that various structural modes of thought—cultural taxonomy, moral morphology, and serial reasoning—all failed to provide viable solutions to the problem of relativism. In the wake of their failure, the idea of historical development emerged as the chief means of explaining the complexity of the world. Although some now argue that the new problem of relativism requires us to jettison this idea—substituting structural modes of thinking in its place—the experience of our parallel age suggests that we might then find ourselves in another intellectual cul-de-sac. Indeed, such may already be the case, given the advent of so many conflicting methodologies in the humanities. The experience of our parallel age, however, also indicates that resolution of the problem may lie in (of all things) a revitalized form of historical understanding.

I would speculate that in this new form of understanding, the issue of the objectivity of historical knowledge will be supplanted by that of its moral utility, by which I mean its ability to provide, not truths about the past, but an orientation in the present. I would further submit that this orientation will necessarily partake of the idea of development. Despite theoretical debates, this idea strangely continues to endure in our everyday lives, as is evidenced by the common response to the question posed at the beginning of the epilogue; indeed, the tendency to view ourselves and our world as developing over time has become second nature. In our new orientation, I imagine that this idea will be regarded, not as the basis for a science, but as the principle for a narrative. And I would like to think that the narratives it inspires will be characterized by a spirit of playfulness that serves, not to relativize values, but to help us understand our own, especially through the irony of unintended consequences.

NOTES

Introduction

1. The French historical school of law and its effect on historical scholarship have been most thoroughly analyzed in J. G. A. Pocock, *The Ancient Constitution and the Feudal Law* (Cambridge: Cambridge University Press, 1957; reissued with a retrospective, 1987), ch. 1; Julian H. Franklin, *Jean Bodin and the Revolution in the Methodology of Law and History* (New York: Columbia University Press, 1963); Donald R. Kelley, *Foundations of Modern Historical Scholarship* (New York: Columbia University Press, 1970); and George Huppert, *The Idea of Perfect History* (Urbana: University of Illinois Press, 1970). Friedrich von Bezold's pioneering essay, "Zur Enstehungsgeschichte der historischen Methodik," reprinted in his *Aus Mittelalter und Renaissance* (Munich: R. Oldenbourg, 1918) is still valuable. For an analysis of the above-cited works, see Schiffman, "Renaissance Historicism Reconsidered," *History and Theory* 24 (1985): 170–82.

2. Francesco Petrarca, *Letters on Familiar Matters (Rerum familiarium libri XVII–XXIV),* trans. Aldo S. Bernardo (Baltimore: Johns Hopkins University Press, 1985), p. 318.

Chapter 1. The Problem of Relativism

1. Lancelot Voisin, sieur de La Popelinière, *L'Histoire des histoires, avec l'idée de l'histoire accomplie. Plus le dessein de l'histoire nouvelle des françois* (Paris, 1599). Because the works in this volume are not paginated consecutively, I refer to them by their separate titles, cited as *Histoire des histoires, Idée,* and *Dessein.* The blueprint for a new history of France is in the *Dessein,* pp. 358–62. La Popelinière describes his new history as *la representation de tout* in *Idée,* pp. 85–86.

2. *Dessein,* pp. 362–64.

3. For an introduction to *copia* in the French Renaissance, see Terence Cave, *The Cornucopian Text* (Oxford: Oxford University Press, 1979).

4. Louis Le Roy, *Proiect ou dessein du royaume de France* . . . and *Les Monarchiques de Loys le Roy* . . . , both bound with and published under the title of Le Roy's *Exhortation aux françois pour vivre en concorde* . . . (Paris, 1570). Nicolas Vignier, *La Bibliotheque historiale* (3 vols.; Paris, 1587).

5. On the role of lists in Rabelais, see Mikhail Bakhtin's extended essay, "Forms of Time and the Chronotope in the Novel," in M. M. Bakhtin, *The Dialogic Imagination: Four Essays,* ed. Michael Holquist, trans. Caryl Emerson and Michael Holquist (Austin: University of Texas Press, 1981).

6. Michel de Montaigne, *Essais,* in *Oeuvres complètes de Montaigne,* ed. Albert Thibaudet and Maurice Rat, Bibliothèque de la Pléiade (Paris: Gallimard, 1962), book 3, ch. 13 (hereafter cited as *Essais* 3.13), pp. 1061–62). All translations from the *Essais* are adapted from *The Complete Works of Montaigne,* trans. Donald M. Frame (Stanford: Stanford University Press, 1958).

7. Montaigne, *Essais,* 1.8, p. 34; 2.18, p. 648.

8. F. P. Bowman makes the same kind of observation about Montaigne's style: "He tries always to catch every shading of his thought, every important aspect of whatever he is discussing. As a result, he tends to double and even triple his adjectives, his verbs, or other descriptive elements. A compulsion to get everything down leads to an accumulation of co-ordinate expressions. Or, indeed, of subordinate ones; Montaigne frequently introduces parenthetical elements in his effort to seize the whole of the *passage,* rather than to catch any oversimplified *essence.* . . . The result is to give the reader the feeling that Montaigne has investigated and expressed every possible aspect of his subject" (F. P. Bowman, *Montaigne: Essays* [London: Edward Arnold, 1965], p. 58).

9. Montaigne, *Essais,* 2.18, p. 648: "I have no more made my book than my book has made me—a book consubstantial with its author, concerned with my own self, an integral part of my own life." See also 2.6, p. 359, "It is not my deeds that I write down; it is myself, it is my essence"; and 3.2, p. 783, "In this case we go hand in hand and at the same pace, my book and I. . . . he who touches the one, touches the other."

10. On lists in general, see Jack Goody, *The Domestication of the Savage Mind* (Cambridge: Cambridge University Press, 1977), ch. 5. Also of interest is Walter J. Ong, S.J., *Orality and Literacy* (London: Methuen, 1982), pp. 123–30. On the broader classificatory impulse in the early modern period, see M. M. Slaughter, *Universal Languages and Scientific Taxonomy in the Seventeenth Century* (Cambridge: Cambridge University Press, 1982). Also of general interest is Michel Foucault's discussion of classification in part 1 of *Les Mots et les choses* (Paris: Gallimard, 1966). Although I obviously agree with Foucault's notion of the "*epistemes*" that underlie and unify the thought of any given period, I depart from him on several fundamental points. (1) Whereas he maintained that a classificatory *episteme* distinguishes the classical period from the Renaissance, I show how both partake of the classificatory view of the world. (2) Whereas he described the transition between *epistemes* in terms of "rupture," I emphasize its evolutionary dimension. (3) Whereas he supplanted historical with structural modes of thought—embodied in his notion of "archaeology"—I argue that, in the past, structural modes of thought failed to provide an adequate orientation amidst the complexity of reality. And (4) whereas he implies that "historical reason"—with its teleological or

"Whiggish" tendencies—cannot transcend itself to grasp the distinctive nature of other *epistemes,* I argue (and, I hope, demonstrate) that this is precisely the function of historical narrative.

11. See Hans Baron, "*Querelle* of Ancients and Moderns," *Journal of the History of Ideas* 20 (1959), reprinted in *Renaissance Essays,* ed. Paul O. Kristeller and Philip P. Wiener (New York: Harper & Row, 1968).

12. On the relationship between the Reformation debates and the rise of skepticism, see Richard H. Popkin, *The History of Scepticism from Erasmus to Spinoza* (Berkeley: University of California Press, 1979), esp. ch. 1.

13. On European reactions to the New World, see J. H. Elliott, *The Old World and the New* (Cambridge: Cambridge University Press, 1970), esp. chs. 1 and 2. Of course, some sixteenth-century travel accounts do attempt to describe the New World in its own terms, but the audience for these accounts does not reach "critical mass" until well into the seventeenth century.

14. Goody, *Domestication,* pp. 37–73; Eric A. Havelock, *Preface to Plato* (Cambridge, Mass.: Harvard University Press, 1963), esp. pp. 215–33, and 290–305; Walter J. Ong, S.J., *Interfaces of the Word* (Ithaca: Cornell University Press, 1977), esp. pp. 17–22 and 121–44; Ong, *The Presence of the Word* (New Haven: Yale University Press, 1967), esp. pp. 17–92; Slaughter, *Universal Languages,* esp. pp. 38–48; and, in general, also see Havelock's *Origins of Western Literacy* (Toronto: Ontario Institute for Studies in Education, 1976), and his *Prologue to Greek Literacy* (Cincinnati: University of Cincinnati, 1971). Michael Heim, *Electric Language* (New Haven: Yale University Press, 1987) offers a summary and philosophical analysis of this "theory of transformative technologies."

15. Ong, *Interfaces,* p. 20.

16. Slaughter, *Universal Languages,* p. 40.

17. Goody, *Domestication,* p. 78.

18. Goody, *Domestication,* p. 6; Slaughter, *Universal Languages,* p. 39.

19. Quoted in Goody, *Domestication,* p. 95.

20. Havelock, *Preface,* pp. 290–305; Havelock, *Origins,* pp. 21–22; Goody, *Domestication,* p. 37. On the relationship between Aristotelian philosophy and decontextualization, see Slaughter, *Universal Languages,* pp. 44–45.

21. Havelock, *Origins,* p. 77.

22. In general, see R. A. Houston, *Literacy in Early Modern Europe* (London: Longman, 1988). Also see David Cressy, *Literacy and the Social Order: Reading and Writing in Tudor and Stuart England* (Cambridge: Cambridge University Press, 1980); Lawrence Stone, "Literacy and Education in England 1640–1900," *Past and Present* 42 (1969): 69–139; François Furet and Jacques Ozouf, *Reading and Writing: Literacy in France from Calvin to Jules Ferry* (Cambridge: Cambridge University Press, 1982); Carlo M. Cipolla, *Literacy and Development in the West* (London: Penguin Books, 1969); Peter Clark, "The Ownership of Books in England, 1560–1640: The Example of Some Kentish Townsfolk," in *Schooling and Society,* ed. Lawrence Stone (Baltimore: Johns Hopkins University Press, 1976); Richard Gawthrop and Gerald Strauss, "Protestantism and Literacy in Early Modern Germany," *Past and Present* 104 (1984): 31–55; *Literacy and Social Development in the West,* ed. Harvey J. Graff (Cambridge: Cambridge University Press, 1981); and Slaughter, *Universal Languages,* pp. 42–43. For a fascinating study of

the relationship between literacy and popular culture, see Carlo Ginzburg, *The Cheese and the Worms: The Cosmos of a Sixteenth-Century Miller,* trans. John and Anne Tedeschi (Baltimore: Johns Hopkins University Press, 1980).

23. Furet and Ozouf, *Reading and Writing,* p. 59.

24. Lawrence Stone, "The Educational Revolution in England, 1560–1640," *Past and Present* 28 (1964): 41–80; J. H. Hexter, "The Education of the Aristocracy in the Renaissance," in his *Reappraisals in History* (New York: Harper & Row, 1961); Gerald Strauss, *Luther's House of Learning* (Baltimore: Johns Hopkins University Press, 1978); George Huppert, *Public Schools in Renaissance France* (Urbana: University of Illinois Press, 1984); and Houston, *Literacy,* ch. 2.

25. See the unpaginated preface to La Popelinière's *La Vraye et entiere histoire des troubles . . . avenues tant en France qu'en Flandres, et pays circonvoisins, depuis l'an 1562* (Basel, 1572), hereafter referred to as *Histoire des troubles.* For a further analysis of this preface, see ch. 2, pp. 28–30. The *Histoire des troubles* formed the nucleus of La Popelinière's life's work, the *Histoire de France.*

26. George Wylie Sypher, "La Popelinière: Historian and Historiographer" (Ph.D. thesis, Cornell University, 1961), pp. 87–88.

27. Ibid., pp. 47–48.

28. On the *Grandes chroniques,* see Denys Hay, *Annalists and Historians* (London: Methuen, 1977), ch. 4. On the myth of the Trojan origins of the Franks and its fate in the sixteenth century, see Huppert, *Perfect History,* esp. ch. 4; and, in general, Claude-Gilbert Dubois, *Celtes et gaulois au XVIe siècle* (Paris: Vrin, 1972).

29. On "cabinets of curios," see Margaret T. Hodgen, *Early Anthropology in the Sixteenth and Seventeenth Centuries* (Philadelphia: University of Pennsylvania Press, 1964), ch. 4. Slaughter describes the proliferation of herbal and zoological lists in *Universal Languages,* esp. pp. 48–64, and her entire work is devoted to schemes for classifying language. On Ramus in particular and place logic in general, see Walter J. Ong, S.J., *Ramus: Method and the Decay of Dialogue* (Cambridge, Mass.: Harvard University Press, 1958). See also Neal Ward Gilbert, *Renaissance Concepts of Method* (New York: Columbia University Press, 1960).

30. On humanist education in general, see Anthony Grafton and Lisa Jardine, *From Humanism to the Humanities* (Cambridge, Mass.: Harvard University Press, 1986).

31. On Renaissance humanism in general, see Hanna H. Gray, "Renaissance Humanism: The Pursuit of Eloquence," *Journal of the History of Ideas* 24 (1963), reprinted in *Renaissance Essays,* ed. Kristeller and Wiener.

32. On *loci, loci communes,* and commonplace thought, see Quirinus Breen, "The Terms *loci communes* and *loci* in Melanchthon," in his *Christianity and Humanism* (Grand Rapids, Mich.: William B. Eerdmans, 1968), pp. 93–105; August Buck, "Die *studia humanitatis* und ihre Methode," in his *Die humanistiche Tradition in der Romania* (Berlin: Gehlen, 1968), pp. 133–50; Wilbur S. Howell, *Logic and Rhetoric in England, 1500–1700* (Princeton: Princeton University Press, 1956); Lisa Jardine, *Francis Bacon: Discovery and the Art of Discourse* (London: Cambridge University Press, 1974), esp. ch. 1; Paul Joachimsen, "*Loci communes:* Eine Untersuchung zur Geistesgeschichte des Humanismus und der Reformation," *Luther-Jahrbuch* 8 (1926): 27–97; George Kennedy, *The Art of Persuasion in Greece* (Princeton: Princeton University Press, 1963), esp. pp. 87–103; Sister Joan Marie

Lechner, O.S.U., *Renaissance Concepts of the Commonplaces* (Westport, Conn.: Greenwood Press, 1974); Alain Michel, *Rhétorique et philosophie chez Cicéron* (Paris: Presses universitaires de France, 1960), esp. pt. 2, ch. 4; Walter J. Ong, "Commonplace Rapsody: Ravisius Textor, Zwinger, and Shakespeare," in *Classical Influences on European Culture, A.D. 1500–1700,* ed. R. R. Bolgar (Cambridge: Cambridge University Press, 1976), pp. 91–126.

33. For the mode of arguing *in utramque partem,* see Michel, *Cicéron,* pp. 158–73; Lisa Jardine, "Lorenzo Valla and the Intellectual Origins of Humanist Dialectic," *Journal of the History of Philosophy* 15 (1977): 149–53 (revised as "Lorenzo Valla: Academic Skepticism and the New Humanist Dialectic," in *The Skeptical Tradition,* ed. Myles Burnyeat [Berkeley: University of California Press, 1983]); Jerrold E. Seigel, *Rhetoric and Philosophy in the Renaissance* (Princeton: Princeton University Press, 1968), esp. ch. 1. See also, in general, Victoria Kahn, *Rhetoric, Prudence, and Skepticism in the Renaissance* (Ithaca: Cornell University Press, 1985); and Joel B. Altman, *The Tudor Play of Mind* (Berkeley: University of California Press, 1978), which traces the role of the argument *in utramque partem* in Elizabethan drama.

34. Michel, *Cicéron,* pp. 201–24.

35. Joachimsen, *"Loci communes,"* pp. 62–63.

36. For the relationship between humanist education and the rise of skepticism, see Schiffman, "Montaigne and the Rise of Skepticism in Early Modern Europe: A Reappraisal," *Journal of the History of Ideas* 45 (1984): 499–516, which forms the nucleus for my analysis of commonplace thought below.

37. Buck, *"Studia humanitatis,"* pp. 141–42; R. R. Bolgar, *The Classical Heritage and Its Beneficiaries* (Cambridge: Cambridge University Press, 1954), pp. 268–72.

38. Desiderius Erasmus, *De copia verborum ac rerum,* ed. Betty I. Knott, in *Opera omnia,* vol. 1, pt. 6 (Amsterdam: North-Holland Publishing Company, 1988), pp. 258–69. A slightly abridged translation of this work has been issued as *On Copia of Words and Ideas,* trans. D. B. King and H. D. Rix (Milwaukee: Marquette University Press, 1963), see esp. pp. 87–97. For analyses of *De copia,* see J. K. Sowards, "Erasmus and the Apologetic Textbook: A Study of the *De duplici copia verborum ac rerum,*" in *Essays on the Northern Renaissance,* ed. Kenneth A. Strand (Ann Arbor: Ann Arbor Publishers, 1968), pp. 92–106; and M. M. Phillips, "Erasmus and the Art of Writing," in *Scrinium Erasmianum,* ed. J. Coppens (2 vols.; Leiden: E. J. Brill, 1969), 1:335–50. Erasmus also emphasized the importance of note-taking in his blueprint for secondary education, *De ratione studii,* ed. Jean-Claude Margolin, in *Opera omnia,* vol. 1, pt. 2 (Amsterdam: North-Holland Publishing Company, 1971), pp. 116–17, 120. Erasmus's role in the development of commonplace thought is analyzed in Joachimsen, *"Loci communes,"* pp. 54–61.

39. Erasmus, *De copia,* p. 261; the translation is from *On Copia,* p. 90; also see Joachimsen, *"Loci communes,"* pp. 57–58.

40. Philip Melanchthon, *De rhetorica libri tres* (Paris, 1529), p. 32v.

41. For Montaigne's education, see Elie Vinet, *Schola Aquitanica: Programme des études du Collège de Guyenne au XVIe siècle,* ed. and trans. Louis Massebieau (Paris: Ch. Delagrave, 1886). Although Vinet wrote his booklet in 1583, he intended it as a record of the educational reforms instituted by Andre Gouvéa around the

time that Montaigne was a student at the Collège. For other accounts of the Collège and its educational program, see Ernest Gaullieur, *Histoire du Collège de Guyenne* (Paris: Sandoz & Fischbacher, 1878); William H. Woodward, *Studies in Education during the Age of the Renaissance* (Cambridge: Cambridge University Press, 1906; reprint ed., New York: Russell & Russell, 1965); Paul Porteau, *Montaigne et la vie pédagogique de son temps* (Paris: Droz, 1935); and Roger Trinquet, *La Jeunesse de Montaigne* (Paris: A. G. Nizet, 1972).

For Descartes's education, see *St. Ignatius and the "Ratio Studiorum,"* ed. Edward A. Fitzpatrick (New York: McGraw-Hill, 1933); this work is a translation of the 1599 edition of the *Ratio,* along with part 4 of the *Constitutiones.* See also P. Camille de Rochemonteix, *Un Collège de Jésuites aux XVIIe et XVIIIe siècles: Le Collège Henri IV de la Flèche,* (4 vols.; Le Mans: Leguicheux, 1889); Georges Snyders, *La Pédagogie en France aux XVIIe et XVIIIe siècles* (Paris: Presses universitaires de France, 1965); Paul Richard Blum, *"Apostolato dei collegi:* On the Integration of Humanism in the Educational Programme of the Jesuits," *History of Universities* 5 (1985): 101–15; and Peter Dear, *Mersenne and the Learning of the Schools* (Ithaca: Cornell University Press, 1988), esp. ch. 2.

42. For classroom practice, see Vinet, *Schola Aquitanica,* p. 19, and *Ratio studiorum,* ed. Fitzpatrick, pp. 201–2. On Montaigne's use of commonplace books, see Porteau, *Montaigne et la vie pédagogique,* pp. 178–89. Trinquet (*Jeunesse de Montaigne,* pp. 445–48) disputes Porteau's conclusion that Montaigne used commonplace books at the Collège; he argues that the *Schola Aquitanica* made no mention of this practice. However, the compilation of commonplace books was not, strictly speaking, part of a humanist school's curriculum; rather, students were expected to undertake this task at home. Also, the *Schola Aquitanica* does describe the use of notebooks with extra space between each line, which traditionally served as the bases for commonplace collections (see Vinet, *Schola Aquitanica,* p. 19, n. 39). Part 4 of the *Constitutiones* proposes that beginning students should use the same kind of notebooks with space between each line, and that advanced students should take class notes on sheets of paper, "and afterwards they should transfer a digest with greater order to paper books which they may wish to keep" (*Ratio studiorum,* ed. Fitzpatrick, pp. 74–75). These compilations were to be indexed; and it was even suggested that good students, with the approval of the teacher, might draw up such compilations for use by their peers (pp. 78–79).

43. Montaigne, *Essais,* 1.26, p. 175.

44. Wilbur Howell's analysis of the relationship between judgment and invention in Thomas Wilson's treatise on dialectic is analogous to my conclusion here: "Wilson justifies himself for placing judgment before invention by saying that you have to know how to order an argument before you seek for it, and that anyway 'a reason is easier found than fashioned.' This attitude is a significant phenomenon in intellectual history. It really is a way of saying that subject matter presents fewer difficulties than organization, so far as composition is concerned. A society which takes such an attitude must be by implication a society that does not stress the virtues of an exhaustive examination of nature so much as the virtues of clarity in form" (Howell, *Logic and Rhetoric,* p. 23).

45. Vinet, *Schola Aquitanica,* pp. 7–9; Porteau, *Montaigne et la vie pédagogique,* pp. 163, 165–66.

46. *Ratio studiorum,* ed. Fitzpatrick, pp. 203–5.

47. On disputation in the Collège de Guyenne, see Vinet, *Schola Aquitanica,* pp. 31, 47; Porteau, *Montaigne et la vie pédagogique,* pp. 165–71, 195–98; Woodward, *Studies in Education,* pp. 153, 225 n. 1. For this practice in Jesuit schools, see *Ratio studiorum,* ed. Fitzpatrick, pp. 75–76, 103, 203–5; Rochemonteix, *Collège de Jésuites,* 2:51–54.

48. "Il se pourroët tirer d'ici le foundemant d'un tel discours: si l'authorite du comandemant paternel pouuoët desobliger le fis de sa promesse. Nostre histoëre nous fournist d'asses d'examples que les papes, les roës, et les magistras le font; mais les peres sount au dessous. Qui me remenra a ste vertu parfaite des anciens romeins et grecs, ie scai bien que ie trouuerrai que le magistrat ne l'antreprenoët jamais, eins au rebours" (R. Dezeimeris, "Annotations inédites de Michel de Montaigne sur les *Annales et chroniques de France* de Nicole Gilles," *Revue d'histoire littéraire de la France* 16 [1909]: 218–22).

49. On the relationship between imitation and anachronism, see G. W. Pigman III, "Versions of Imitation in the Renaissance," *Renaissance Quarterly* 33 (1980): 1–32, esp. pp. 29–32; and Thomas M. Greene, *The Light in Troy* (New Haven: Yale University Press, 1982), ch. 3. Also of interest is Pigman, "Imitation and the Renaissance Sense of the Past: The Reception of Erasmus's *Ciceronianus,*" *Journal of Medieval and Renaissance Studies* 9 (1979): 155–77. For a general discussion of imitation, especially in relationship to Ciceronianism, see Cave, *Cornucopian Text,* ch. 2.

50. On the development of humanist philology, see Anthony Grafton, *Joseph Scaliger: A Study in the History of Classical Scholarship* (Oxford: Oxford University Press, 1983); Jerry H. Bentley, *The Humanists and Holy Writ* (Princeton: Princeton University Press, 1983); and John F. D'Amico, *Theory and Practice in Renaissance Textual Criticism: Beatus Rhenanus between Conjecture and History* (Berkeley: University of California Press, 1988). For the application of philology to the study of Roman law, see Franklin, *Jean Bodin,* and Kelley, *Foundations.*

51. In addition to the above-cited works by Franklin and Kelley, see also Louis Delaruelle, *Guillaume Budé: Les origines, les débuts, les idées maitresse* (Paris, 1907; reprint, Geneva: Slatkine, 1970); and David O. McNeil, *Guillaume Budé and Humanism in the Reign of Francis I* (Geneva: Droz, 1975).

52. In addition to the above-cited works by Franklin and Kelley, see also Coleman Phillipson's separate essays on Alciato and Cujas in *Great Jurists of the World,* ed. John Macdonell and Edward Manson (Boston: Little, Brown, 1914).

53. On the notion of the discontinuity between past and present introduced by legal humanism, see J. G. A. Pocock, "The Origins of the Study of the Past: A Comparative Approach," *Comparative Studies in Society and History* 4 (1961–62): 209–46.

54. For the broader context of this fear, see William J. Bouwsma, "Anxiety and the Formation of Early Modern Culture," reprinted in his *A Usable Past: Essays in European Cultural History* (Berkeley: University of California Press, 1990), pp. 157–89, esp. p. 172: "No objective system of boundaries could now supply either security or effective guidance. When man still clung to the old culture, he seemed to have become, in spite of himself, a trespasser against the order of the universe, a violator of its sacred limits, the reluctant inhabitant of precisely those dangerous

borderlands—literally no man's land—he had been conditioned to avoid. But his predicament was even worse if this experience had taught him to doubt the very existence of boundaries. He seemed thrown, disoriented, back into the void from which it was the task of culture to rescue him. And this, I suggest, is the immediate explanation for the extraordinary anxiety of this period. It was an inevitable response to the growing inability of an inherited culture to invest experience with meaning."

55. François Hotman, *Antitribonian* (Paris, 1603; facsimile ed. in Images et temoins de l'age classique, no. 9 [Saint-Etienne, 1980]). The *Antitribonian* has been analyzed in the above-cited works of Franklin and Kelley, as well as in Pocock, *Ancient Constitution,* ch. 1. See also Pierre Mesnard, "François Hotman et le complexe de Tribonian," *Bulletin de la société de l'histoire du protestantisme français* 101 (1955): 117–37; and Ralph E. Giesey, "When and Why Hotman Wrote the *Francogallia,*" *Bibliothèque d'humanisme et renaissance* 29 (1967): 581–611, esp. pp. 596–604. Giesey's interpretation of the work is the most cogent, and his article provides an extensive bibliography on Hotman. Also of interest is Donald R. Kelley, *François Hotman: A Revolutionary's Ordeal* (Princeton: Princeton University Press, 1973).

56. Hotman, *Antitribonian,* p. 12; the reference to the "seasons" alludes to the natural cycle of growth and decay in the life of a state.

57. Ibid., pp. 17–18, 32–38.

58. Ibid., pp. 77–99.

59. Ibid., pp. 150–59.

60. Giesey, "When and Why," pp. 599–604; and E. Fournol, "Sur quelques traites de droit publique du XVIe siècle," *Nouvelle revue de droit français et etranger,* 3d ser., 21 (1897): 298–325, see esp. pp. 319–20.

61. Hotman, *Antitribonian,* pp. 154–55.

62. Giesey, "When and Why," p. 604.

63. Hotman, *Antitribonian,* pp. 28–29. Hotman devoted chs. 4–9 to a detailed comparison of Roman and French private law that was very relativistic. At one point he even exclaimed that a jurist trained solely in Roman law would, upon finding himself in a French court, no doubt feel as if he had landed among the savages of the New World (see *Antitribonian,* p. 36).

64. François Hotman, *Francogallia,* ed. Ralph E. Giesey and J. H. M. Salmon (Cambridge: Cambridge University Press, 1972). In addition to the editors' excellent introduction to this work, see Giesey, "When and Why"; Julian H. Franklin, *Constituutionalism and Resistance in the Sixteenth Century* (New York: Pegasus, 1969), pp. 19–30; Nannerl O. Keohane, *Philosophy and the State in France* (Princeton: Princeton University Press, 1980), pp. 49–53; Dubois, *Celtes et gaulois,* pp. 110–15; and Kelley, *Hotman,* pp. 238–60.

65. Hotman, *Francogallia,* pp. 287–331.

66. Pocock, *Ancient Constitution,* pp. 23–25.

67. Jean Bodin, *Method for the Easy Comprehension of History,* trans. Beatrice Reynolds (New York: Columbia University Press, 1945), p. 28.

68. Ibid., pp. 29–40.

Chapter 2. The Order of History

1. José Ortega y Gasset has aptly termed this intellectual system the "traditional way of thinking"; see his *The Idea of Principle in Leibnitz and the Evolution of Deductive Theory,* trans. Mildred Adams (New York: Norton, 1970), which, despite its title, is largely about Aristotelianism. For cogent analyses of this way of thinking, see Ernst Cassirer, *Substance and Function, and Einstein's Theory of Relativity,* trans. William and Marie Swabey (New York: Dover, 1923), pp. 3–9; and Michael E. Hobart, *Science and Religion in the Thought of Nicolas Malebranche* (Chapel Hill: University of North Carolina Press, 1982), pp. 9–13. In general, see also Etienne Gilson, *The Spirit of Mediaeval Philosophy,* trans. A. H. C. Downes (New York: Charles Scribner's Sons, 1936).

2. On the four causes, see John Herman Randall, Jr., *Aristotle* (New York: Columbia University Press, 1960), ch. 6.

3. See the unpaginated "Epistre à la noblesse," in the *Histoire des troubles;* and *Idée,* p. 104. On the four causes in sixteenth-century legal theory, see A. London Fell, *Origins of Legislative Sovereignty and the Legislative State* (2 vols.; Königstein: Athenäum, 1983).

4. On Agrippa and Patrizi, see Franklin, *Jean Bodin,* pp. 89–102; on Ruelle, see John L. Brown, *The "Methodus ad facilem historiarum cognitionem" of Jean Bodin* (Washington, D.C.: Catholic University of America Press, 1939), pp. 163–65. See also Giorgio Spini's analysis of Patrizi in his article "Historiography: The Art of History in the Italian Counter Reformation," in *The Late Italian Renaissance,* ed. Eric Cochrane (New York: Harper & Row, 1970), esp. pp. 100–109.

5. The best single source of information about La Popelinière's life remains George Wylie Sypher's unpublished dissertation "La Popelinière"; also see his "La Popelinière's *Histoire de France:* A Case of Historical Objectivity and Religious Censorship," *Journal of the History of Ideas* 24 (1963): 41–54. La Popelinière mentioned studying with Adrien Turnèbe in *Idée,* p. 259.

6. For a portrait of the law school at Toulouse around 1560, see Pierre Mesnard, "Jean Bodin à Toulouse," *Bibliothèque d'humanisme et renaissance* 12 (1950): 31–59.

7. See above, ch. 1, n. 1. On the possibility that La Popelinière was seeking royal patronage, see Orest Ranum, *Artisans of Glory* (Chapel Hill: University of North Carolina Press, 1980), pp. 90–91. See also Bernard de Girard, seigneur du Haillan, *De la fortune et vertu de la France, ensemble un sommaire discourse sur le desseing de l'histoire de France* (Rouen, 1571). Aside from paying lip service to the myth of the Trojan origins of the Franks (even though admitting that he no longer believed in it), Du Haillan seems to have anticipated some of the broad social and institutional scope of La Popelinière's *Dessein.*

8. For analyses of La Popelinière, in addition to the above-cited works of Sypher, see Donald R. Kelley, "History as a Calling: The Case of La Popelinière," *Renaissance Studies in Honor of Hans Baron,* ed. Anthony Molho and John A. Tedeschi (De Kalb: Northern Illinois University Press, 1971), pp. 771–89; Huppert, *Idea of Perfect History,* ch. 8; Myriam Yardeni, "La Conception de l'histoire dans l'oeuvres de La Popelinière," *Revue d'histoire moderne et contemporaine* 11 (1964): 109–26; Claude-Gilbert Dubois, *La Conception de l'histoire en France au XVIe siè-*

cle (Paris: Nizet, 1977), pp. 124–53; Erich Hassinger, *Empirisch-rationaler Historismus* (Bern: Franke Verlag, 1978), pp. 110–19; and Schiffman, "An Anatomy of the Historical Revolution in Renaissance France," *Renaissance Quarterly* 42 (1989): 507–33, esp. pp. 514–24, on which my account is chiefly based.

9. *Histoire des histoires,* pp. 21–48, 137–57, 158–59.

10. Ibid., pp. 6, 8.

11. *Idée,* pp. 20–22.

12. Ibid., p. 36.

13. Ibid., p. 82.

14. Ibid., p. 85, my emphasis.

15. Ibid., p. 76.

16. Ibid., p. 103. On Patrizi's formulation of this notion, and its status as a commonplace, see John Racin, *Sir Walter Raleigh as Historian* (Salzburg: Institut für Englische Sprache und Literatur, 1974), p. 61.

17. *Idée,* pp. 103–4.

18. Franklin, *Jean Bodin,* pp. 116–19; Donald R. Kelley, "*Historia integra:* François Baudouin and His Conception of History," *Journal of the History of Ideas* 25 (1964): 35–57; and Adalbert Klempt, *Die Säkularisierung der universalhistorischer Auffassung* (Göttingen: Musterschmidt, 1960), esp. pp. 64–69.

19. The very terms with which Baudouin denoted universal history, such as *historia integra* and *historia perfecta,* derived from the study of Roman law; see Michael Erbe, *François Baudouin* (Gutersloh: Mohn, 1978), p. 111.

20. For the role of origins in French Renaissance literature—and especially for their embodiment of essences that endure despite change—see Marian Rothstein, "Etymology, Genealogy and the Immutability of Origins," *Renaissance Quarterly* 43 (1990): 332–47.

21. *Idée,* pp. 104–5.

22. *Dessein,* pp. 354–55.

23. La Popelinière's proposal (*Dessein,* p. 354) begins by outlining the geography of Gaul and the customs of its inhabitants; it continues as follows: "En apres d'escrire la forme de l'estat, la police, religion, justice, finance, traffic, et autres façons de vivre. Soub l'entretien et continuë desquelles, les Romains et autres nations, vindrent pour telles occasions, par tels endroicts, tels moyens et succez renverser ce premiere estat Gaulois, et en son lieu y en establit un autre, auquel ils donnerent la forme qu'on representeroit par le menu et briefvement, jusques à ce que les Germains, et entre autres les Francs entrez és Gaules . . . essayerent à diverse fois, premierement de l'esbransler puis abattre, pour y planter une nouvelle forme de seigneurie." Passages like this one—reiterating the need to study the successive forms of the state—abound throughout the *Dessein.*

24. For the text of this letter, see Huppert, *Perfect History,* pp. 194–97.

25. This expression appears repeatedly throughout La Popelinière's writings on historical theory. In addition to the above-quoted passage from the *Dessein* (pp. 354–55), see also the *Idée,* pp. 30, 95, 104, and 190. The notion of "origins and progress" figures prominently not only in La Popelinière's work but also in that of his contemporaries, especially in Estienne Pasquier's *Recherches de la France.*

26. The expression is Julian Franklin's, in *Jean Bodin,* pp. 118–19; here he also notes: "This idea of the 'indivisibility' of history, together with the idea of con-

tinuity and the divorce of history and nature, is often uncannily suggestive of the historicism of the nineteenth century."

27. *Idée,* p. 114: "Les choses qu'on veut narrer trouvees, faudra faire comme le bon Architecte, qui suivant le dessein ja tracé de son ouvrage: jette les fondemens premieres, puis y bastit les murailles qu'il y esleve comme bon luy semble. . . . Ainsi l'Historien . . . preparera premierement les chose plus generales d'icelles. Puis disposera les particulieres, selon les temps et les lieux esquel elles sont advenues . . . suyvant la forme Annalitique des anciens." Other references to this architectural metaphor appear in *Idée,* p. 113, and *Dessein,* pp. 357 and 364.

28. *Dessein,* pp. 350–51.

29. Nicolas Vignier, *La Bibliothèque historiale* (3 vols.; Paris, 1587), 1:Preface; all subsequent references to the *Bibliothèque* are drawn from the unpaginated preface to volume one. A fourth, posthumous volume, including a biography of Vignier, was published in 1650. On Vignier, see Huppert, *Perfect History,* ch. 7; and Schiffman, "Anatomy," pp. 524–27, on which my analysis here is chiefly based. Also of interest is the preface to Vignier's *Sommaire de l'histoire des françois* (Paris, 1579), which contains some variations on the statements made in the later work.

30. On Eusebius in general, and his chronology in particular, see F. J. Foakes-Jackson, *Eusebius Pamphili* (Cambridge: W. Heffer & Sons, 1933); Robert M. Grant, *Eusebius as Church Historian* (Oxford: Oxford University Press, 1980); and Eusebius, *The Bodleian Manuscript of Jerome's Version of the Chronicle of Eusebius,* intro. J. K. Fotheringham (Oxford: Oxford University Press, 1905).

31. Estienne Pasquier, *Les Recherches de la France* (Paris, 1611), book 4, ch. 1, (hereafter cited as *Recherches* 4.1), p. 421. Unless otherwise indicated, all references are to the 1611 edition of the *Recherches,* which was the last edition published during Pasquier's lifetime. For the editions of the *Recherches,* see D. Thickett, *Bibliographie des oeuvres d'Estienne Pasquier* (Geneva: Droz, 1956).

32. For Pasquier's life, see D. Thickett, *Estienne Pasquier* (London: Regency Press, 1979). For analyses of his writings, see Kelley, *Foundations of Modern Historical Scholarship,* ch. 10; Huppert, *Perfect History,* ch. 3; P. Bouteiller, "Un Historien du XVIe siècle: Etienne Pasquier," *Bibliothèque d'humanisme et renaissance* 6 (1945): 357–92; L. Clark Keating, *Etienne Pasquier* (New York: Twayne, 1972); Margaret J. Moore, *Estienne Pasquier, historien de la poésie et de la langue françaises* (Poitiers: Société française d'imprimerie et de librairie, 1934); Robert Bütler, *Nationales und universales Denken im Werke Etienne Pasquier* (Basel: Helbing & Lichtenhahn, 1948); Joan Crow, "Estienne Pasquier, Literary Historian," *French Studies* 22 (1968): 1–8; Myriam Yardeni, *La Conscience nationale en France pendant les guerres de religion* (Louvain: Nauwelaerts, 1971), pp. 64–66; Keohane, *Philosophy and the State in France,* pp. 42–49; Schiffman, "Estienne Pasquier and the Problem of Historical Relativism," *Sixteenth-Century Journal* 18 (1987): 505–17, and "Anatomy," pp. 527–32. My analysis of Pasquier is largely based on the material in the last two articles.

33. Estienne Pasquier, *Les Oeuvres d'Estienne Pasquier* (2 vols.; Amsterdam, 1723), 2:293. The first volume of this work contains a complete edition of the *Recherches,* including several posthumous books, and the second volume contains his collected letters.

34. Ibid., 2:37–38.

35. *Recherches* 1.1, pp. 5–6, and 1, Introduction, pp. 2–3. Although Pasquier did not make the systematic distinction between primary and secondary sources that characterizes modern historical scholarship, he did try to rank his sources in a hierarchy of merit. The best ones were those written at the time of the events described, preferably by eyewitnesses. If these were unavailable, he moved on to consult sources written close to the time of the events. And in lieu of these, he sometimes had to rely on the reports of chroniclers far removed from events. For Pasquier's use of sources, see Bouteiller, "Pasquier," and Huppert, *Perfect History,* ch. 3. For a general assessment of French historical scholarship at this time, see Bezold, "Entstehungsgeschichte der historischen Methodik," esp. pp. 379–82.

36. *Recherches* 1.2, p. 8.

37. *Recherches* 1.1, p. 4; and 7.13, p. 840.

38. *Recherches* 1.2, p. 9.

39. *Recherches* 1.6, p. 24; 1.7, p. 27; and 2.11, p. 135.

40. Pasquier was even more fond of this expression for historical change than La Popelinière; see, for example, *Recherches* 6.1, p. 712, where he says he will recount the "origin, antiquity, and progress" of French poetry. Also see Bouteiller, "Pasquier," p. 362.

41. *Recherches* 2.1, p. 55.

42. Ibid., pp. 55–57.

43. *Recherches* 2.2, pp. 57–60.

44. Ibid., pp. 59–60.

45. *Recherches* 3.11, p. 256.

46. See, for example, Victor Martin, *Les Origines du Gallicanism* (2 vols.; Paris: Bloud & Gay, 1939), 1:38.

47. *Recherches* 3.6, pp. 223–24.

48. *Recherches* 3.16, p. 282.

49. *Recherches* 3.21, p. 306.

50. *Recherches* 6.1, pp. 712–13. For an analysis of the books on poetry and language, and their scholarly context, see Moore, *Pasquier.*

51. For Pasquier's account of the mutation of language and the germination of French, see *Recherches* 7.1.

52. "J'ay voûé ce mein premier Livre en passant, pour quelques discours des Gaulois, & aussi de l'habitation des premiers François, ensemble de quelques autres peuples qui nous touchent, que nous ne recognoissons (par maniere de dire) qu'à tatons: mon second, à la deduction de la commune police, qui a esté diversement observee selon le temps, non seulement és choses prophanes, mais aussi Ecclesiastiques: le tiers, à quelques anciennetez, qui ne concernent tant l'estat public, que des personnes privee: & le quatriesme, en la commemoration de quelques notables examples, que je voy ou n'estre deduites par le commun de noz Croniqueurs, ou passees si legerement qu'elles sont à plusieurs incognues: Et pour le regard du cinquiesme, je me le suis reservé à l'explication de quelques proverbes antique, qui ont eu vogue jusques à nous: estendant quelquesfois mes propos, mesme à l'origine & usage de quelque parolle, de marque" (Estienne Pasquier, *Des Recherches de la France* [Paris, 1560], p. 5r–v).

53. Of the two additional books on historical figures, one (book 10) consisted of

twenty-five chapters that Pasquier probably intended to add to book 5; they were, however, discovered too late to be put in their appropriate place in the first complete edition of the *Recherches,* published posthumously in 1621. They were incorporated into book 5 in subsequent editions.

54. This pattern of thinking is discussed throughout Ong's *Ramus,* as well as in Kenneth D. McRae, "Ramist Tendencies in the Thought of Jean Bodin," *Journal of the History of Ideas* 16 (1955). Also see Donald R. Kelley, "The Development and Context of Bodin's Method," in *Jean Bodin,* ed. Horst Denzer (Munich: C. H. Beck, 1973).

55. Hotman, *Francogallia,* pp. 287–349.

56. Ibid., p. 293.

57. Ibid., p. 217.

58. *Recherches* 2.2, p. 57.

59. Hotman, *Francogallia,* pp. 377–89, 531. For a discussion of the distinction between between "unfolding" and "development," see Karl J. Weintraub, "Autobiography and Historical Consciousness," *Critical Inquiry* 1 (1975), esp. pp. 829–34. See also Weintraub's *The Value of the Individual* (Chicago: University of Chicago Press, 1978), esp. pp. 275–78, and Schiffman, "Renaissance Historicism Reconsidered."

60. *Essais* 3.11, pp. 1003–4.

Chapter 3. The Order of the Self

1. For the order of composition of the *Essais,* see Pierre Villey, *Les Sources et l'évolution des Essais de Montaigne,* 2d ed. (2 vols.; Paris: Hachette, 1933).

2. On the relationship between the *Essais* and the genre of commonplace literature, see Peter M. Schon, *Vorformen des Essays in Antike und Humanismus* (Wiesbaden: Franz Steiner, 1954), pp. 63–89, and esp. p. 73; also see Pierre Villey, *Sources et évolution des Essais,* 2:3–33.

3. The *Essais* contain three different layers, or strata, of composition: the "A" stratum comprising the first edition of 1580; the "B" stratum comprising the additions made to the fifth edition of 1588; and the "C" stratum comprising the additions made between 1588 and 1592, when Montaigne died. My analysis is of the 1580 version of this essay; in subsequent editions, Montaigne expanded his point with an extended meditation on Alexander's disdain for the bravery of his opponents. My interpretation of this essay is based on Schiffman, "Montaigne and the Rise of Skepticism," pp. 500–502. For related interpretations, see Hugo Friedrich, *Montaigne,* trans. Robert Rovini (Paris: Gallimard, 1968), pp. 158–63; Weintraub, *Value of the Individual,* pp. 170–72; and Karlheinz Stierle, "Geschichte als Exemplum—Exemplum als Geschichte," in *Geschichte—Ereignis und Erzählung,* ed. Reinhart Koselleck and Wolf-Dieter Stempel (Munich: Wilhelm Fink Verlag, 1973), pp. 370–71. My interpretation of the essays in books 1 and 2 is based on their original form in the 1580 edition.

4. For an analysis of Montaigne's skepticism, see Schiffman, "Montaigne and the Rise of Skepticism," which argues that the roots of Montaigne's skepticism lay not in his reading of Sextus Empiricus—as is usually maintained—but rather in his

reaction to his humanist education at the Collège de Guyenne. For the influence of Sextus on Montaigne, see Popkin, *History of Scepticism,* ch. 3. For the influence of Cicero's Academic skepticism, see Elaine Limbrick, "Was Montaigne Really a Pyrrhonian?" *Bibliothèque d'humanisme et renaissance* 39 (1977): 67–80.

5. *Essais* 2.17, p. 637; see also Philip P. Hallie, *The Scar of Montaigne* (Middletown, Conn.: Wesleyan University Press, 1966).

6. The standard account of Montaigne's life remains Donald M. Frame's *Montaigne: A Biography* (New York: Harcourt, Brace & World, 1965). Roger Trinquet's, *La Jeunesse de Montaigne* (Paris: A. G. Nizet, 1972) adds some interesting details, as well as offering new interpretations, not all of which are convincing. Fortunat Strowski's, *Montaigne: Sa vie publique et privée* (Paris: Editions de la Nouvelle revue critique, 1938) remains a valuable work.

7. All the poets of the Pléiade, for example, studied law. Trinquet (*Jeunesse,* ch. 15) suggests that Montaigne never went to law school at all and that, instead, he studied Greek in Paris with Turnèbe. But there is not much evidence to support this conjecture, which, furthermore, runs counter to the practice of the new nobility in the sixteenth century.

8. *Essais* 1.28, p. 192.

9. For the inscription commemorating Montaigne's retirement, see Frame, *Montaigne,* p. 115.

10. Compare *Essais* 1.19, p. 79, with Montaigne's letter to his father about La Boétie's death (*Oeuvres complètes,* p. 1353).

11. *Essais* 2.1, p. 316. On the influence of Seneca, see Camilla Hill Hay, *Montaigne: Lecteur et imitateur de Sénèque* (Poitiers: Société française d'imprimerie et de librairie, 1938). See also Léontine Zanta, *La Renaissance du stoicisme au XVIe siècle* (Paris: Librairie ancienne Honoré Champion, 1914).

12. *Essais* 1.8, p. 34.

13. Erich Auerbach, *Mimesis,* trans. Willard R. Trask (Princeton: Princeton University Press, 1968), p. 344; this observation, made in regard to Don Quijote's idealism, applies equally well to Montaigne's.

14. *Essais* 3.4, p. 814; see also Montaigne's remark in his "Journal de Voyage en Italie," *Oeuvre complètes,* p. 1270.

15. Villey described "Of Sadness" as one of Montaigne's earliest essays. It is first in a large block of early essays, all written around 1572; and Villey concluded that Montaigne usually published the essays in such blocks in their order of composition. Thus, although "Of Sadness" is the second essay, it was probably composed first (1.1 having been written around 1578)—see Villey, *Sources et évolution des Essais,* 1:349, 395. Regardless of whether "Of Sadness" was actually Montaigne's very first composition, we shall see that all his early essays reflect the same intellectual

16. Donald M. Frame, *Montaigne's Discovery of Man* (New York: Columbia University Press, 1955), p. 38. See also Frame, *Montaigne,* pp. 142–44; Jean Plattard, *Montaigne et son temps* (Paris: Boivin, 1933), pp. 121–41; Strowski, *Montaigne: Sa vie,* pp. 125–27.

17. *Essais* 1.8, p. 34.

18. Edme Champion first sketched the evolution of Montaigne's thought in his *Introduction aux Essais de Montaigne* (Paris: Colin, 1900). Six years later Fortunat

Strowski described the three basic stages of Montaigne's thought—termed "Stoic," "Skeptic," and "Epicurian"—in his study *Montaigne* (Paris: Alcan, 1906). Working independently of Strowski, Pierre Villey confirmed this pattern of evolution in his *Sources et évolution des Essais* (first published in 1908). Villey also managed to date the composition of virtually every essay by identifying Montaigne's sources; his work remains the most thorough analysis of the evolution of the *Essais*. Villey assumed, however, that Montaigne's readings had provided the impetus for his thought—Seneca inspired his "Stoicism," Sextus Empiricus incited his "Skepticism," and Plutarch influenced his "Epicurianism." Reacting to this somewhat bookish interpretation, F. J. Billeskov Jansen made a psychological study of the evolution of Montaigne's thought in his *Sources vives de la pensée de Montaigne* (Copenhagen: Levin & Munksgaard, 1935). Donald M. Frame further revised Villey's thesis by examining the evolution of Montaigne's thought in the context of his life and times. This biographical approach revealed yet another stage of development—corresponding to Montaigne's composition of book 3—which Frame characterized as the acceptance of the universal brotherhood of man and epitomized in the title of *Montaigne's Discovery of Man*.

19. *Essais* 1.39, p. 242.

20. Ibid., p. 238.

21. *Essais* 1.23, p. 116.

22. *Essais* 2.1, p. 317.

23. Ibid., p. 316.

24. *Essais* 1.37, p. 225.

25. The term *creatural*, derived from the German *kreaturlich*, was coined by twentieth-century scholars to signify the medieval Christian view of man's suffering as a mortal creature. In *Mimesis*, Erich Auerbach has described how Rabelais transformed the creatural view of man into a celebration of "the vitalistic-dynamic triumph of the physical body and its functions" (p. 276). Mikhail Bakhtin has shown how creaturalism can also be associated with the "grotesque realism" characteristic of medieval popular culture—see *Rabelais and His World*, trans. Helene Iswolsky (Cambridge, Mass.: MIT Press, 1968). Both interpretations are useful for understanding the creatural view of man inherited by Montaigne, which blends Christian moral elements with grotesque realism.

26. For the dating of the accident, see Villey, *Sources et évolution des Essais*, 1:371.

27. *Essais* 2.6, pp. 356–57.

28. *Essais* 2.2, p. 328.

29. Ibid., p. 324. In the first edition, Montaigne confused Cato the Younger with Cato the Censor, who had a reputation for drinking.

30. *Essais* 2.3, p. 330.

31. *Essais* 2.2, p. 328.

32. Villey suggested that Montaigne did not pay much attention to the "Life of Pyrrho" until after reading Sextus around 1576 (*Sources et évolution des Essais*, 1:126–27).

33. On the translation of Sextus and the diffusion of his doctrines, see Popkin, *History of Scepticism*, ch. 2. On the pervasive influence of the *Academica*, see Charles B. Schmidt, *Cicero Scepticus: A Study of the Influence of the "Academica"*

in the Renaissance (The Hague: Martinus Nijhoff, 1972). For the Pyrrhonian inscriptions on the ceiling of Montaigne's library, see Frame, *Montaigne*, pp. 174–75.

34. *Essais* 2.12, p. 485.

35. Strowski has convincingly described Montaigne's translation of Sebond as the spiritual counterpart to the civil plan for religious reconciliation laid out by La Boétie in his *Mémoire sur l'édit de janvier 1562* (*Montaigne: Sa vie*, pp. 86–89, 95–96).

36. *Essais* 2.12, p. 496.

37. Ibid., p. 548.

38. Ibid.

39. For Popkin's analysis of the impact of Montaigne's skepticism, see *History of Scepticism*, pp. 52–54.

40. *Essais* 2.12, p. 548.

41. *Essais* 2.17, p. 640–41.

42. On the theory of imitation, see Pigman, "Versions of Imitation," and Greene, *Light in Troy*, ch. 3. For the relationship between the theory of imitation and modes of self-expression, see Phillips, "Erasmus and the Art of Writing."

43. For Montaigne's meditations on this process, see *Essais* 1.50, pp. 289–90.

44. For an evocative description of Montaigne's conversational style of writing, see Auerbach, *Mimesis*, pp. 290–91.

45. *Essais* 3.13, p. 1058.

46. *Essais* 3.12, p. 1026.

47. *Essais* 3.10, p. 987. On Montaigne's idea of habit as second nature, see Schiffman, "Montaigne and the Problem of Machiavellism," *Journal of Medieval and Renaissance Studies* 12 (1982): 237–58, esp. pp. 254–55.

48. *Essais* 3.13, p. 1094.

49. *Essais* 3.2, p. 782.

50. Ibid.

51. Ibid., p. 789.

52. *Essais* 3.3, p. 802.

53. In the seventeenth century this informal notion would contribute to the formation of a new social norm for French court culture; see M. Magendie, *La Politesse mondaine et les théories de l'honnêteté en France au XVIIe siècle* (2 vols.; Paris: Alcan, 1925).

54. See Richard L. Regosin, *The Matter of My Book: Montaigne's Essais as the Book of the Self* (Berkeley: University of California Press, 1977), esp. p. 62.

55. *Essais* 3.9, p. 941.

56. Weintraub, "Autobiography," pp. 824–26. In general, also see Claudio Guillén, "On the Concept and Metaphor of Perspective," in his *Literature as System* (Princeton: Princeton University Press, 1971).

57. The "here and now" even dominated Montaigne's thinking about the past. He described himself as "frequenting" the ancients, using the verb *practiquer* to denote his "presence" with them. See *Essais* 1.26, p. 155.

58. Duns Scotus had coined this term to describe the quality by virtue of which a thing or occurrence is unique, denoted as *this* particular thing or occurrence. He defined *haecceitas* as a qualitative rather than quantitative distinction: that is, he regarded Socrates as an individual by virtue not of his accidents (height, hair color,

and so on) but of his *haecceitas,* his individual "form," which existed apart from his "matter." I am introducing this term, not to imply that Montaigne was a nominalist or that he was directly influenced by scholasticism, but rather to offer a substitute for the traditional vocabulary used to describe Montaigne's perception, which emphasizes its "presentness." Georges Poulet, among others, has described how Montaigne portrayed himself in the "here and now," the emphasis on which enabled him to transcend the moment and dwell in an "eternal present," to ascend, in other words, from a state of "passage" to one of "being." This vocabulary tends to emphasize the state of mind of the perceiver rather than the nature of his perception, which is the subject of my inquiry. See Poulet, *Etudes sur le temps humain* (Edinburgh: Edinburgh University Press, 1949), ch. 1.

59. See Peter Burke, *Montaigne* (New York: Hill & Wang, 1981), p. 41; in general, see also Ian J. Winter, "L'Emploi du mot 'forme' dans les *Essais* de Montaigne," in *Montaigne et les Essais,* ed. Pierre Michel (Geneva: Slatkine, 1983), pp. 261–68.

60. *Essais* 3.2, p. 782.

61. *Essais* 1.50, p. 290. Note that Montaigne's *maistresse forme* should not be confused with his *forme maistresse.* The former expression signifies a particular personal quality ("ignorance"), whereas the latter signifies the collection of such qualities constituting the "ruling pattern" of his self.

62. *Essais* 3.10, p. 988.

63. For other uses of the word *forme,* see *Essais* 1.50, p. 290 ("Our character drags fortune in its train and molds her in its own form"); 2.37, p. 764 ("I have put all my efforts into forming my life"); and 2.18, pp. 647–48 ("In modeling this figure upon myself, I have had to fashion and compose myself so often to bring myself out, that the model itself has to some extent grown firm and taken shape [*que le patron s'en est fermy et aucunement formé soy-mesmes*]").

64. See Regosin, *Matter of My Book,* p. 110: "*Donner corp* and *mettre en registre* are the same act."

65. *Essais* 2.6, p. 359.

66. See Frances A. Yates, *The Art of Memory* (Chicago: University of Chicago Press, 1966), which clarifies the relationship between memory theaters and commonplace thought.

67. Ong, *Ramus,* pp. 262–63.

68. *Essais* 2.6, p. 359.

69. *Essais* 3.2, p. 782. On the subject of time, see Poulet, *Etudes sur le temps humain;* Bakhtin, "Forms of Time and of the Chronotope in the Novel"; Richard Glasser, *Time in French Life and Thought,* trans. C. G. Pearson (Towanda, N.J.: Rowman & Littlefield, 1972); Ricardo J. Quinones, *The Renaissance Discovery of Time* (Cambridge, Mass.: Harvard University Press, 1972); and, Donald J. Wilcox, *The Measure of Times Past* (Chicago: University of Chicago Press, 1987), esp. chs. 6 and 7.

70. *Essais* 1.43, p. 261. In general, see Frieda S. Brown, *Religious and Political Conservatism in the "Essais" of Montaigne* (Geneva: Droz, 1963).

71. *Essais* 3.13, p. 1049.

72. *Essais* 1.43, p. 261; see also 2.12, p. 567, and 1.23, p. 115, for the same sentiments.

73. Poulet, *Etudes sur le temps humain,* p. 44.
74. *Essais* 3.11, p. 1006.
75. Quoted in Frame, *Montaigne,* pp. 310–11.

Chapter 4. The Moral Order

1. The translation is from Montesquieu, *Persian Letters,* trans. C. J. Betts (Harmondsworth: Penguin Books, 1973), pp. 151–52 (letter 75).
2. *Essais* 2.12, p. 422.
3. The most important analysis of Charron's life and work remains J. B. Sabrié, *De l'humanisme au rationalisme: Pierre Charron (1541–1603)* (Paris: Alcan, 1913); see also Renée Kogel, *Pierre Charron* (Geneva: Droz, 1972); Jean Daniel Charron, *The "Wisdom" of Pierre Charron* (Chapel Hill: University of North Carolina Press, 1961); Eugene F. Rice, Jr., *The Renaissance Idea of Wisdom* (Cambridge, Mass.: Harvard University Press, 1958), esp. ch. 7; Günter Abel, *Stoizismus und frühe Neuzeit* (Berlin: Walter de Gruyter, 1978), esp. ch. 6; Alan M. Boase, *The Fortunes of Montaigne* (London: Methuen, 1935), chs. 6–7; Popkin, *History of Scepticism,* esp. ch 3; Paul Grendler, "The Enigma of 'Wisdom' in Pierre Charron," *Romance Notes* 4 (1962): 46–50, and "Pierre Charron: Precursor to Hobbes," *Review of Politics* 25 (1963): 212–24. Also of interest are Henri Busson, *La Pensée religieuse française de Charron à Pascal* (Paris: Vrin, 1933); René Pintard, *Le Libertinage érudit dans la première moitié du XVIIe siècle* (Paris: Boivin, 1943); and Gerhard Oestreich, *Neostoicism and the Early Modern State,* trans. David McLintock (Cambridge: Cambridge University Press, 1982).
4. The "Discours chrestien" is published in Pierre Charron, *De La Sagesse,* ed. Amaury Duval, 3 vols. (Paris, 1824; reprint, Geneva: Slatkine, 1968), 3:349–58; see esp. p. 351. This edition of the *Sagesse* also includes the *Petit Traicté de sagesse.* All references to Charron's writings are to this edition.
5. Charron, *Sagesse,* Preface (1601 version), p. xxxiv. Duval's critical edition of the *Sagesse* is based on the 1604 version, with variants from the 1601 version given in the notes. My analysis concentrates on the original 1601 version of the *Sagesse,* which I identify as such in the notes whenever it differs significantly from the 1604 version.
6. In his *"Wisdom" of Charron,* Jean Charron has speculated that the structural similarity between the two works indicates that the *Sagesse* was an attempt to continue the anti-Protestant argument in *Les Trois Veritez* by another means, leading Huguenots via the path of human wisdom back into the fold of the Roman Church. This interpretation disregards Charron's explicit and constantly reiterated distinction between religion and ethics.
7. *Sagesse,* Preface (1601), p. xxxiv.
8. Ibid.
9. *Sagesse,* Preface, p. xliii.
10. See *Sagesse,* book 2, ch. 4, hereafter cited as *Sagesse* 2.4.
11. This theme is lifted almost whole from the *Essais.* For example, *Sagesse* 2.3 is a pastiche of borrowings from *Essais* 3.12, Montaigne's most extensive treatment of the idea of living according to nature.

12. For the elaboration of these arguments, see *Sagesse* 1.41, pp. 298–301, and 3.14, pp. 87–93; also see Boase, *Fortunes of Montaigne,* pp. 85–86.
13. *Sagesse,* Preface, pp. lii–liii.
14. Ibid., p. xliv.
15. *Sagesse* 2, introduction, pp. 5–7.
16. Ibid., p. 4.
17. *Sagesse* 2.2, p. 53.
18. Ibid., pp. 30–32.
19. Ibid., p. 50. In the *Petit Traicté* (4.4, p. 308), Charron explained that his form of Academic skepticism, with its emphasis on the establishment of verisimilitude, was entirely different from Pyrrhonism. Eugene Rice (*Renaissance Idea of Wisdom,* p. 184) advises us not to take this disclaimer too seriously; but as we shall see, it lies at the very heart of Charron's method in the *Sagesse.*
20. *Sagesse* 2.3, p. 82–83; see also Preface, p. xliii, for similar terminology. Boase (*Fortunes of Montaigne,* p. 95) discusses the influence of civil and canon law on Charron's conception of nature.
21. *Sagesse* 2.3, p. 86.
22. *Essais* 3.13, p. 1068.
23. The expression is from Kogel, *Charron,* pp. 92–93.
24. *Sagesse* 2.5 (1601), pp. 156–57.
25. Ibid., p. 120; Charron suppressed this passage in the 1604 edition, but the one he substituted in its place was hardly more palatable to devout Christians.
26. *Sagesse* 2.5, p. 126.
27. *Sagesse* 2.5 (1601), p. 127.
28. Ibid., pp. 129–30.
29. Ibid., p. 139; in the 1604 version of this passage, he found himself forced to declare that he did not condone idolatry.
30. *Sagesse* 2.5, p. 134.
31. Ibid., pp. 151–52.
32. Ibid., pp. 155–56.
33. *Sagesse* 2.2, p. 57.
34. See *Sagesse* 1.37 (references are to the chapter numbers of Duval's critical edition, based on the 1604 version of the *Sagesse*; I shall later describe how Charron drastically revised the form of book 1, placing the initial chapters in the center of the book).
35. This suggestion is made in Boase, *Fortunes of Montaigne,* pp. 81–82.
36. *Sagesse* 1.39 (1601), p. 253.
37. Ibid., p. 259.
38. *Sagesse* 1.42, p. 306.
39. Ibid., p. 308.
40. Ibid., p. 314.
41. Ibid., pp. 317–18.
42. *Sagesse* 1.35, p. 222.
43. *Sagesse* 1.8 (1601), p. 45.
44. See ibid., p. 49 for Charron's application of humor theory.
45. *Sagesse* 1.43, pp. 318–22.
46. For Charron's use of climate theory, see *Sagesse* 1.44.

47. Ibid., p. 333.

48. See *Sagesse* 1.45.

49. See *Sagesse* 1.46, which begins with a dichotomized table that lays out Charron's subject spatially, in the manner of place logic and the classificatory view of the world that underlay it.

50. *Sagesse,* Preface, p. xlii.

51. *Sagesse* 1.19, p. 148.

52. *Sagesse* 3.1, p. 285. Note that this conclusion is analogous to Montaigne's in the first chapter of the *Essais,* that "it is hard to found any constant and uniform judgment" on man.

53. *Sagesse* 3.14, pp. 108–9.

54. *Sagesse* 2.18, pp. 198–200. The whole third chapter of the *Petit traicté* is set up as an argument *in utramque partem,* in which Charron attempted to define the sage by contrasting him with his opposite.

55. Grendler discusses this charge against Charron in "Engima of 'Wisdom,'" p. 49.

56. *Sagesse,* Preface (1601), p. xxxii.

57. *Sagesse* 3.2, pp. 302–3.

58. In general, see Grendler, "Charron: Precursor to Hobbes."

59. *Sagesse* 2.5, pp. 129–30.

60. For contemporary reactions to *Sagesse,* see—in addition to the above-cited works of Sabrié, Kogel, and Jean Charron—Boase, *Fortunes of Montaigne,* ch. 13, and Popkin, *History of Scepticism,* chs. 5 and 6.

Chapter 5. The Order of the Sciences

1. Descartes's only reference to Montaigne and Charron was in a letter to the marquess of Newcastle (23 November 1646) in which he attacked their view that animals behaved rationally. See Descartes, *Philosophical Letters,* trans. and ed. Anthony Kenny (Oxford: Oxford University Press, 1970), pp. 205–8.

2. See Kogel, *Charron,* p. 170: "The guideposts of Descartes's moral system—conformity, consistency, and self-control—evolve easily from the ethics of Charron's wise man"; see also ibid., p. 117; and, Sabrié, *Charron,* p. 322. For other resonances with Montaigne and Charron, see the extensive commentary in *René Descartes: Discours de la méthode, texte et commentaire,* ed. Etienne Gilson (Paris: Vrin, 1925); and, in general, see Léon Brunschvicg, *Descartes et Pascal, lecteurs de Montaigne* (Paris: Vrin, 1944).

3. For some of those who have doubted the veracity of Descartes's autobiographical account, see *Discours,* ed. Gilson, pp. 98–100.

4. For accounts of Descartes's life, see Charles Adam, "Vie de Descartes," in vol. 12 of René Descartes, *Oeuvres,* ed. Charles Adam and Paul Tannery (12 vols.; Paris: Vrin, 1896–1910); Elizabeth S. Haldane, *Descartes: His Life and Times* (London: Murray, 1905); and Jack Rochford Vrooman, *René Descartes: A Biography* (New York: Putnam, 1970). One should also consult the classic work of Adrien Baillet, *La Vie de Monsieur Des-Cartes* (2 vols.; Paris, 1691; reprint, Geneva: Slat-

kine, 1970), which has almost attained the status of a primary source and, despite some inaccuracies, is all the more interesting for having been written by a near contemporary.

5. Accounts vary as to when Descartes attended the Collège; see *Discours,* ed. Gilson, pp. 103–5; and J. Sirven, *Les Années d'apprentissage de Descartes* (Albi: Imprimerie coopérative du sud-ouest, 1928), pp. 25–27, 41–43.

6. *Ratio studiorum,* ed. Fitzpatrick, pp. 25–33. In general, see ch. 1, n. 41, above.

7. *Ratio studiorum,* ed. Fitzpatrick, p. 68; in general, see Blum, "*Apostolato dei collegi.*"

8. Rochemonteix, *Collège de Jésuites,* 2:104, 121–24, 140–41.

9. For the philosophy curriculum at the Collège de La Flèche before its revision in 1626, see Rochemonteix, *Collège de Jésuites,* 4:21–22, 32; *Discours,* ed. Gilson, pp. 117–19; and, Sirven, *Années d'apprentissage,* pp. 33–36.

10. Third-year students disputed among themselves or with their professors. For the pattern of instruction in the philosophy curriculum, see Rochemonteix, *Collège de Jésuites,* 4:22–26.

11. The *Ratio* of 1599 explicitly discouraged intellectual innovation: "Even in matters where there is no risk to faith and devotion, no one shall introduce new questions in matters of great moment, or any opinion which does not have suitable authority, without first consulting his superiors; he shall not teach anything opposed to the axioms of learned men or the general belief of scholars" (*Ratio studiorum,* ed. Fitzpatrick, p. 151). All Jesuit students were thus trained to be strong defenders of the established order. For the political agenda of Jesuit education, see Blum, "*Apostolato dei collegi.*"

12. *Ratio studiorum,* ed. Fitzpatrick, pp. 130, 175. See also Rochemonteix, *Collège de Jésuites,* 4:36–49; after the revision of the philosophy curriculum in 1626, when physics and metaphysics were studied in second year and mathematics alone in the third, instruction in mathematics included (in addition to arithmetic and geometry) astronomy, chronology, geography, music, optics, and civil and military architecture.

13. Blum, "*Apostolato dei collegi,*" pp. 109–10.

14. Descartes, *Oeuvres,* ed. Adam and Tannery, 1:383, 2:377–79. All references to Descartes's works will be to this edition, hereafter cited as AT, with the appropriate volume and page numbers.

15. For the daily routine at the Collège, see Rochemonteix, *Collège de Jésuites,* 2:28–40.

16. AT, 6:4; see also *Discours,* ed. Gilson, pp. 100–103. Unless otherwise indicated, all translations are from *The Philosophical Writings of Descartes,* trans. John Cottingham, Robert Stoothoff, and Dugald Murdoch (2 vols.; Cambridge: Cambridge University Press, 1984–85).

17. AT, 6:7.

18. AT, 6:9.

19. For example, see Popkin, *History of Scepticism,* pp. 172–76.

20. *Discours,* ed. Gilson, pp. 143–44.

21. AT, 6:10.

22. For an assessment of Beeckman's influence on Descartes, see Henri Gouhier, *Les Premières Pensées de Descartes* (Paris: Vrin, 1958), p. 29; this work is invaluable for understanding Descartes's early thought and writings.

23. Gouhier, *Premières Pensées,* pp. 21–22.

24. AT, 10:156.

25. AT, 10:164–65; see also *Discours,* ed. Gilson, pp. 185–86.

26. See Descartes's reference to the Rosicrucians in one of his earliest notebooks, in AT, 10:214.

27. For an analysis of Schenkel, and Descartes's reaction to him, see Yates, *Art of Memory,* pp. 300–302, 373–74; see also pp. 114–21 and 129–172 for a discussion of traditional and occult mnemonics.

28. On the probable dates for the composition of "Parnassus," see Gouhier, *Premières Pensées,* pp. 24, 66.

29. AT, 10:230 (translation adapted from that in Yates, *Art of Memory,* p. 373). The complaint that Schenkel's art uses up too much paper underscores Descartes's attraction to mathematics.

30. According to Baillet, Descartes recorded his vision and dreams in an early notebook, under the rubric "Olympica," or "Olympian matters." The contents of the original notebook (to which Baillet had access when writing his biography) survive only in a partial copy made by Leibniz, who did not include the portion describing the vision and dreams. We are thus dependent solely on Baillet for this information, which he fortunately recorded in great detail. The appropriate section of Baillet's biography is reproduced in AT, 10:180–88. An English translation of this material is in John Cottingham, *Descartes* (Oxford: Basil Blackwell, 1986), pp. 161–64. For analyses of this seminal experience, see J. Maritain, *The Dream of Descartes,* trans. Maybelle L. Audison (London: Editions Poetry, 1946); and Poulet, *Etudes sur le temps humain,* ch. 2.

31. For Descartes's conception of a *mathesis universalis,* see AT, 10:377–78.

32. AT, 10:213–15. See Gouhier, *Premières Pensées,* pp. 66–69, for the dating and analysis of these notes.

33. AT, 10:215.

34. AT, 6:19.

35. AT, 10:215.

36. AT, 6:22.

37. Ibid. Gouhier (*Premières Pensées,* pp. 63–65) maintains that Descartes adopted some tentative form of provisional morality just after his experience in the *poêle.* Descartes elaborated on the provisional nature of his moral code in a letter of April 1638: "I apply this rule mainly to actions in life which admit of no delay, and I use it only provisionally, intending to change my opinions as soon as I can find better, and to lose no opportunity for looking for such" (*Philosophical Letters,* p. 50).

38. For analyses of the *Regulae,* see L. J. Beck, *The Method of Descartes: A Study of the "Regulae"* (London: Oxford University Press, 1952); Harold H. Joachim, *Descartes's Rules for the Direction of the Mind,* ed. Errol E. Harris (London: George Allen & Unwin, 1957); Brian E. O'Neil, *Epistemological Direct Realism in Descartes' Philosophy* (Albuquerque: University of New Mexico Press, 1974); and S. V. Keeling, *Descartes,* 2d ed. (London: Oxford University Press, 1968), esp. ch. 3.

In *Descartes against the Skeptics* (Cambridge, Mass.: Harvard University Press, 1978), E. M. Curley argues that Descartes's method in the *Regulae* is fundamentally different from that in the *Discours,* due to the effect of a *crise pyrrhonienne* around 1628 (Curley subscribes to the traditional interpretation that Descartes underwent such a skeptical crisis). Although there are important differences between the two works, Descartes's terminology in the *Discours* can be clarified by reference to the *Regulae;* and (as we shall see) such a comparison reveals how his thought evolved in response less to a specific skeptical crisis than to the more general problem of relativism.

39. AT, 10:368; also see Rules Six, Eleven, and Twelve for further discussion of intuition. The terms "clear" and "distinct" used throughout Descartes's writings have technical meanings. According to Joachim (*Descartes's Rules,* p. 32), "to perceive anything clearly means that what is perceived is present and open to the mind attending to it, just as objects of sight are clear to the eye when they strike it *satis fortiter et aperte.* To perceive distinctly means (in addition to perceiving clearly) that one has before one's mind precisely what is relevant, no more and no less."

40. AT, 10:368

41. Ibid., pp. 381–87.

42. Tom Sorell, *Descartes* (Oxford: Oxford University Press, 1987), pp. 18–19; see also Beck, *Method of Descartes,* p. 172.

43. AT, 10:381.

44. Ibid., pp. 439–40.

45. Ibid., p. 451. For a cogent analysis of Descartes's serial reasoning and concept of unity, see Hobart, *Malebranche,* ch. 2. I am much indebted to this work, which is not only about Malebranche in particular but about the mentality of the Scientific Revolution in general.

46. AT, 10:421–22.

47. AT, 7:140–41.

48. AT, 5:147; the translation is from *Descartes's Conversation with Burman,* trans. John Cottingham, (Oxford: Oxford University Press, 1976), p. 4.

49. Beck, *Method of Descartes,* p. 109.

50. AT, 10:365.

51. Ibid., p. 408.

52. Ibid., p. 409; see also Rule Seven, pp. 387–88, for a further description of how to combat the weakness of memory.

53. AT, 10:405–6. Other critiques of syllogistic reasoning and scholasticism are in the *Discours* (AT, 6:17) and the *Recherche de la vérité par la lumière naturelle* (AT, 10:515–17). See also Beck, *Method of Descartes,* pp. 107–110, for an analysis of the Cartesian critique of syllogistic reasoning.

54. AT, 10:381, 418–19, and 368. For analyses of the concept of simple natures, see O'Neil, *Epistemological Realism,* ch. 1; Beck, *Method of Descartes,* ch. 5; Joachim, *Descartes's Rules,* pp. 28–37; and Keeling, *Descartes,* pp. 67–73.

55. Keeling, *Descartes,* pp. 67–70, 258; Joachim, *Descartes's Rules,* pp. 41–42. See also Beck, *Method of Descartes,* pp. 72–73.

56. Joachim, *Descartes's Rules,* pp. 36–37.

57. See O'Neil, *Epistemological Realism,* p. 15, and Joachim, *Descartes's Rules,* p. 36.

58. See Hobart, *Malebranche,* chs. 1–2, for a description of Descartes's insight in terms of an implicit model of "number" versus the traditional one of "substance."

59. Hobart, *Malebranche,* pp. 24, 27.

60. AT, 9B:14, 18. On the order of Descartes's tree of knowledge, see Hiram Caton, *The Origin of Subjectivity* (New Haven: Yale University Press, 1973), ch. 1.

61. See Richard A. Watson, *The Downfall of Cartesianism* (The Hague: Martinus Nijhoff, 1966), which attributes the decline of Cartesianism to the conflict between its quantitative and qualitative assumptions.

62. Cottingham, *Descartes,* p. 36. I am following the "existential" interpretation of the *cogito,* although there are a host of others; see, for example, the various interpretations in *Descartes: A Collection of Critical Essays,* ed. Willis Doney (Garden City, N.Y.: Doubleday, 1967).

63. See the *Meditationes,* AT, 7:27; see also the *Principia philosophiae,* AT, 8A:7, "It is a contradiction to suppose that what thinks does not, at the very time when it is thinking, exist."

64. Descartes, *Philosophical Letters,* 154–59; see also his letter of 28 June 1643 to Princess Elizabeth of Bohemia (ibid., pp. 140–43), which expresses the same notion about the "unity" of body and soul. For a commentary on this notion, see Hobart, *Malebranche,* pp. 40–41.

65. AT, 7:54; see also Hobart, *Malebranche,* p. 41.

66. AT, 6:32–33 (my emphasis).

67. Gilson, *Mediaeval Philosophy,* p. 86. This notion of "transitive causation" also implies a hierarchy of substances, which can be differentiated according to genus and species. Although Descartes would ultimately reduce the myriad of traditional substances to only two—thought and matter—they nonetheless represented generic concepts of classification.

68. In general, see Hobart, *Malebranche,* pp. 35–38.

69. AT, 6:35–36.

70. AT, 6:37–39.

71. AT, 7:140. On the Cartesian Circle in general, see Cottingham, *Descartes,* pp. 66–73.

72. For this point, see Hobart, *Malebranche,* pp. 42–44.

73. See O'Neil's analysis of early Cartesian realism (*Epistemological Realism,* esp. ch. 2), where he describes how Descartes was trying to use epistemology to "clean up" the traditional Aristotelian notion of sense perception.

74. AT, 6:4.

75. On the history of autobiography in general, and on intellectual autobiography in particular, see Weintraub, *Value of the Individual.*

76. See Dalia Judovitz, *Subjectivity and Representation in Descartes* (Cambridge: Cambridge University Press, 1988), ch. 3.

Epilogue

1. For this question and its historiographical repercussions, I am much indebted to Karl J. Weintraub's work on the history of autobiography; in particular see his "Autobiography and Historical Consciousness," pp. 829–34.

2. Some of the arcane intellectual context of the *Scienza nuova* is described in Paolo Rossi, *The Dark Abyss of Time,* trans. Lydia G. Cochrane (Chicago: University of Chicago Press, 1984).

3. The contemporary Neapolitan interest in feudal law is described in Peter Burke, *Vico* (Oxford: Oxford University Press, 1985), pp. 37–38.

4. Isaiah Berlin, *Vico and Herder* (New York: Viking Press, 1976), pp. 125–42, esp. pp. 131–32.

5. Giambattista Vico, *Autobiography,* trans. Max Harold Fisch and Thomas Goddard Bergin (Ithaca: Cornell University Press, 1944), pp. 128–30.

6. Giambattista Vico, *New Science,* trans. Thomas Goddard Bergin and Max Harold Fisch (Ithaca: Cornell University Press, 1968), par. 331 (as is customary, all references will be to the system of paragraph numbers established by Fausto Nicolini in his standard edition of the *Scienza nuova*).

7. This passage from *De antiquissima Italorum sapientia* (1710) is quoted in Vico, *Autobiography,* p. 38.

8. A. Robert Caponigri, *Time and Idea: The Theory of History in Giambattista Vico* (Chicago: Regnery, 1953), p. 150.

9. On the origins of this notion, see the essays on Vico in Isaiah Berlin, *Against the Current* (New York: Penguin Books, 1982), esp. pp. 94, 116.

10. Ibid., p. 117.

11. For Montaigne's analysis of Cato's suicide, see *Essais* 2.11, pp. 403–4. On the role of historical imagination in the *Essais,* see Regosin, *Matter of My Book,* pp. 158–59.

12. *Essais* 2.10, p. 396.

13. *New Science,* pars. 186–87.

14. Ibid., par. 34.

15. Ibid., par. 338.

16. Ibid., pars. 137–40.

17. Ibid., par. 349.

18. Berlin, *Vico and Herder,* pp. 64–67.

19. *New Science,* par. 1108.

20. Friedrich Meinecke, *Historism,* trans. J. E. Anderson (New York: Herder & Herder, 1972), p. 47.

21. For this distinction, see Isaiah Berlin, "Note on Alleged Relativism in Eighteenth-Century European Thought," in *Substance and Form in History,* ed. L. Pompa and W. H. Dray (Edinburgh: University of Edinburgh Press, 1981), pp. 1–14.

INDEX

Agricola, Rudolf, 13
Agrippa, Cornelius, 26
Alciato, Andrea, 19, 39
Aristotelianism, 25–27, 32, 57, 66, 107, 119; causation in, 26, 27, 32–33, 52, 164 n. 67; classification in, 8, 25, 27, 46–49, 52, 164 n. 67; substance in, 26, 72. *See also* Charron; Descartes; La Popelinière; Montaigne; Pasquier; Vignier
Aristotle, 12, 23, 25, 26, 55; and argument *in utramque partem,* 12
Auerbach, Erich, 154 n. 13, 155 n. 25, 156 n. 44
Augustine, Saint, 126

Baillet, Adrien, 160 n. 4, 162 n. 30
Bakhtin, Mikhail, 155 n. 25
Bartolus of Sassoferrato, 19
Baudouin, François, 32, 35, 39, 131, 150 n. 19; causation in, 32
Beeckman, Isaac, 111, 112
Berlin, Isaiah, 130–31
Bodin, Jean, 23–24, 28, 35, 82, 93, 94, 130; causation in, 32; classification in, 23–24, 35
Bordeaux, parlement of, 56
Bourges, University of, 19, 20, 80
Bouwsma, William J., 147 n. 54
Bowman, F. P., 142 n. 8
Bruni, Leonardo, 5, 13
Budé, Guillaume, 19

Caesar, Julius, 41
Capet, Hugues, 42
Cartesian Circle, 124
Cartesianism, xiv, 122, 131, 164 n. 61
Catholic League, 74, 80
Cato the Younger, 60, 61, 62, 97, 132, 133, 155 n. 29
Champion, Edme, 154 n. 18
Charlemagne, 42
Charron, Jean, 158 n. 6
Charron, Pierre, xiv, 79–102, 103–4, 110, 128; argument *in utramque partem* in, 84–85, 89, 95–97, 160 n. 54; casuistry, avoidance of, 97; classification in, 79, 82, 93, 94–95, 96, 98, 100–102, 160 n. 49; climate theory in, 94; commonplace thought in, 81–82; education of, 79–80; fideism in, 81, 86, 87, 89–90, 98–99, 101; on "following nature," 85–86, 101; habit, role of, 83, 87, 88, 89, 92, 99–100; on human nature, 90–95; humor theory in, 93–94; on "law of reason," 82, 83, 85, 88, 89–90; Montaigne, influence of, 79, 82–83, 84–86, 88, 89, 90–91, 92, 93; on piety, 86–89; on political morality, 95–98; on *preud'hommie,* 83–84, 86, 88–89, 90, 97; on religion and politics, 80–81, 83, 89, 95, 158 n. 6; revision of *Sagesse,* 98–101; on *science* and *sagesse,* 83, 104; skepticism in, 84–85, 89, 90, 95, 98–99, 101, 159 n. 19. Works: *Discours chrestien,* 80; *Petit Traicté,* 81, 90, 159 n. 19, 160 n. 54; *Sagesse,* 81–102; *Trois Veritez,* 81, 87
Cicero, xiii, 12, 23, 26, 55, 63; and argument *in utramque partem,* 12

Clovis, 42, 43, 44, 48, 51
Collège de Guyenne, 14–15, 16, 17, 55, 146 n. 42, 153 n. 4
Collège de La Flèche, 14, 104, 105–6, 107–8, 118, 119, 161 nn. 9, 10, 12
Collège de Presles, 39, 48
Commonplace books. See *liber locorum rerum*
Commonplace thought, intellectual system of, 12–13, 17, 25, 55, 109, 121. See also *In utramque partem*, argument; *Loci*
Commonplaces. See *Loci*
Concordat of Bologna, 44
Constitutiones Societatis Jesu, 14, 106, 146 n. 42. *See also* Education, Jesuit
Copia, theory of, 2
Coras, Jean de, 28
Corpus juris civilis, 19, 21, 22, 109. *See also* Legal scholarship, humanist
Corruption, idea of, 50–51, 74–75
Council of Constance, 44
Crusades, 44
Cujas, Jacques, 19, 22, 28, 39, 80, 130
Curley, E. M., 163 n. 38

Dante, 137
Decontextualization: effects of, 10–11, 20, 23, 27, 73, 137; theory of, defined, 7–8
Descartes, René, xiv, 102, 104–28, 129, 131–32; on analytical geometry, 111, 113; Aristotelianism in, 122–24, 125, 164 n. 73; autobiography of, 105, 125–26; classification in, 113, 164 n. 67; clear and distinct ideas in, 115, 120, 124, 163 n. 39; *cogito* in, 117, 120, 122, 123, 124, 126, 127, 131, 164 n. 62; cognitive moment in, xiv, 104, 117–18, 121, 126, 128, 130; criterion of truth in, 110, 121; education of, 14–15, 104–10; idea of God in, 117, 123–25; influence of Charron, 104–5, 122, 160 n. 1; influence of Montaigne, 104–5, 109–10, 119–20, 121, 160 n. 1; intuition in, 115; memory, on weakness of, 117; military career of, 110–11; on mnemonics, 112–13, 114, 162 n. 29; pineal gland, theory of, 127; *poêle,* experience in, 111, 113, 115, 126; on provisional morality, 114–15, 162 n. 37; Pyrrhonism in, 109–10; on *science* and *sagesse,* 104, 114–15, 121–22, 126, 127; serial reasoning in, 116; simple natures in, 115, 116, 118–20; on syllogistic logic, 118; unit/unity, idea of, 116–17, 120, 122–23, 125, 126; universal mathematics, on, 113. Works: *Conversations with Burman,* 117; *Discours,* 104–5, 108, 109, 114, 115, 116, 120, 121, 122, 123, 125, 126–27, 163 n. 38; *Meditationes,* 123, 124, 127; "Parnassus," 112; *Passions,* 127; "Praeambula," 113–14; *Principles of Philosophy,* 127; *Regulae,* 115–20, 122, 123, 125, 126, 163 n. 38. *See also* Vico
Development, idea of, xi–xii, xiv–xv, 51–52, 74, 75–76, 104, 128, 129–30, 138–39
Diogenes Laertius, 63
Druids, 41, 42, 43, 45, 47, 48
Du Haillan, Bernard de Girard, seigneur, 30, 149 n. 7
Duns Scotus, 156 n. 58
Du Vair, Guillaume, 82

Education, humanist, 6, 11–18, 23, 55–56, 106–7, 110; commonplace books in, 13–15; disputation in, 15–17; rhetoric in, 11–12, 13
Education, Jesuit, 14–15, 16, 105, 106–7, 161 n. 11
Einstein, Albert, 77
Elizabeth of Bohemia, 164 n. 64
Epaminondas, 54
Erasmus, Desiderius, 2, 13–14, 18, 67
Estienne, Henri, 46, 63
Eusebius, 37

Fauchet, Claude, 43, 46
Fell, A. London, 149 n. 3
Ferdinand II, 113
Foucault, Michel, 142 n. 10
Frame, Donald M., 155 n. 18
Freud, Sigmund, 137

Galileo, 125
Garasse, François, 101
Gassendi, Pierre, 101
Gilles, Nicole, 17
Gilson, Etienne, 105, 123
Gouvéa, Andre, 55, 145 n. 41
Grandes chroniques de France, 10
Great Schism, 43, 44
Grotius, Hugo, 130
Guarino da Verona, 13
Guise(s), 58, 80

Haecceitas, concept of, 71, 73, 129, 134, 136, 156 n. 58
Henri III, 80
Henri IV, 106
Herodotus, 31
Historia magistra vitae, concept of, 3, 19, 28, 31, 109
Historicism, xii, 150 n. 26
Hobart, Michael E., 163 n. 45, 164 n. 58

Hobbes, Thomas, 98
Homer, 137
Hotman, François, 20–23, 32, 39, 50, 74, 75, 76, 130, 131; and the ancient constitution, 22–23, 50. Works: *Antitribonian,* 20–22, 148 n. 63; *Francogallia,* 22–23, 50
Howell, Wilbur S., 146 n. 44
Huarte, Juan, 82, 93
Human sciences, 104, 122, 127, 137, 138

Imitatio, theory of, 18, 67
In utramque partem, argument, 12–13, 17. *See also* Charron; Montaigne

Jansen, F. J. Billeskov, 155 n. 18
Jus naturale, concept of, 85

La Boétie, Estienne de, 56, 57, 156 n. 35
La Popelinière, Lancelot Voisin de, xi, xii, xiv, 9, 10, 27–36, 38–39, 49, 52, 54, 73, 74, 103, 113, 135; causation in, 26, 32–34; classification in, 24, 35; Divine Providence in, 135; education of, 27–28; historical Pyrrhonism in, 28–29; lists in, 1–3, 5, 24, 34, 35; perfect history, idea of, xi, 2–3, 10, 27, 29–30, 33–36, 49; on "substance" of history, 26, 31–35; on Trojan origins of Franks, 2; on Vignier, 36. Works: *Dessein,* 1–3, 24, 30, 33–34, 35; *Histoire de France,* 9–10, 28, 30, 144 n. 25; *Histoire des histoires,* 30–31; *Histoire des troubles,* 9, 26, 28–30, 144 n. 25; *Idée,* 26, 30, 31–33, 34–35
La Ruelle, Charles de, 26
Legal scholarship, humanist, xi–xii, 6, 18–24
Leibniz, Gottfried Wilhelm von, 162 n. 30
Le Roy, Louis, 3
L'Hôpital, Michel de, 21
Liber locorum rerum, 13–15, 17, 23–24, 55, 107, 146 n. 42. *See also* Education, humanist
Lipsius, Justus, 82, 98
Lists and list-making, 1–5, 73. *See also* Decontextualization, effects of
Literacy, impact of, 6, 7–9, 10, 11, 13, 20, 23, 73. *See also* Decontextualization
Loci, theory of, 10, 12, 13–14, 15, 24, 35, 37, 73, 112. *See also* Charron, classification in; La Popelinière, classification in; Montaigne, classification in; Pasquier, classification in; Vignier, classification in
Louis Debonnaire, 42
Louis XI, 50
Loyola, Ignatius, 106, 107
Lull, Raymond, 111–12

Machiavelli, Niccolò, 98
Malebranche, Nicolas, 127
Maurice of Nassau, 110
Marx, Karl, 137
Maximilian, Duke of Bavaria, 110, 113
Meinecke, Friedrich, 136
Melanchthon, Philip, 14
Mersenne, Marin, 101
Mesland, Denis, 122
Montaigne, Michel de, xi, xii, xiii, xiv, 3–4, 17–18, 52, 53–77, 78–79, 80, 95, 96, 102, 103, 104, 110, 128, 129, 130, 132–33; annotations to Gilles, 17; argument *in utramque partem* in, 54–56, 58–59, 62–63, 64, 68; on causation, 52; classification in, 70, 72–74; cognitive moment in, xiv, 68–70, 71, 75, 104, 130, 132, 156 n. 57; commonplace thought in, 54–55, 57, 58–59; composition of *Essais,* 4, 53, 58, 68, 154 n. 15; conservatism in, 74–75; "creatural" view in, 61–62, 65, 155 n. 25; development, idea of, 70–71, 72, 129; education of, 14–15, 55–56; essay, idea of, 67–70; evolution of his thought, 59–60, 153 n. 3, 154 n. 18; fideism in, 65–66, 86; on "following nature," 66, 69, 85; on *forme maistresse,* 69, 72–73, 157 n. 61; on habit, 60–61, 68–69, 75, 77, 156 n. 47; on *honnêteté,* 70, 156 n. 53; lists in, 3–4, 5; Pyrrhonism in, 63–66, 119; on reason, 64–65, 69; retirement of, 56–57; sage, ideal of, 56–57, 60–63; on self-study, xi, 66–67, 69, 71; selfhood, idea of, 70–74, 76–77; time in, 74–76. *See also* Charron; Descartes; Pasquier; Vico
Montesquieu, 78, 79

Naudé, Gabriel, 101
Neo-Bartolism, 21, 23–24, 25, 26, 27, 35, 103
New World, impact of, 5, 7, 11, 143 n. 13
Nietzsche, Friedrich, 137

Occasionalism, theory of, 127
Ochino, Bernardino, 80
Ong, Walter J., 73
Ortega y Gasset, José, 149 n. 1

Paris, University of, 79, 106
Pasquier, Estienne, xiv, 27, 38–49, 50–52, 74, 76, 103, 150 n. 25; causation in, 38–39; classification in, 46–49; Divine Providence in, 48, 135; education of, 39; on Franks, 41; on Gallican church, 43–45; on Gauls, 41–46; on historical Pyrrhonism, 39–40; historical scholarship in, 40, 49, 152 n. 35; on language,

39, 45–46; on Montaigne, 76; on parlement, 42–43; on perfect history, 38; plan of *Recherches*, 46, 152 n. 53; on poetry, 45; on Trojan origins of Franks, 40
Patin, Guy, 101
Patrizi, Francesco, 26, 28, 32, 150 n. 16
Paul, Saint, 91
Pelopidas, 54
Pepin, 42, 44
Petrarch, xiii, 5, 13
Philology, impact of, 5, 6, 7, 10, 18–19, 20, 23, 73
Pithou, Pierre, 43
Place logic. See *Loci*
Plato, 8, 23
Pléiade, 45, 154 n. 7
Plutarch, 64, 82
Poitiers, University of, 109
Poliziano, Angelo, 18
Polybius, 23, 32
Pompey, 54, 55
Popkin, Richard, 66
Poulet, Georges, 157 n. 58
Pragmatic Sanction of Bourges, 44
Pragmatic Sanction of Saint Louis, 44
Psammenitus, 58
Pufendorf, Samuel, 130
Pyrrhonism, historical, 26, 28–29, 109. *See also* Descartes; Pasquier; Skepticism; Vignier

Quadrivium, 113

Rabelais, François, 3
Ramus, Peter, 10–11, 39, 48, 49, 73, 79
Ratio studiorum, 14, 106, 108, 161 n. 11. *See also* Education, Jesuit
Reformation, impact of, 5, 6, 9, 11
Relativism, xii–xiii
Rhodes, Knights of, 44
Rice, Eugene F., Jr., 159 n. 19
Ronsard, Pierre, 45
Rosicrucians, 112

Scaliger, J. J., 34
Schenkel, Lambert, 112, 162 n. 29
Schiffman, Z. S., 153 n. 4
Schola Aquitanica, 14, 146 n. 42. *See also* Collège de Guyenne
Sebond, Raymond, 64, 156 n. 35
Selden, John, 130
Seneca, 56, 57, 82
Sextus Empiricus, 63, 64, 153 n. 4
Skepticism: Academic, 12, 55, 63, 64, 84, 107; Pyrrhonian, 63, 64, 84, 110, 163 n. 38
Strowski, Fortunat, 154 n. 18
Sulla, 54, 55

Templars, 44
Toulouse, University of, 27–28, 39, 56
Tribonian, 20, 21
Trinquet, Roger, 146 n. 42, 154 nn. 6, 7
Turnèbe, Adrien, 27, 154 n. 7

Unfolding, idea of, 27, 49–52, 74, 76, 134–35

Valla, Lorenzo, 18
Vico, Giambattista, xiv, 130–37; on childhood, 133; cognitive moment in, 132–33, 136; *corsi* and *ricorsi*, ideas of, 134, 135, 137; on Descartes, 131–32, 136; development, idea of, 130, 131, 132–33, 134–36; Divine Providence in, 134, 135; on "ideal eternal history," 134, 135; individuality in, 136; on "modifications of mind," 131–33, 136, 138; Montaigne, compared with, 132–33; on "philologico-philosophical" method, 133–34; on Roman history, 134, 136
Vignier, Nicolas, xiv, 3, 27, 36–38, 49, 52, 74, 103, 135; chronology in, 36–38; classification in, 37; Divine Providence in, 36, 37, 135; historical Pyrrhonism in, 36; on perfect history, 36, 38, 49; on "substance" of history, 37. Works: *Bibliothèque*, 36–37; *Sommaire*, 36, 37
Villey, Pierre, 154 n. 15, 155 nn. 18, 32
Vinet, Elie, 145 n. 41

Watson, Richard A., 164 n. 61
Weintraub, Karl J., 164 nn. 74, 1
Whig history, 138, 143 n. 10
Wilson, Thomas, 146 n. 44

Designed by Pat Crowder. Composed by Professional Book Compositors, Inc. in Baskerville text and display. Printed on 60 lb. Warren's Olde Style and bound in Holliston Roxite A50475 linen finish by Thomson-Shore, Inc.